A question I've often asked people: Are you open-minded?

If you quickly answer yes, then most likely you are not.

Part of being open-minded, by definition, includes being open to the possibility that you are not open-minded at all, because fundamentally, how can we ever really know?

— Adam Unlisted

Morally Grey

CONFESSIONS OF A CAREER DRUG DEALER

A Mildly Autistic Perspective

ADAM UNLISTED

Contents

Author's Preface:		IX
Introduction:		1
Chapter 1:	Far Divorced From Normality	5
Chapter 2:	A Group Home And New Directions	13
Chapter 3:	The Changing Of Residences	23
Chapter 4:	A Caper With A Plot Like A Movie	27
Chapter 5:	Restrained Enlightenment	33
Chapter 6:	Free And Unclear	41
Chapter 7:	After All My Hours	45
Chapter 8:	Suddenly Different	49
Chapter 9:	My First Love And A Painful Good-Lie	53
Chapter 10:	A Moment Of Reflection	59
Chapter 11:	Teenage Toilet Training	61
Chapter 12:	The Final Alternative	65
Chapter 13:	Attempting A Startup	67
Chapter 14:	Oh K; Not Okay	69
Chapter 15:	It's Oh K, It's A Good Friday	73
Chapter 16:	Another Beginning	77
Chapter 17:	Ottawa; A New City, A New Life	79
Chapter 18:	A Mother Confrontation	85
Chapter 19:	A Trip Off The Bus	89
Chapter 20:	A New Apartment; A New Kind of Ending	93
Chapter 21:	Room For A New Mate	97
Chapter 22:	Anxiously Distracted	101
Chapter 23:	Inappropriately; "Inappropriate And Serious"	113
Chapter 24:	The Canadian Tire Incident	117
Chapter 25:	The Second Cup Scenario	121
Chapter 26:	Re-Dealing	127
Chapter 27:	A Hard Thing To Sleep On	129
Chapter 28:	An Oily Landscape	131
Chapter 29:	A Different Kind Of Job, From A Different Kind Of Loan	135
Chapter 30:	A Highway Hard-Knock	141
Chapter 31:	Nick, A Peach And A Rockstar Punch	145

Chapter 32:	Rico Sauve	149
Chapter 33:	On A Drunk Lady's Hood	159
Chapter 34:	Ass Grab Head Butt	163
Chapter 35:	Ready, Aim, The Fire Works	167
Chapter 36:	A Mechanical Push	169
Chapter 37:	A Damsel In Distress	173
Chapter 38:	A Flex To My Moral Perspective	177
Chapter 39:	The 40 Foot Jump	183
Chapter 40:	A Decisive Moment	191
Chapter 41:	Which Way Should I Turn Away?	195
Chapter 42:	The Die Has Been Cast	199
Chapter 43:	A License To Sell	205
Chapter 44:	Unexpected Freedom	211
Chapter 45:	A Club To The Side Of The Head	213
Chapter 46:	A New Kind Of Club	221
Chapter 47:	By(what?)Law	227
Chapter 48:	The Rights Preparation	231
Chapter 49:	A Short Recess	233
Chapter 50:	A Table, A Tablet, And Too Much Talk	235
Chapter 51:	Studio Unlisted	239
Chapter 52:	Actuatedly Misunderstood	241
Chapter 53:	Empty Threats And A Tip	245
Chapter 54:	Progressive Restrictions	247
Chapter 55:	Don't Dee Dishonest	251
Chapter 56:	The House Dose Not Always Win	255
Chapter 57:	Illegal Entry Of The Law	263
Chapter 58:	Accidental Break And Entering	269
Chapter 59:	My Friend Dan The Cop And I	273
Chapter 60:	A Few Random Events	277
Chapter 61:	Officer Simon's Unexpected Trip	279
Chapter 62:	Illegal Arrest And Assault	285
Chapter 63:	Charter Application - Round Deux	289
Chapter 64:	Love And Regrets	295
Chapter 65:	Our Last Fight; My Catalyst To Change	305

Chapter 66: Moments Of Time 309
Chapter 67: Eternal Love; Forever Lost, A Trauma Leading To Change 313
Chapter 68: Bittersweet Changes; Musically Minor In Key 337

PREFACE

Twenty Years ago, when I was nineteen, I already had a fairly crazy life that taught me a lot about myself. This resulted in a number of distinct periods of rapid, permanent changes to my personality and behavior. Even at that age, I felt there were enough stories that were both interesting and insightful enough to share, which might help others to look at their own problems differently; this is what inspired me to first consider writing a book. Not only did that idea never go away, but because of the strong sense of justice, which is very common in people who are mildly autistic, the next twenty years of my life, were even more interesting and crazy, as a result of the countless times when I have stood up to people who I felt were either exceptionally selfish, because of something they did, or something that I knew was unjust.

One of the big life-changing events that had a huge positive impact on me, was spending ten months in jail when I was seventeen. In addition to the positive impact it had on me, it was during this time when I first developed an interest in law; more specifically, constitutional law and the Charter of Rights. As I would eventually discover, not only did I have an exceptional natural talent for law, but by the time I was twenty, I realized I had discovered a new way to challenge drug laws in Canada, that's never been attempted before. After getting caught for drug trafficking about eight years ago, it only made sense to represent myself in court. Considering no other lawyer has ever discovered what I had, I knew I was more of an expert in the constitutional argument that I was going to present.

After I first got arrested, I had no choice but to admit the bag of drugs was mine, since it was the only way to prevent my friend from being charged as well; this was obviously the morally right thing to do. Because I had essentially admitted to drug dealing, my entire legal defense was based on this new way I had discovered in the Charter of Rights. Over the next eight months, as I began educating myself, and learning everything I needed to know so that I could properly present my argument in court, I ended up learning something even more profound about this new constitutional argument that I had discovered; not only has Section 1 never been used to challenge drug laws, but Section 1 has never been used defensively, ever. In Canada, Section 1 of the Charter of Rights is supreme law; all other law must conform to it.

As soon as I discovered that Section 1 has never been used defensively, I immediately realized that even if I'd lost the Charter argument with respect to drug laws, the case would still set precedent, and the Charter Application that I had written could be used as a template, to easily allow Section 1 to be used defensively, for all sorts of different issues. Ultimately, I never formally submitted the Charter Application, because two months after I gave the Federal Prosecutor a courtesy copy, before I would have needed to officially submit it, and despite admitting the bag was mine, the charges against me were suddenly dropped; no reason given as to why. If you heard about this book because of an interest in these legal details, I've intentionally kept them separate from my story, and all the details can be found at www.daffa.org

My life has always been difficult for as long as I can remember. I only found out about a month ago that I'm mildly autistic, but when I found that out, it suddenly explained so much of the difficulties I experienced, and why I was always a magnet for bullies. Up until I started school, I was always a very polite, respectful, and calm kid; I hated conflict and confrontation, but being forced to stand up to those bullies changed everything.

I was, and have always been, very polite and respectful, but after the bullying, if I'm pushed too far, my strong sense of moral justice usually kicks in, and tends to become a primary motivator. The behavioral problems I ended up developing, eventually landed me in a group home, and then jail when I was 17. Both of those experiences ended up having wonderful and lasting positive effects on me, but there has always been one lingering issue I've never been able to figure out.

About 5 months before finishing this book, that last issue I was still haunted by from my childhood, ended up pushing away my fiancé of five years, shortly before the COVID-19 lock-down. Alone, and with nothing to do, over the next few months, I slowly fell into a mental hell, as my autistic mind endlessly and obsessively searched for answers. After a trip to the hospital to get something to calm me down, because of the months of hell that was only getting worse, I was eventually able to focus clearly again. Over the following couple of months, I was surprised I managed to write over 100 000 words and finish this book. But because I have a very detailed and clear memory from a very young age, as I relived my past in great detail, I was shocked to end up discovering just how many suppressed memories I had, which were the cause of the issue I've never been able to resolve before.

Like with any good fictional story, I have met many interesting characters along the away, experienced countless moments of conflict and despair, as well as moments of success and personal growth, and by the time I finished writing, I suddenly found myself realizing, I was not quite the same person who initially started writing this book.

INTRODUCTION

There have been times in my life when I've questioned if I'm a good person or not; recently has been one of those times. It wasn't my career as a Drug Dealer for almost 20 years that causes me to question myself, it's not even that I think this all the time, or even very often, in fact, most of the time I don't think this at all. But the moments when I do, I tend to be very critical of myself; sometimes to the point of having strong suicidal thoughts. Thankfully, my intense empathy and love for others has always prevented me from following through with such thoughts, and in fact, it's the only reason I'm still alive today.

Like most people, I'm far from perfect, but the reason why I question myself at times, is because of a specific combination of character traits I have, and when they start resonating all together due to negative or unjust situations I'm confronted with, it can lead to some extreme and excessive reactions from me, some of which I later regret, and others that make me smile. Regardless of how my reactions are perceived, such reactions have resulted in a lot of crazy and interesting stories.

For the most part, I'm a very calm, easy going person that can always find a positive thing to say about any situation. I tend to be very forgiving and not the type who can really hold a grudge against someone. But a close friend once described me best by saying: *"You are one of the calmest persons that I know and can stay calm even when faced with a lot of crap from another person, but only up to a certain point. It takes a whole lot to push you to that point, but once you are pushed past that point, whoever pushed you that far, better watch out, because they will likely end up regretting it."*

The essence of this book, is essentially a collection of stories from my life, when for one reason or another, I felt pushed to the point where I decided to take action. Some of the stories will be of things I regret and am not proud of, and others I feel were completely justified.

Along the way, down this bumpy road that's been my life, there has been an interesting chain of events that has led me to this point in my life, and if any one of those things had gone differently, it's quite likely I wouldn't be writing this book right now.

I first started getting bullied not long after I began school, and from kindergarten through grade 4, very few school days were free from it. Because of the intense bullying I experienced, and the impact it had on my behavior, when my parents got divorced at the end of grade 7, my behavior became even worse, and I started getting into trouble with the police quite often. Eventually my behavior became so bad, when my mom finally had enough of me not listening to her, she decided to drop all of my things off in my dad's driveway, while I was with him visiting family. When I got home late that night, and realized what had happened, I grabbed the first thing I saw, went upstairs, and threw it at my mom's ass while she was sleeping. This led to me being sent to a group home. Even though the group home did have a lot of positive effects on me, I knew I still had a bunch of unresolved issues when I was finally discharged.

Those remaining issues still continued to cause problems, and eventually I would end up in jail for 10 months. Like with the group home, going to jail was a very good thing for me, which also completely changed certain things about myself, and also first sparked my interest in law, but there were still some remaining personal issues when I got out of jail. All, except one, were related to social anxieties, and if I hadn't started taking the club drug, ecstasy, I doubt I would have ever understood what was causing those anxieties, and I would be a very different person than I am today.

Eventually, because the city I grew up in only had a population of 200 000 people, and most of the police officers knew me from all the trouble I had gotten into over the years, when I had an opportunity to move to Ottawa after I finished high school, I didn't hesitate for a moment.

I've always struggled with school my whole life. I technically failed every year up until grade 8, because I rarely ever did any homework. But because it was very apparent that I was intelligent and understood what had been taught, I got 50% in more classes than I can remember, and surprisingly, I was never held back a grade.

When I got to high school, things were obviously different, and there was no way I was going to get my diploma without doing the work.

I was never able to do well in a normal high school, and the only reason I was able to get my diploma, was because I got almost all my credits from alternative schools, where I could work at my own pace.

After I moved to Ottawa, I decided to take computer engineering at one of the colleges, and although I did well in my first semester, the work load by the third semester finally became too much, and at the rate I was proceeding, I realized how much student debt I was going to have by the time I finished. The thought of being in debt for 20 years made dropping out the obvious choice.

I've always had problems falling asleep and waking up on time, which was always an issue with school, but when I started working full time, it caused me to be fired from one job after another.

I also started selling weed while I was in college to make a little extra money, and be able to smoke weed basically for free. After losing one too many jobs, I decided to start selling drugs full time. I never sold to other dealers or ever made all that much money, but it was enough for me to live on, not have much stress in my life, and continue learning how to become a computer engineer on my own, and according to my own sleep schedule. I knew I didn't want to work for anyone, so the diploma didn't matter.

Eventually, after about 10 years of selling drugs, I would end up getting caught and charged with drug trafficking. Because of what I had learned about the Charter of Rights, I was able to successfully defend myself in court, even after admitting to drug dealing. Not long after the trafficking charges were dropped, a friend of mine approached me with an opportunity to buy the local after-hours dance club.

He was friends with the owner, and found out that his buddy was just going to close the club; after not being able to find anyone to buy it, due to the legal issues with owning such a place, as well as issues relating to the local biker gang. Because of all the bullying I've had to deal with, the way it forced me to learn how to defend myself and not accept bullshit from anyone, is the reason why my buddy accurately said to his friend, "I know the perfect person!"

Owning the club would lead to its own chain of events, one of which was meeting the only girl I've ever met, that I knew I wanted to spend the rest of my life with, and said yes when I asked her to marry me. Sadly, I would end up scaring her away, because of that one remaining behavior issue that still haunted me, from all those years of being bullied. It took a trauma as intense as knowing I scared away the most beautiful girl, who redefined my definition of love, to cause my mind to finally start obsessively trying to figure out this last remaining issue.

After she left, there was a few months of mental hell, a trip to the hospital to get something for the stress, after it got really bad, writing this book, and a random comment from the doctor asking me if there was any history of autism in my family, for me to finally find the answers.

Hearing the doctor's question, led to me asking my mom if anyone ever suspected that I might be slightly autistic when I was younger, and to my surprise, my parents actually went to many doctors because they were pretty sure that I was. But in the early 80's, autism was only seen as either yes or no, and nothing was understood about the whole spectrum of severity; of course all the doctors they went to said no.

The only two positive things that have come from my ex leaving, is that I finally started, and finished this book. Next, between what I realized about myself from writing in detail, regarding what I experienced as a kid, and the way my mildly autistic mind will endlessly obsess, when I've done something that causes me some kind of intense trauma, it thankfully led to some key realizations.

If any one of those key events didn't happen, my life would be very different right now. If only one doctor had realized I was slightly autistic, then my parents would have told the school, and when I started my first day of kindergarten, the teacher would have known too. When she came up to me and touched my arm because I was so nervous and didn't stop playing with the toys when she asked, I'm sure I would have still completely freaked out, if she still touched my arm in that moment, but she wouldn't have grabbed me by the arm after and dragged me down to the office, kicking and screaming the whole time, thinking I just had a behavior problem. If that didn't happen, the whole school wouldn't have been looking out of the classrooms wondering what was going on, I never would have become an instant target for the bullies; most likely, none of those key events in my life would have ever happened, and I wouldn't be left with this deep loss, knowing I will always love my ex.

Now, if I ever get a chance just to be able to hang out with her enough, so she can see for herself these changes that have happened, and I get another chance with her, then everything that has happened in my life would have all been worth it.

FAR DIVORCED FROM NORMALITY

My morally questionable activities began at a fairly young age, around the time my parents divorced when I was 11 years old. When my parents split up, my dad moved only a few blocks away so that he could still be close to us, but he worked as a truck driver at the time, and was often gone anyway. My older sister and I stayed living with our mother in the house we grew up in, and as child support, our dad continued to pay the mortgage payments, to ensure that my sister and I would always have a roof over our heads. My dad was actually my mom's first boyfriend, so initially the divorce had a heavy emotional impact on her. She also had essentially no work experience, which resulted in the three of us living off of welfare, and to make matters worse, my mom was never very good at managing money.

Both of my parents were always very supportive and would do anything for my sister and I, but emotional distress has a way of causing people to do some rather irrational things at times. During this time, my mother was no exception and I was no exception either. Within the first few months of being on welfare, there was one month when my mom took the entire monthly welfare check and spent the whole amount on earrings, and cork boards to hang all her new earrings up in her bedroom. Needless to say, this left no money for important things, such as food.

During those first few years, it wasn't uncommon for the hydro or gas to be shut off due to non-payment, and sometimes, both would be shut off at the same time. Additionally, my mother would also be gone a lot, quite often for days at a time, and as a consequence, this resulted in my 13-year-old sister and my 11-year-old self, essentially left to our own accord. I understand how easy it is to do irrational things when emotionally overwhelmed, even for someone like me, who is normally a very rational person. Even if she didn't leave for days at a time, and was great at managing money, I was good with math, and knew the welfare check still wasn't enough. Because of how screwed up I was from the bullying, I'm sure that wouldn't have made much difference to how my life has turned out. Most likely, if my behavior didn't get as bad as it did, I may not have ended up in the group home or went to jail, and because I know how much those experiences helped me, I'm glad those things happened. I've never thought any less of my mom, and if I had, I would have felt like the biggest hypocrite, after how irrational I was for months after my ex left, and unlike my mom, she wasn't even close to being my first girlfriend, just the only one I was ever afraid of losing.

The house we lived in was on a double lot, with a detached two car garage, and after my dad moved out, I quickly took over the garage and turned it into my own little club house. Having this new space to hang out in, and left with very little adult supervision, my new garage quickly became the popular place to hang out for all the neighborhood kids, and I suddenly found myself experiencing a new sense of social acceptance that I had never experienced before. I say a new "sense of", because even though it felt that way, eventually I started to realize that most of these new "friends", were not good people, and so not really friends at all; pretty much all of those "friends" that I had at the time, at one point or another, eventually ended up betraying me. Many of them were quite sketchy characters, and most, at the very least, were not opposed to stealing things, even if only rarely. And so it began, my life of crime, at the young age of 11.

Being the empathetic kid that I was, I always felt bad about stealing, especially at first, but when poor at that age, with essentially no rules, and high from the fact that suddenly so many people actually wanted to hang out with me, it quickly became easy to ignore any sense of guilt I had. Much of what I stole I would end up selling, and pretty much all of that money, I would end up spending on food. There were also a lot of times when we would just steel food directly, and there were pretty much only two different ways we would do this.

During the day, our preferred tactic involved driving our bicycles in front of a gas station, which had shelves of chips and pop outside in front of the store, and we would simply grab what we could as we drove by, without ever stopping. At night, when most of the gas stations were closed, we had another easy way to steal food that wasn't usually an option during the day. About a half a block from where I lived, there was a bakery that made pita bread, and like most bakeries, they would bake their bread at night. Conveniently, there was an alley way behind the bakery, and because of how hot it gets inside, they would almost always leave the big garage style loading door open, which made it very easy to quickly run inside and grab some fresh, still puffed up pitas, directly off the conveyer belt.

Over the next few years, stealing was essentially the only type of crime I would commit. I would never, and have never robbed anyone (as in face to face). When it came to stealing other things, there were quite a few different things we would regularly do.

Behind my house, there was a rather large parking lot for one of the largest banquet halls in the city. There was also a strip of bushes and trees between my back fence and the start of the parking lot. Large events, when the parking lot was full, always presented a big enough opportunity, for us to work together as a group, generally the more of us, the better and less risky it was. Ideally, 2 or 3 of us would climb up the trees behind my back fence, which provided an ideal view of the whole parking lot, to watch for anyone walking to their car. The rest of us would climb over the fence and down into the parking lot. We'd crouch down, always stay between the two rows of parking spaces, and only ever cross the space between the rows, by staying hidden in the bushes along the fence that we would climb over. If anyone started walking towards the cars we were around, someone watching from the trees would make a loud crow sound, to warn us that someone was coming. Most of the time we would just check every car door handle, and take anything of value from any unlocked car we found.

Besides looking for unlocked cars, sometimes we'd also look for any nice aftermarket valve stem caps from the wheels, either to put on our bikes, or sell at school. At one point, someone I sold some caps to at school, asked me if I could get any hood ornaments, and so for a short period of time, we started taking them off cars as well. It was surprising how many kids in grade 8 were willing to pay for specific ornaments; so many, I actually had to make a list.

When the parking lot was full, that was usually our priority. Most of the time, there were no big events in the banquet halls and the only cars in the parking lot belonged to either the regular staff, or members of the private club aspect of the business, which were always parked too close to the building and too few cars to make it worth the risk.

Another car related scheme we often did, was something we only did at night, and one of the most common things we did if we were out stealing at night, which also involved looking for unlocked cars. This was best done with only two people, and was as simple as walking down streets, one person walking on the road, pulling each door handle, and the other person walking on the curb side checking the other door handles.

Lastly, of all the ways we'd frequently look for things to steal, and definitely what we did the most, was often a two-step process. The reason we did this the most was because it was usually the most profitable, but only worked because of the way a lot of the city is laid out. First of all, Windsor is essentially completely flat, and because of that, all of the streets create one large grid. The majority of the residential blocks, share the same basic layout, and most still have alley ways behind the houses, back from the horse and buggy days.

During the day, we'd ride our bikes up and down alley after alley, checking out people's back yards, mostly looking for nice bikes. We'd also come across garages with the big car door open, all of which faced the alley, and were often left open by people who went to do some errands during the day. Tools were the most common score, but anything of value that we could carry on our bikes would also be taken.

Our main objective was always bikes. Rarely would we ever go into a back yard and steal a bike during the day. Instead, our preferred method would be to come back at night, and most of the time the bikes would just be left in the back yard unlocked. After finding a few targets during the day, we'd meet back up that night at my place. We'd leave the big car gates to the back yard open, and one of my garage doors open as well. A minimum of one person would stay in the garage, with the lights off, and then at least two of us would leave on one bike, with the second person standing on the foot pegs on the back, while holding on to the shoulders of the person who was driving. We'd then ride to where the target was, and if the bike was still in the back yard, the person on the back would hop off, grab it from the back yard, and we would then ride back to my place. We did it this way, because if any cops saw us, it would seem like we were just riding around at night with our own bikes, instead of how suspicious it looks when one person is riding one bike, while also holding on to a second one.

Once we got back to my place, we'd drive straight into the garage. The person who stayed behind, would then quickly close the door behind us, and then turn on the lights. At this point, we'd all grab tools, and within 2 or 3 minutes, at most, we'd have the entire bike taken apart, and the serial number ground off. If we found more than one target during the day, we'd then go right back out and do the same thing again.

The parts would be split between us. Sometimes we sold parts on their own, and sometimes we'd take parts from different bikes and build a new bike and sell that, being sure to repaint the bare metal where the serial number use to be. At one point, there were enough parts, either in the garage or in the yard, to build close to 100 complete bikes.

Eventually, even my mom called the cops on me, but when the cops came during the day to question me, I simply said I found them all. Obviously, the cops knew that was bullshit. Despite how many times they asked where I found a specific bike, I always had a quick response. Because of how many bikes they questioned me about, I started saying a lot of the same places, and when they decided to questioned me about that, I even said, "Ya, we find a lot of bikes there. Maybe you guys should keep an eye on that area, you might see who keeps leaving them there." Without any serial numbers, there was no way for them to identify any of them as stolen, and to the shock and dismay of my mother, after that bit of attitude I gave them, they left empty handed.

During all these adrenaline inducing crime sprees, at some point a few of my friends and I started enjoying the adrenaline rush so much, sometimes, when we were just bored late at night, instead of stealing, we'd just drive our bikes a few blocks away to a major intersection and wait. When a police car drove by, we'd start yelling at the police, calling them pigs or whatever we could just to get them to chase us. Once the chase began, we'd all take off in different directions, so at the very worst, only one of us could ever get caught. Thankfully I never got caught, because one time, when they caught one of my friends in an alley, they took out a phone book, put it against his stomach and hit him a bunch of times with their billy-clubs. You would think that would have discouraged us from doing that any more, but if anything, it just pissed my buddy off, and made the thrill of doing it again that much more enticing.

All these events took place with in about a year and a half after the divorce. After about the first year of such chaos, my mom started making sure she was home a lot more often, and started trying to enforce rules upon us once again. However, after running completely wild for that long, I really had very little respect for my mom's authority, and when she would attempt to ground me from leaving the house, I'd simply be like, "Ya, ok. I'm going for a bike ride, be back later." …then off I'd go. As long as she was home, she was at least able to prevent me and my sketchy friends from hanging out in the garage, which definitely had an impact on how often we would go out stealing things, but even though we were on welfare, she wasn't able to stay home all the time.

Years before the divorce, when I was around 7, my dad took my sister and I to a nearby nature reserve to go biking, and while we were there, we found an injured duck. My dad knew of a non-profit wildlife rescue and rehabilitation group, that the wife of one of his co-workers was involved in, so we took the duck home and contacted the group. Shortly after this, my mom started volunteering for the group as well. Initially, she started fostering a single litter of baby squirrels, then a few more, and in no time at all, our house turned into quite the wildlife zoo, then eventually, she became heavily involved with the group.

Starting from just a few baby squirrels, to being chair-person on the board of directors. Over the 13 years or so that she was with the group, at one point or another, she held just about every position there was. This was a great experience to have while growing up, and for many years, I was also very active in the group. In grade 6, I fostered a litter of baby raccoons, but before I was allowed to, my mom made it very clear that they would be completely my responsibility. Even at that young age, I was quite fearless of being bitten, and because of my small size, I was often recruited to get animals out of places, such as crawl spaces under a house, up trees, or in attics. Because of my mom's responsibilities with the group, this was one of the main reasons why she was not able to stay home as often as she likely wanted to.

Ultimately, the lack of respect I had for my mom's authority, came to a point that caused my mom to take drastic action. One particular time when I was grounded, I did my usual, "See you later mom, I'm going with dad to visit family in the states." When I got home late at night, around 2 A.M, or so, I went up to my bedroom, and discovered all of my stuff was gone. I checked in the basement, in a room I had with a bunch of model trains set up, and even looked out in the garage, but my stuff was nowhere to be found. A few minutes later, as I was standing there, literally scratching my head, wondering where my things were at, I saw my dad backing his truck up into the drive way, with all my things in the back. As it turned out, while I was away with him, my mom packed up all my stuff, and dumped it on his front lawn; needless to say, I was immediately pissed!

I grabbed the first thing I saw, which was a pint sized paint can, went straight upstairs, and threw it at my mom's ass while she was sleeping. Needless to say, this was definitely a morally wrong thing to do, and I did end up regretting it, because of how much I love my mom, and I knew it was an impulsive thing done out of anger. However, looking back at it now, it's not quite something I'd call regret, per se, because of the positive way it ended up affecting my life, and what ended up happening as a result.

Two days later, a couple of detectives showed up at my place and asked me about the paint can incident. After telling them the truth, they "asked" me if I would be willing to go with them to the hospital, to talk with a doctor who wanted to ask me a few questions. They told me it would only be a few hours and I had a strong feeling if I said no, that they would have insisted, so I reluctantly agreed. After talking with a doctor about what happened, I was told they were going to keep me overnight, and at this point it was made clear that I had no choice. So the few hours turned into 24 hours, and then the 24 hours turned in to "a few days", but in the end, I was in the psych ward for a full month, after which I was transferred to a group home for other problematic kids. When I got to the group home, I was told I'd be there a month, but ultimately, I was in the group home for about a year and a half.

It's not that my mom just dropped her problems off to someone else, or anything like that. Clearly some kind of intervention was needed, considering how out of control I was, and she was actually very involved and supportive the whole time I was there. Within the first two months of being at the group home, and showing no interest in doing any school work in the on sight school they had, my unit manager asked me if they allowed me to go back to my previous high school during the day, would I agree to actually doing my school work, which of course I agreed to. At least this gave me some freedom, and as promised, I did do my school work.

At this point in my life, when I first went to the hospital, I was 14, and in my first semester of grade 9. Even though it was clear to everyone that I was very intelligent and loved to learn, I'd never really done very well in school. Starting as early as kindergarten, I was always having issues in school. I was definitely very A.D.D. but was not hyperactive, so despite all the counselors I'd seen over the years, surprisingly, no one ever realized this about me. I usually had no problems paying attention to lessons in class, but when it came to actually doing work on my own, either in school or at home, I rarely ever did any. I can't remember how many times my mom would sit down with me at our dining room table for hours, trying to get me to at least start writing even a single thing. It wasn't even that I didn't want to do it, but rather, it felt like I couldn't do it. I never understood why, all I remember is feeling immense pressure, which was completely overwhelming, and would cause me to disconnect from the world around me, only to get lost inside of my own thoughts.

I pretty much failed every class except gym, up until grade 8, but surprisingly was never held back any years. Teachers would often notice I wasn't looking at the chalk board while lessons would be taught, but when they would tell me to look upfront and pay attention, I'd usually tell them that I was paying attention, since I knew I was. But when they would ask me a question in front of the class about what was being taught, I'd get that same overwhelming feeling, and my eyes would lose focus on any one thing, and all I could see with my peripheral vision, was the whole class looking at me simultaneously. This would always prevent me from being able to say anything, even though I usually knew the answer. After a lesson, when a teacher would take me aside to ask me questions about it, I'd usually be able to answer then. I've always assumed this is why I was never held back, since they realized I paid attention and understood enough to pass, despite the almost complete lack of any written work handed in.

My sister was two grades ahead of me, and rather ironically, I was often very interested in what she had to do for homework, and I'd often help with her math homework, even though I wouldn't even do my own. Additionally, I was almost always late, even though we lived a block away from the school. Because I was getting bullied almost daily starting in kindergarten, understandably I didn't want to be at school, and because of the social issues I had, I was often getting suspended. I absolutely hated when random people unexpectedly touched or grabbed me, and would completely freak out when someone did. This made everyone think that I simply had a problem with my temper, but as I would only find out recently, that wasn't at all what the issue was. The first time I got suspended was in grade 1, and it only went downhill from there.

A GROUP HOME AND NEW DIRECTIONS

I was not much different when I started high school, but clearly no high school is going to tolerate any student who was late almost every day, and didn't do any of the assignments. Thankfully, when I started at a new school, at least I was no longer being bullied, but I did still get teased sometimes. The main issues I had was with attendance, and not doing the work, rather than any behavioral issues as well. I only lasted at a normal high school for about a month, but because I showed promise, and wasn't having any other behavior problems, I was given the option to either be expelled, or transferred to a new experimental high school program the school board had called Directions. It was a small pilot project that accepted only 21 kids from the whole city, and had only two teachers, and a child and youth worker for staff. After meeting with the 3 of them, I was accepted into the program, and because the school work was done at our own pace, I actually did surprisingly well.

    To give you a better idea of how many problems I had in school up until grade 8, after being at the new school for a few months, and getting to know the two teachers and youth worker, at one point during a lunch break, while I was casually chatting with the staff, they told me something that was surprising even to me. They mentioned that before I first came for the interview, they were sent my entire school file, and that of all of the files they had ever seen, they had never seen one so thick. They even showed it to me, and it was easily 4-5 inches thick. After reading it, all three of them imagined I'd be some huge kid with a really bad attitude, and before meeting me, didn't think they would actually accept me into the program. When they first met me, they were shocked that I was this skinny kid, and one of the shortest kids, even in the normal high school I was at. They were even more shocked at how polite and innocent looking I was.

By the time I was first sent to the hospital, I had only been at the new school for a few weeks, and it was clear I was enjoying the new school. So when I suddenly disappeared, because no one had told them why I stopped coming to class, they actually thought I might have died in an accident or something. When they finally found out that I had been sent to the group home, to my surprise, they actually came and visited me, despite the fact that I had only been going to the school for a couple of weeks. It had only been about a month and a half when they came to see me in the group home, but the moment they saw me walking towards the visiting room, all three of them were shocked at how much I had grown in that short period of time; I hadn't even realized I grew at all. Clearly being fed properly and having enough to eat, had a big impact, because I actually grew at least a foot taller in only a month and a half; to this day, I still have vertical stretch marks just below my hips from that rapid growth spurt. I also slowly started noticing it was becoming more and more easy for me to concentrate on my school work, and as a result, for the first time in my life, I actually started doing very well in school.

Despite all of the criminal issues that I had up to that point in my life, surprisingly, alcohol and drugs were things I had never tried yet, but like most kids in the program, I did smoke cigarettes regularly. The whole topic of drugs, alcohol and addiction, wasn't even a conversation I'd ever had with anyone or even thought about before; the first time I did, left a lasting impression that would eventually help shape my views on addiction that I still have to this very day.

Initially, when a group of recovering addicts from a local A.A. center came into the school, to talk about drug and alcohol addiction, I actually had no interest in listening to them. Because it was an issue that did not at all concern me, I was annoyed I was being forced to listen to them instead of being allowed to do my school work. So I quietly sat there in class, reluctantly listening, and as the conversation progressed, I slowly became more and more annoyed that I was being forced to listen to things, which sounded ridiculous to me. The fact that pretty much all the other kids actually seemed to agree, and relate to everything being said, was even more annoying.

Eventually, as I quietly sat there, the teacher clearly noticed something was on my mind, and ended up dragging me into the conversation by saying, "Adam, it looks like something is on your mind. Would you mind sharing it with everyone here?" Realizing how confrontational my thoughts would be, I initially declined, but he politely insisted, and because I liked the teacher, out of respect, I reluctantly shared my thoughts with the room.

    The main issue I disagreed with, had to do with the way they were talking about addiction, and how no one chooses to be an addict. The concept that they had no choice to drink, or do drugs, was completely ridiculous to me. After sharing that view with everyone, the first thing someone said was, "Well clearly you only think that because you've never been addicted to anything." But that didn't make any sense either, so I explained, "That has nothing to do with it. It just doesn't make sense. No one is forcing anyone to put something in their mouth; it's obviously something a person chooses to do, because they want to." So then someone asked, if I had ever tried drugs or alcohol. After I told them "No, I haven't", one of my classmates pointed out the fact that I smoke cigarettes. Then someone said, "Oh, well that's not good for you, so why don't you quit?" So I told them, "Because I don't want to." Then someone said, "So you're addicted then." At that point, I kind of shook my head, because it seemed like they didn't hear what I just said, so I replied, "What? Did you not hear what I just said? I choose to smoke, because I like smoking!" But yet again, someone dismissed what I said by saying, "That means you are addicted. If you were not addicted, you'd be able to stop." At that point, the same person asked everyone to raise their hands if they smoke. Considering this wasn't a normal high school, and that all 21 of us were delinquents, an abnormally high percentage of us smoked. Next, when he asked how many of them would like to quit, all of the same people put their hands back up. Finally, one of my class mates said in a very, matter-of-fact kind of tone, "You're obviously addicted. If you weren't addicted, you'd prove it by throwing your pack of smokes in the garbage right now." At this point, seeing that my logic was going nowhere, I paused, and thought for a moment.

    Realizing there was an important point to be made here, I made a choice. So I pulled out my pack of smokes, held it up to the class, and told everyone, "Fine then, I'll prove it. I'll quit for exactly one month." Then turned and threw my pack of smokes into the trash. But still, someone laughed and dismissively said, "Oh, it's probably almost empty. You'll just get a new pack later, and we'll see you smoking again by tomorrow." It wasn't empty though, and I told them, "Actually, I just bought that pack this morning, there's only two missing." At that point, everyone looked at me for a moment, clearly wondering if I was being honest. After a moment, two of the male students looked at each other, and then suddenly jumped up and ran across the room, each trying to get the pack before the other. And so for the next month, I didn't have a single smoke, not at school, not at all.

Finally, 32 days later (deciding to emphasize the point by using a full 31-day month), I did something I normally wouldn't do, and went to school two buses before the bus I usually took, which got me to school consistently 5 minutes late. I bought a pack of smokes on the way, but waited until I got to school before opening them. As I walked towards the school, there were already a few students outside smoking, who all started looking at me, wondering who was walking up. As I got closer, I could hear them talking, followed by surprised reactions, and then finally when I walked up next to them, someone asked, "What the heck are you doing here so early?" I just smiled and said, "Oh, I just felt like coming in early." I then waited a moment for their attention to go back to each other, and then very purposefully, pulled out my new, unopened pack of smokes, slowly unwrapped them, took out a smoke, put it in my mouth, and despite having a lighter in my pocket, I then leaned in towards the group and asked, "Anyone got a light?"

After not seeing me outside smoking for a month, they all looked at me, paused for a moment with confused looks on their faces, and then one of them said, "What? Didn't you quit?" So I reminded them, "Yes I did. I said I would quit for a month, and it's been a month, so now I'm making the choice to smoke again, because I like smoking." There was then an odd moment of silence that was broken when one of the girls said, "Stupid. So stupid. You quit!" Now usually that girl had always been polite towards me, so I was a bit surprised by her reaction, and because of my history with being picked on, I stood there for a moment wondering if she was actually calling me stupid, or if it was just a figure of speech. While I was contemplating that, one of the other girls suddenly exclaimed, "Fuck this shit!" Then tossed away her smoke and walked inside the school. That girl also had always been nice to me, but now I was standing there thinking I somehow offended her too. Not long after, the other students finished their smokes and then walked inside as well. Stunned, I just stood there, wondering what had just happened!?

When I first decided to prove that point to everyone, I didn't have any expectations at all; it was really just a matter of principle and because of the way I had been treated by others in school most of my life, there was also a strong element of self-respect that had motivated me as well. After the reactions from the other students when the A.A. people came to the school, I definitely didn't think my demonstration would have any kind of influence on anyone, so I was quite surprised when I later found out why the one girl said "Fuck this shit!" At first I thought she meant it towards me, like she was also calling me stupid, but it turned out she was talking about smoking, and decided to quit right then and there. As other students heard that I started smoking again, and learned that the one girl decided to quit, quite a number of other students also made the choice to quit smoking. For a while, it even turned into a bit of a friendly competition between some of them. Unsurprisingly, most eventually started smoking again, but there was at least one who stopped at least for as long as we were in school together. I'd never realized how much a single choice one person makes could affect so many others; the entire situation was extremely profound and would leave a lasting impact on me.

As the months went by, and I was in the group home longer, eventually I completely stopped talking to almost every single one of my old "friends", and with that, most of my criminal activities stopped as well. The smoking situation from school also continued to linger in my mind. I couldn't stop thinking about how great of a feeling it was to have had a positive effect on other people the way I did, which was such a contrast to the latent guilt I was accustomed to feeling, when stealing so much in the past.

The year and a half I spent in the group home, wasn't without issues. After having been completely wild and following no rules leading up to the group home, suddenly having very strict rules imposed upon me, definitely took some adjustment. I also started feeling very socially isolated again, and eventually I took off from the group home and went on the run. Because I knew I didn't feel good about stealing, especially all the bikes I stole, the only friends I continued to hang out with were people I didn't have an extensive criminal history with, and it was with these few friends, where I often found sanctuary during the times I was on the run. But just because I felt really bad for stealing bikes, doesn't mean my days of stealing were over. Like before, and even though it was morally questionable, I never really felt bad about stealing food, or taking what change I could find from unlocked cars, since what little money I did get this way, was always spent completely on food, and so this is something I continued to do during the times when I was on the run. I always knew how expensive it would be to replace a broken window on a car, and the guilt I knew I would feel if I did something like that, just for a bit of change, was always enough to discourage me from doing any such thing.

Even though I was never a very revengeful person, like most things in life, there are usually some exceptions to every "rule". One such exception, related to someone I had been friends with since I first moved into the neighborhood, when I was 3, and for the longest time, I considered him to be my best friend. Even though we were not at all poor while my parents were still together, his dad had a unionized job at a GM car factory, and financially were definitely a lot more well-off. They had a pool, a cottage, and always had the coolest new things as soon as they came out, but despite this, I still remember the first time he stole something from me.

It was only a single "micro-machine" toy car, no bigger than an inch long, and was a hot new fad at the time. He and his two brothers had a box full of them, but I only had two that were given to me by a cousin of mine. He must have taken it when he brought his cars to my place to play with them together. He knew I was looking everywhere for it, because I even asked him to check his box to see if he "accidentally" took it when he brought his home. He told me it wasn't in there, and I even asked him to check again when I couldn't find it in my room, but he still told me it wasn't with his. Then one day, weeks or months later, while I was at his house playing, I saw it in their collection. He tried telling me they recently got that one, but I knew it was mine because of a specific scratch that was on it. He still tried to deny it was mine, but then tried to make himself look good by "giving" it to me, "since they had so many anyway."

This incident caused me to start questioning something else that had happened, sometime within the previous year, involving a new orange ball of mine that got lost while playing with it together in the park. While at the park, he suggested we play a game, which involved one of us turning around with our eyes closed, the other burying the ball in the sand pit, and then the other one, who had their eyes closed would then try to find the ball. After doing this to each other a number of times, when it was my turn to try to find the ball, despite digging essentially everywhere in the sand pit, ultimately, I was never able to find it. At the time, it had never occurred to me that he took it, but after the micro-machine incident, I started to think maybe he had. Then one day, maybe a year or two after he stole the toy car, I ended up seeing a beat up orange ball in his yard, that his dog had been playing with. I never said anything, but I was pretty sure it was the same orange ball.

Because I didn't really have very many friends, we still continued to be "friends" for many more years, and was one of the friends that were often involved when we started stealing, although most of the time he'd just help keep a look out for people and rarely ever stole things himself. Eventually, during the summer before I went to the group home, either him or another kid from the neighborhood stole a really nice bike that I had stolen by myself, and was such a nice bike, I decided to keep it together and only paint it a different color. I suspected he was involved, so when I knew no one was home at his place, I went looking in his yard, and sure enough, I found it. Shortly after I took it back, someone called the cops, and because I had told my friends where I stole it from, the cops took it and returned it to the owner. Surprisingly, I never got charged, but between that and the other times he stole from me, I was mad enough to actually hold a grudge against him and would eventually get my revenge.

    I finally got even with him, during one of the times when I was on the run from the group home. I knew he was away with his whole family, because both their car and camping trailer were gone. At the time, he had a very small, racing style, mini motorcycle. It wasn't big enough to drive on a highway, and the seat was only about 2 feet above the ground, but it was road legal, so unlike a home built mini bike, I knew I'd be able to drive it around for a while, without some random person calling the police, to report a kid driving around on an illegal motor bike. So that one night, I broke into his shed and stole it. I had no doubt at all he would know it was me, since not very many people knew where he hid the key. I only drove the bike around for about a week or two, because I didn't want to get caught by the police, but I knew from the beginning it would only be a short term thing. After getting chased by the police one night, I knew it was time to get rid of it. But because of the motivation for stealing it in the first place, instead of simply pushing it into a ditch, where it most likely would be found, and eventually returned to him, I spent the next day taking the whole bike apart, then scattered the parts all over the place. This was my way of saying to him, "Fuck you!" for all those years of being such a shitty friend to me.

    Even though it was clearly a crime, from a moral point of view, I've never felt bad about it at all. I'm not saying it was right, but I definitely don't feel it was wrong. Although I'd never heard the word karma before, I still had an understanding of the concept because of a term my mom would often say, any time I got hurt doing something I knew I wasn't supposed to be doing; "A God a getch ya" is what she'd say.

    During another time when I was on the run from the group home, was the first time I ever had any suicidal thoughts over something I had done. And even though looking back at it now, I don't feel I did anything morally wrong, because it was just an instinctual response to physical pain, but at the time, I felt tremendous guilt about what had happened. After taking off from the group home once again, I went straight home to get a few things before I went to a friend's place to stay.

    When I got home, I patiently waited in the park across the street for my mom to leave. Surprisingly, I didn't need to wait long. After I saw my mom leave, I went to the house to get my things. I was only inside a few minutes, when I saw some car lights through the window. I looked out to see my mom's truck pull into the driveway, followed by a police car. I ended up hiding in the attic, and figured that would be the last place she'd ever think to look. After waiting a while once I saw the police had left, eventually I came out of the attic and went downstairs. Needless to say my mom was shocked, but to my surprise, she did something she had never done before and tried to prevent me from leaving. Neither of my parents ever had any drug or alcohol problems, which is why the whole concept of addiction was quite new to me, when it came up at school, so I never realized what is quite obvious now. My mom was very addicted to food, and at the time, she weighed over 300 lbs. Compared to my 120lb self, when wet, I definitely knew I couldn't push my way past her. Up until this point in my life, my mom had never laid a hand on me or even tried to physically restrain me, but I could tell just from the look in her eyes that she was completely prepared to do that. I knew that my only advantage was speed, and so I kept running back and forth around the house, trying to open up a clear path to either one of the doors. As I was trying to escape, she ended up getting a hold of me and wrestled me to the ground, but because she was holding on to me, there was no way for her to call the police, and so we ended up struggling on the floor for a while.

Eventually, I ended up tiring her out enough to be able to slip free, but as I went to take off, I suddenly felt this intense pain from her nails digging into my waist, as she grabbed a hold of my belt. Her nails dug into me deep enough, to end up leaving some scars that took a while before finally fading away. Despite the fact I had never hit either of my parents ever before, the pain was intense enough, to cause me to instinctually turn around quickly, and swing at the source of the pain; not realizing that it was my mother who I would end up hitting. After I hit her, and she fell to the ground, I was in such a state of shock and panic, that I took off running, and ran like I had never even ran from the cops before.

Because of the shock and guilt that I felt over what had just happened, instead of running to a friend's place like I had planned, I ran where no one would find me. After running as fast as I could for as long as I could, eventually I stopped some place no one would see me, took a break, and then slowly walked around for hours. For the most part, I walked along some train tracks that I knew led from my place all the way to the group home. Windsor actually has a lot of train tracks going all over the city, and some even lead into a tunnel that goes under the river and into Detroit. I knew where all the tracks went very well, from years of hitching rides on trains and using it as my own private expressway to get all over the place in the city. So I just walked around aimlessly, for hours, during this cold and rainy night, which is why I wanted to go home and get clothes in the first place.

I came up to the entrance to the train tunnel, seriously considering running away to Detroit, but I knew I couldn't just show up at any of my cousins' places. So instead I climbed up onto a very high bridge, for some other tracks, that went over the tracks that led into the tunnel. I must have sat on the edge of that bridge with my feet hanging off for hours, crying like I never had before, seriously thinking about jumping off, which was easily high enough to have killed me. At the time, I wasn't sure if it was high enough, and that was part of what stopped me from jumping. Eventually, I got up and started walking again, but the thoughts of killing myself didn't end, nor did the intense sorrow I felt. As I walked, the thoughts of suicide continued along with the guilt. Instead of jumping, my thoughts turned to a throwing knife I had strapped to my leg.

I walked all the way along the tracks and ended up next to the group home. I sat there for couple hours, sitting on one track, staring off into infinity while holding the knife in my hand thinking about the best way to shove it into my body. Finally, after all those hours outside, soaking wet and colder than I had ever been before, I realized I couldn't kill myself and decided to turn myself into the group home. After changing into dry clothes and laying down in bed, I'm not sure how long I was there before the police came to arrest me, for assaulting my mother, and I still felt just as cold when the cops came. This just made that horrible night even worse, because I knew how cold the holding cells were in the jail, but despite how much I pleaded my case to the police, and tried explaining the unintentional nature of what had happened, they still arrested me, brought me to the police station, and charged me with assault.

When I had to go to court, I'll never forget how afraid I was, because I already had a number of past convictions for stealing, which I had only ever received probation for. I knew my mom was asking for some jail time, but the lawyer I had was always good at presenting the whole "child of a broken home" case, and together with my most innocent of looks, to my surprise, I once again got only probation.

I'm not sure how long it took for my mom to finally forgive me, but that moment was a definite turning point, and after a while of doing really well in the group home, eventually she started talking to me again, and even started allowing me to come home on the weekends. When things became really good, I was finally discharged from the group home during the summer, about 6 months before my 16th birthday.

When the following school year started, I continued to attend the alternative school I was at, and over the next school year, things at home and at school, for the most part, went really well. During this time, my mom started renting out one of the rooms in our house to a friend and her boyfriend. At first we all got along quite well, but eventually some friction started to develop, mostly relating to the use of the new computer we had, which I quickly became quite addicted to.

During this time, AOL started sending out the countless CD's they would send everywhere for a free month of internet access, but the only catch, was that it required a credit card to use. Initially, I was able to activate the free trails, using a credit card generator program I got from a hacker friend, but eventually that stopped working, and I found myself left with this new addiction to the internet. My mom didn't have a credit card, but her friend who was staying with us did. I thought about asking, but I always felt too anxious to ask, so of course, I just went into her purse and copied down her credit card details to get on to the internet without anyone knowing. Because I used a real credit card this time, and forgot to cancel the free trial before the month ended, I was eventually caught, when the first bill showed up on her card. This all happened near the end of the following school year, when I was 16, and I quickly found myself being kicked out of my mom's house.

At the time, my sister was living with my dad, in the only extra bedroom of his apartment, so I had no other choice but to go live in the Salvation Army's men's shelter downtown. I lived there for a number of months, but then towards the end of that school year, a friend of mine, who was 17, and had a really well paying co-op job working at a machine shop, wanted to get an apartment. Under the assumption I'd be able to get welfare, while I tried to find a job, him and I found a place and moved in together at the beginning of June of that year.

THE CHANGING OF RESIDENCES

During the first weekend after moving in, all with his money, we went to the beer store with some fake I.D.'s we had hitched hiked to Toronto to get. He looked quite old for his age, so we ended up successfully getting 9 cases of beer to throw our first house warming party. Needless to say that summer turned into quite a mess. I'd also started smoking weed the year before, and also tried LSD for the first time that summer.

As the days went by, and things got more and more crazy, tension between my friend and I started to develop after my welfare application was denied, because of what my mom had told the welfare office when they called. Rather than telling them that I was kicked out and not allowed to live there, which was in fact the truth, instead she told them that I was allowed to live there if I followed the rules, despite the fact that she wouldn't actually allow me to come back to live there, even if I promised to follow the rules. Technicalities aside, I was left with no job, no money, and this quickly caused a lot of problems with my friend who was paying all the bills.

Towards the end of the summer, the fake I.D.'s eventually stopped working, and drugs were becoming hard to find, but we did find ourselves with a kitchen filled with cases of empty beer bottles, since my roommate wanted to keep them as a symbol of how much we partied that summer. Then one day, after talking to the "cool" superintendent for our building, we were able to exchange the empty cases of beer, for random pharmaceutical pills that he had. To this day I have no clue what any of them were, but we gobbled them down anyway like they were candy from some stranger we got on Halloween.

Within a few hours, we were completely messed up out of our minds, high in a way I'd never been before, or since, when I found myself home alone for a period of time, and feeling very depressed from all of the tension between my friend and I. We also had a bunch of black lights in our apartment, and I had discovered one day, when I accidentally hurt myself, that blood looks quite interesting under a black light. Although I wasn't feeling at all suicidal, I was still depressed, and in that state of mind, for whatever reason, I decided to take a box cutter that was on the shelf next to me, and started poking small cuts on my wrist, just because I wanted to see the blood under the black light. I eventually got bored of this, and fell asleep with the knife still in my hand, and blood on my wrist.

I was awoken some time later, when my roommate came home with another friend. When he saw me, he kind of turned to the other friend and said, "Look at Mr. Suicidal over there." Everything was so foggy from the pills we had taken, I don't even remember how it started, but eventually we got into a shoving match and after that short confrontation ended, I found myself still holding the knife. As I walked towards the door to leave, without really thinking about it, I rested my arm on a low shelf by the door and said, "That's not suicidal; THIS, is suicidal!", and then stabbed the knife directly into my wrist, so hard, that the tip came through the other side. Dazed, and very confused, I pulled the knife out of my wrist, and slowly walked towards the exit of the apartment building.

When I got downstairs to go outside, as I passed the superintendent's apartment, he had obviously heard the commotion, because he was standing in the hall looking at me walking towards him. When I got down the stairs, he asked, "What the heck just happened?" I kind of looked at him in that dazed state I was in, raised my hands slightly next to me and shrugged my shoulders, as I just kind of muttered, "I donno". When he saw the knife, he asked me if he could have it, which I calmly gave him, and few minutes later, an ambulance arrived to bring me to the hospital. By some surprise, thankfully I didn't cut anything serious, despite the blade going all the way through my wrist.

As the doctor stitched me up, between seeing that I was obviously high on something, and me telling him what happened, it was enough to convince him that I really wasn't suicidal. When I walked out of the emergency room, and outside into the parking lot, I was greeted by two *very* unhappy parents, and it was the first time I had seen the two of them together in years.

What happened next is very unclear, but for someone like myself, who has very clear and continuous memories going back to as early as three, not remembering at all, is a very unsettling experience. The last thing I remember from that night was walking away from my two arguing parents, and onto the street. To this day, I have absolutely no idea where I went from there.

My next memory is from a day or so later, of driving my bike and wiping out after I drove onto some gravel. Then again, no more memory at all until a very fuzzy conversation with my parents that turned into me having no choice but to go live with my dad. I remember sleeping for what seemed like forever, until when I finally awoke, and found myself now living with my dad.

With the next school year not far away, and being too old to continue to attend the alternative high school, I was doing so well at, I was left with no choice but to return to a normal high school. I knew I didn't want to attend the high school that was closest to my house. Instead, I wanted to attend a technical oriented school that had a machine shop, and welding classes, that my district high school didn't have. Being that it wasn't my district school, it took a bit of convincing to be accepted, but with the support of the staff from the alternative school I was at the previous year, I was eventually accepted on a probationary status.

However, despite how well I did at the alternative school, my old bad habits of being frequently late in the morning, and not doing my homework, were still things I struggled with. Once again, I was on the verge of being expelled. The final moment that eventually led to me being expelled, involved an incident in my welding class, involving me trying to make a grappling hook.

"A CAPER WITH A PLOT LIKE A MOVIE"

The story as to why I wanted to make a grappling hook, involved one of those decisions that would end up forever changing my life, and this book would never have been written, if it wasn't for this choice that I made.

After the insanity of what happened during the prior months of the summer before, the friendship with my old roommate was beyond repair. I found myself hanging out with a mostly new group of friends, that I had met through one of my old female friends I was still in contact with. Her boyfriend was also into computers and after we first met, the two of us quickly became best of friends.

While sleeping over at his place one night, after watching a movie that involved a high tech bank robbery, for whatever reason, as a joke, I said to him, "Do you know how easy your school would be to break into?" To my astonishment, he turned to me with a surprised look and said, "You know, I was just thinking the exact same thing!" We then, in a not at all serious way, started talking about how we could do it, "if" we were to, as we played a game of chess. What initially started out as a playful mental exercise, soon turned into serious plans as we started realizing how easy it would be to do.

The design of his school was such, that the first floor, which is the only floor that had motion sensors for the alarm system, was a half a floor above ground, and the entire building was three and a half stories all the way around. So initially, we thought about using a grappling hook to somehow throw to the top of the building, but after I got expelled for trying to make one in school, and us also realizing that it was impossible for us to be able to ever throw it up that high, we eventually developed a new plan, that would work because of another design feature of the building. The building had an unusual, castle like layout to it, parts of which formed some narrow spaces, where the outside walls came close enough to each other to allow us to shimmy up, and reach a second floor window, which was hidden from the road. This window became our entrance point, and we thoroughly developed a very detailed plan. We had radios to communicate with a driver outside, who would also keep watch for any police, and practiced way to talk over the radios, in code, that would only seem weird to anyone who may hear the conversation on a scanner. We had a backpack oxygen/propane cutting torch, to "quietly" cut through the window, instead of breaking it, and making a loud distinct noise. We had cordless drills, and a whole lot of large hockey bags. So with a plan in hand, we set a date during the two week Christmas break, to hopefully make it harder for the police to know when the break-in happened; then we waited for the day to come.

When the day finally came, we went, shimmied up the wall, and I took out the torch to cut the window out. Moments after the flame touched the glass, the most unexpected thing happen, when the window suddenly exploded and sent glass flying directly at us. I immediately understood why, and felt I should have anticipated that happening; the moment the flame cut though the outer window, the space between the two panes of glass, instantly became so hot, it caused the outer window to explode towards us, and the inner window into the class room, and ended up being much louder than breaking the window would have been; thankfully I managed to close my eyes, just before the glass hit me. After the window was gone, we went into the class room. A few minutes later, we heard a coded message from the driver outside, that indicated the police were driving around. Because the window couldn't actually be seen from the road, eventually the police left, and we quickly abandoned our attempt. But of course, the story doesn't end here!

The next day, my buddy and I took a walk by the school, to see if anyone had noticed. To our surprise, after having a chance encounter and short conversation with one of my friend's teachers, and seeing nothing unusual, we realized that we could go back again that night and make another attempt. This time, because the window was already broken, we were able to quickly and quietly get back into the school. Once inside, we proceeded to disassemble 44 computer towers between two computer rooms. Due to the logistics, we only took the valuable parts from inside the computers, such as the mother boards, hard drives and accessory cards. We then packed up the parts, carefully lowered the bags out the window with rope, loaded up the car, and got away with our score; over the next couple months, we eventually sold everything.

Now, this is one of the rare things I have done, while certainly a wrong thing to do, and I definitely would not ever do anything like that again, it still has always been something I find hard to feel bad about, at least from an empathetic point of view. Partly because we didn't steal anything from an individual, or any small business, it was really just the insurance company who lost money. No one really got hurt, and I'm sure the insurance company didn't miss the money either. We also knew that the teachers were actually happy about it, because they ended up getting all brand new, much nicer computers, and for the same reason, the students were happy as well. …at least that's what we told ourselves.

Since my friend went to the school, and was also very close with the computer teachers, and like me, was a most innocent looking kid, that no one would ever suspect of being involved with something like that, he was actually able to find out a lot of detailed information, regarding what they knew, again, so we thought. Details such as, the school and police thinking the theft happened during a basketball tournament, which took place during the Christmas break. They thought the window was broken from the inside, due to the way the heat from the torch, unexpectedly caused the window to explode in both directions, and since that room was for drama classes, the raised floor of the mini stage, which was on the other side of the window, was slightly higher than the bottom of the window frame, so we swept most of the glass out the window, just because it was really slippery. Due to that incorrect assumption, the school didn't upgrade their alarm system, and instead only installed a camera that pointed at the two computer rooms.

After selling all the parts from the first heist, and no longer having money all the time, when the school got all brand new computers, I got greedy and decided to go back during the March break. One difference though, was that the window we went into the first time, was replaced with a thick aluminum plate, which meant a slightly new plan was needed. This time, my friend decided he didn't want to go into the building, so I decided to go in alone. He was still involved, but instead decided to wait in the car with the driver, and only helped to carry the bags to the car, once I lowered them outside.

This time, to get into the building, required that I shimmy up three and a half stories, all the way up to the top of the building. When I got onto the very top, I had to reach for a slightly higher ledge, that was about six and a half feet higher. Because it was just an overhanging ledge, there was no wall for me to push my feet against. Being weighed down with a 50-foot rope, tools, and a bag full of bags, as I reached for the very top ledge, I actually dislocated my shoulder from an old injury I had! That still didn't stop me, I just put my shoulder back in place, took a moment to relax, and eventually lifted myself to the top. I then went over to the edge of a courtyard, and after lowering the bag of supplies down, I looped the rope around a ventilation pipe for the plumbing system, tossed the two ends of the rope down into the court yard, slowly scaled down two stories, then simply pulled on one of the lengths of rope to get it down. Next, I simply slid open one of the hallway windows, which my friend made sure to unlatch the Friday before the March break, and quietly entered the building. No sign of forced entry, and the police never did figure out how I got into the building that time. Once in the hall, I was able to go up behind the camera, and simply cut the wire, before going about taking the computers apart. This time, because I was alone, I was only able to take apart 26 computers. After doing so, I went to a class room that was behind the building, where no one from the street could see very well. Once I lowered the bags out, then using the same technique of looping the rope around the leg of a desk, I climbed outside, leaving the window open only wide enough for the rope, lowered myself to the ground, and then pulled the rope down. Again, we loaded up the car, brought the stuff to friend's place, and then we both went home to bed; once again getting away with the score.

Admittedly, at the time I was rather disappointed that my friend decided not to go in, a few days before the second round, because of a part of that original plan we came up with. When we were planning to go in together, we were going to bring his camcorder, tap into the wire of the camera facing the computer rooms and record the hallway. While we waited, we were going to take off one of the sky-lights for the library, which was under the court yard, lower down with the rope, and take a rather expensive main-frame computer. After, we would have played the recording of the hallway from the camcorder, and then cut the camera feed, so when they would look at the recording later, they simply would have seen just the hallway. Sure, that would have served no practical purpose, but we saw it done in the bank robbery movie that inspired the first break-in, and I was already good enough with electronics at the time to know how easily that could have been done; we figured it would be an amusing homage to the movie.

I was awoken by a call from my friend, only to find out that the police had just left his place, and questioned him about the theft. When he called, he "casually" mentioned the police had just left, and he was standing there with his mom. He was only able to say, "uh huh" and "nuh uh", which sound very similar, and limited me to asking just yes and no questions.

Because of that, I came to the incorrect conclusion, that the police knew where the stuff was being stored.

I got on my bike, and rushed over to my friend's house where the computer parts were stashed, to quickly get them out of her basement, so she didn't get in trouble. To my delight, the cops hadn't been there yet, which as I later found out, was because I misunderstood, and in fact, the police had no idea where the parts were being stored. But I didn't know that, so I left with the parts anyway. At this point, the logical thing to do, would have been to go ditch the parts in a pond nearby, but remember, it was greed that motivated going back in the first place, and greed once again motivated me to keep them.

My plan was to bring them to my mom's house, since she would be at work. From all the years of growing up in that house, and hanging around with thieves who had no issue stealing from me, I had all sorts of secret hiding spots inside the walls of the house, which I knew would be enough space to store the parts for as long as I needed to. I decided to come up from the parking lot behind my mom's house, and lift the bags over the fence, to reduce the chance of any neighbors seeing me. Well when I got to my mom's house, to my surprise, I saw that her truck was still there, instead of being away at work, like she should have been. I ended up just leaving the bags of parts behind the garage, and planned to return the next day to hide them.

Later in the evening, my friend, myself, and a few other close friends, were hanging out at our usual coffee shop, to have a better conversation. That's when I found out that they didn't actually know where the stuff was being stored, but at that point, it was too late. And as luck would have it, the next door neighbor to my mom's, just happened to be a retired police officer. After seeing me lifting the bags over the back fence, and knowing my criminal history, after I had left, he decided to go take a look.

It wasn't long after we got to the coffee shop, when we were stunned to see my dad walk in, knowing we were likely there. He walked up to our table and said to us, "There are some gentlemen outside who would like to speak with the two of you." My friend and I looked at each other, each with a look on our faces, that said to the other, "Oh! Fuck!" As we walked outside, we saw only a pickup truck, and for a moment, I had a brief feeling of "maybe not". As we walked towards the truck, and saw the bags of computer parts in the back, we knew the gig was up; that was the last time I would be free for the next 9 months and 25 days.

RESTRAINED ENLIGHTENMENT

When we got to the county jail, surprisingly they put us both in the same cell. Due to my record, I knew I was going to be spending time in jail no matter what, and since he didn't have a record at all, we got our stories together, and I agreed to take as much blame as I could, hoping to spare him the same fate I knew awaited me. He was only there a few days before his parents bailed him out. Ultimately, he got lucky, and only received a period of house arrest, followed by probation. But neither of my parents were willing to bail me out, not even until my court date, because they knew I needed to go to jail. Of course I hated and regretted what I had done at the time, but as I mentioned earlier, "As luck would have it, the next door neighbor saw me." I actually learned to appreciate those very difficult months I spent in jail, because it finally would put a welcomed end to all those years of stealing, and leave a lasting positive effect on my life.

Those months in jail were beyond difficult. Not only because I was isolated from everyone I knew, which was made even worse, after I was moved to a long term facility about 4 hours away, but also because once again, I started being bullied by countless other kids, because of my innocent and passive demeanor, and it started the first day after my friend posted bail.

I awoke to a punch in the face. But to the guy's surprise, I actually knew how to defend myself, from all the years of being bullied in the past. I was sleeping on the lower bed when I was hit, and by the time the guards came and broke it up, I was actually starting to get the upper hand, after I was able to get my feet under him, and started slamming him into the steel bunk bed above us. I'm sure I would have won, but it was not obvious to anyone else. While it did earn me a slight bit of respect from the other kids at first, but because it wasn't clear who would have won, it still only encouraged them to continue testing me over the following weeks. Each time anyone got into a fight, whoever was involved, would then spend 3 days locked in their cell. So pretty much every three days, I'd be allowed out of my cell again, and then someone else would start a fight with me. They would take turns spending 3 days in their cells, which led to me being locked in mine most of the time. I'd wake up to all sorts of things being thrown at me, including pee.

Eventually, due to safety reasons, the guards had no choice but to place me in solitary confinement; in a yellow room, with a yellowish light that was on during the day, which would change to a slightly less bright, amber light at night. I would end up spending over a month in that room by myself; slowly feeling like I was going to lose my mind. At one point, I started banging my head off the brick wall, trying to knock myself out, in the hopes that I would be able to at least get out of there for a few hours, and spend some time in the hospital. Despite how hard I hit my head off the wall, it just ended up giving me a really bad headache.

In hindsight, I should have realized it would be impossible to knock myself out. I wasn't even knocked out after a car hit me on my bike one day, without a helmet, and my head went straight into the windshield, as the car was traveling at least 50km/h; after leaving a half-a-head-sized hole, I rolled off the car, got up right away, went straight over to my buddy and said to him, "Hey man, guess I really need to fix those brakes!"

Following that failed attempt to knock myself out, I went on a hunger strike, and didn't eat or drink a single thing for almost a week. When I was about to be taken to the hospital, if I didn't end the hunger strike, the guards made me an offer, and said if I started eating, they would allow me to spend a few hours out of the cell at night, to play some games on a computer; I promptly agreed and started eating again.

After I was sentenced, I was quickly transferred out of there. First to the Hamilton county jail, and then finally a much nicer place, which I would have otherwise not been transferred to, if I hadn't been transferred to Hamilton first. Of course, I am forever grateful for that, because the other long term facility, was a much harsher place, than where I was able to serve most of my time at. The place had a full high school: computer class, wood working shop, auto repair shop, home education (which taught sewing and cooking, allowed us to make our own clothes, and even make food we could bring back to our rooms.) There were four "lodges", instead of ranges: with a common room that had games, a T.V., a fridge and tables to play the games at. There was even a pool table and a ping pong table, that kids who were on the highest levels of 3 and 4, were allowed to use. The rooms really were rooms, rather than cells, and none of the doors even had locks on them. Instead, if someone was not behaving, they would just be brought to a solitary cell in another part of the building. We could even wear our own clothes, when on levels 3 and 4, could have a Walkman, as well as other privileges, such as being allowed to go out with an adult in the city, and even home for some weekends, if one was really well behaved. Over all, it wasn't that bad of a place, but jail is still jail.

Because I lived 4 hours away, I rarely got any visits, and never able to go home for any weekends. They did however, have a volunteer from the area, come in every week to spend some time with me. I forget his name, but he was really nice. He was in charge of a power generating facility, and was even able to take me on a tour one time, but usually, we would play chess. It was lot of fun, and because of how much I played chess while in jail, I became quite good at it. It was also during this time in jail, when I discovered, I was a lot better at writing than I realized before. Over all, I learned a lot while I was there, especially about myself. But one of the most life changing things that happened, is when I realized I have an exceptional, natural talent for law.

It all started when a new guy came into our lodge. He was Muslim, and so unlike the rest of us, didn't have to follow the no facial hair rule, and was allowed to keep his beard. At the time, I liked having my mustache and goatee, and even though I didn't know anything about law or the Charter of Rights, I just felt that this didn't feel right. It bothered me so much, one day, while I was in English class, the teacher noticed something was bothering me. After a little prodding, he got me to talk about what was distracting me from doing my work. He was one of those awesome teachers you never forget, and after I told him what was bugging me, he suggested I go check out the Criminal Code from the library and read the Charter of Rights. With little else to do, and all the time in the world to do it, I would eventually spend countless hours learning and understanding the Charter of Rights. Ultimately, I would come to realize that my understanding of the Charter, actually exceeds that of the average lawyer.

With this new powerful knowledge in hand, I ended up challenging the shaving policy. I attempted to exercise one of my rights that grants me "Freedom of Religion", by proclaiming that I now identified as Muslim, and therefore was no longer required to shave. Well, needless to say, that did not go over well. I was quickly sent to an isolation cell, and was not allowed out, until I agreed to shave, so that's where I was for the next few weeks.

To make matters worse, when you're in there, you have no mattress, no pillow, no real blanket, and no clothes. Instead, all you have, is a steel bed, a steel toilet, two 5 foot by 5 foot "blankets" that are basically an oven mitt like material, but not nearly as soft, and feels much more like plastic than cloth. Instead of clothes, you get a poncho made out of the same material; yet still, I was determined to stand up for my rights!

During this time of protest, I experienced a very interesting and special moment, that I'll never forget. Because there's only so much a person can sleep, especially when lacking common comforts, such as clothes. This one day, I found myself just lying there, staring at the wall, with nothing else to do, but wait. When the sun came up, and cast a line on the wall, between daylight and shadow, I couldn't help but think of how fitting of a metaphor it was; sunny on one side of the window, and feeling very dark inside. So I just laid there, staring at the wall; not moving, and blinking so infrequently, someone could easily think I was dead. When it comes to not blinking, well put it this way, I've never lost a staring contest, and have even been known to fall asleep with my eyes open, from time to time. So there I lay, the whole day, staring at that line. As I got into a trance like state, eventually, I started seeing the light from the sun, ever-so-slowly, yet fluidly, moving across the wall; quite like the flow of time while locked in jail. It was one of the most beautiful moments I'd ever experienced. Just lying there, realizing that it was the spin of the earth, which was causing this subtlest, yet perfectly fluid, motion of light, I was seeing on the wall that wonderful day.

After a few weeks of this protest and seeing the determination I had to continue, as I waited for a reply to my complaint I filled with the ombudsman, regarding the violation of rights I felt was taking place, the supervisor of my lodge, and the head of the entire facility came to see me. They essentially blackmailed me, into agreeing to rescind my formal complaint. They told me, if I followed through with my complaint, that it "likely" wouldn't look very good on my review to the judge, when I became eligible for early release. Although I still feel that was a morally wrong thing for them to do, I'm not stupid, so that ended that protest, right then and there. They did however, make a comment about how much they respected my determination on the matter. That left me with a distinct and lasting impression, that there was definitely merit in what I had done, which to this day, still makes me feel it was completely worth those few weeks of discomfort, and the following month it took, to get back up to level three and get my Walkman back.

One of the great things that came from my time in jail, was the AutoCAD experience I gained while in school there. I had first started learning AutoCAD while in grade 9, and that was one of the only classes I actually did really well in, during the first month, before being transferred to the alternative school. While I was in jail, not only did I finish all of the official high school level classes they had for AutoCAD, but the computer teacher let me continue learning even more, and gave me an extra random credit towards my diploma. For the extra work, I took a Special Edition of Popular Science, which had detailed pictures of the International Space Station, that I was able to take scaled measurements from, then start creating a 3D model of the entire station. The teacher was so impressed, that he even submitted the design into the biggest high school drafting competition in the country. I didn't even want to submit it, since it was incomplete, due to the file becoming too big for the computers we had in the school. But he insisted, and to my surprise, I ended up coming in first place, which was the first time in my life I had ever came in first with anything; it's a skill I've continued to use over the years to design all sorts of cool things, before building them.

For the most part, the time I spent there was good, but there was one dark moment that I'll never forget, and one of the closest times I ever came to dying. It happened earlier on when I was there, shortly after the whole newness of the place was over. I fell in a period of deep depression, and suicidal thoughts once again entered my mind. This led to me sneaking a sewing needle back from school, and that night while in my room, I slowly picked away around a vein in my arm. After completely exposing the vein, I shoved the needle straight through and pulled until it ripped apart. As I let the blood flow out into my garbage can, eventually losing about 2 liters of blood (which is about 40% of the blood in the average human body), and as I could actually feel the life slowly draining from me, once again I found myself saved by empathy. All I could think of was how much it would hurt my family, and those who loved me, so I applied pressure, and stopped the bleeding.

The next morning while cleaning my room, I carefully hid the red color in the small, white plastic trash can, and then threw the whole container into the larger garbage without anyone seeing. Shortly after, while standing in line waiting to go to breakfast, one of the kids standing next to me looked at me and asked, "Hey man, you feeling ok? You look like a ghost!" I was also very light headed, in a daze, and extremely weak, which took many weeks to fully recover from. Eventually, I was forced to tell the staff what I had done, when I saw the wound was becoming infected. I knew from my years of experience working with the animals in the wildlife center, that if left untreated, there was a very real possibility of losing most of my arm. But the deed had been done, and it left a deep mark, not just physically, but psychologically as well.

After that, things slowly started to get better for me. One memorable thing that helped me realize that my life wasn't really all that bad, had to do with one of the other kids in my lodge. It was the first time I'd ever met someone who was very schizophrenic. My first real experience talking with him, one-on-one, was in the cafeteria while eating one day. He started rambling on about space, and eventually started saying something about the base that NASA has on Mars. Because I knew a lot about such things, I attempted to correct him by explaining that it was a robotic rover that NASA has on Mars, and not actually a base with any Humans on it. He reacted by saying, "No, this is real, I saw it on TV!." Not wanting to cause any trouble, especially knowing that he was in jail for killing someone, I just kind of agreed with him by saying "Oh, I didn't know about that."

Later that day, while playing chess with another kid, I made a comment about the conversation, and that is when I found out that he was schizophrenic. I was also told that at one point, the schizophrenic guy had a pet comb, but it was best not to ever bring the topic up. He told me that one time, when the comb was not behaving, there was some kind of fight that led to the schizophrenic guy killing the comb, and after, he felt really bad about the whole thing. As the months went by, eventually he felt that he was ready to have another pet, and while watching TV one day, he brought the comb out to show everyone. He even made a little tiny pillow and blanket in school, and had made a nice cozy bed for the comb inside an empty tissue box. An experience like that is a hard thing to forget, and really helps put your own problems into perspective; no matter how bad you think you have it, chances are, it's not as bad as some of the problems other people face in life.

Getting back to a more positive note, one last great thing that came from jail, and has helped me understand myself better over the years, has to do with 40 hours of psychological and aptitude testing that was done on me, over the course of 7 days. Out of the 24 or so kids in each lodge, they only did this amount of testing on two of us from each of the 4 lodges, at least during the time I was there. Not only did I find the psychological tests to be rather interesting and very accurate, but the amount of very specific aptitude sub-tests that I took, has proved to be quite insightful and practical over the years, especially when it comes to my lowest scores. Understanding these areas of weakness, has allowed me to target those areas with specific mental exercises, and actually improve upon a great deal over the years. I also want to share the specifics of my highest score, not to gloat about in anyway what-so-ever, but rather, to help put into perspective, as to why I have a natural talent when it comes to law, and also, because of how it relates to key events that I have not yet shared, which are a fundamental aspect, relating to my motivation for writing this book.

First off, before I get into the details, I want to quickly bring up a controversial aspect relating to I.Q. tests. On one hand, I agree there is definitely merit in the argument that, I.Q. tests can fail to show aptitude with in certain demographics, even though someone may actually be quite adept in the area being tested. However, on the other hand, a person cannot possibly score high in a specific area, if they are not very adept in that area.

Having said that, my highest score was 183, and to quote the report: "Was earned on a Verbal subtest which requires practical social judgment, the ability to organize facts and relationships, and superior abstract thinking. It tests the examinee's ability to respond and adapt to situations by dealing with a specific problem in an efficient and socially acceptable manner." If we stop and think about this for a moment, and ask what type of profession this specific skill would be highly useful in, a lawyer is just such a profession. To put the score into perspective, based on the current world population of 7.53 billion people, what that score means, statistically speaking, is there's approximately 12 000 people who would score that high or higher when it comes to that specific type of ability. On one hand, such a specific ability can be quite useful at times. It has allowed me to be able to learn all sorts of different things, that I set my mind on learning, and has been especially helpful, when it comes to being able to make fundamental changes about myself. On the other hand, I also realize that this exact "gift", is also directly related to why I had such tremendous social difficulties when I was younger, and still often makes it hard to really connect with and relate to others. When I do get emotionally overwhelmed, it is also this exact ability that causes me so much turmoil. Because of this, rather than seeing this as a gift, sometimes it feels like a curse.

Another positive aspect of this ability, is how it relates to why I was able to eventually understand the Charter of Rights the way I have, and is also why I stated that eventually I would come to understand the Charter better than the average lawyer. This ability, combined with how much free time I had while in jail, allowed me to spend countless hours, simply trying to fully understand what Section 1 of the Charter really means. Section 1 is only a single sentence, but because it is the most important law in Canada, I literally spent *countless* hours reading it again and again. With a dictionary next to me, I looked up each word, and thinking about every nuance, of every single, slightly different definition of each word, and how each one relates to all the other words in Section 1.

FREE AND UNCLEAR

After I got out of jail, in Feb of 1999, I completely stopped hanging around with all of the old friends. Instead, my sister introduced me to some of her friends, at a coffee shop downtown they would often hang out at. It was during this time when I first started DJ'ing at the coffee shop. They only had two regular CD players and a very basic mixer, so it wasn't possible to actually mix tracks, but it was still a lot of fun, and sparked a new interest in music that would stay with me to this day. It was also during this time, when I met someone who would eventually become one of the few best friends I've had over the years. His name was Nick, he was half Bosnian, half Croatian, and came to Canada as a refugee when he was about 12, due to the Croat–Bosniak War. Hearing some of his stories from living in the war, such as a time when him and his friends were out playing, just being kids, when one of his friends stepped on a landmine, which ended up blowing up. After seeing the restrained intensity of his emotions, as he told me that story, it was one of those moments that would make most people realize, their life has really never been that bad.

Additionally, because of how turbulent my life had been over the last few years, and the frequent difficulty I experienced in school, I still hadn't yet finished my high school diploma. I still needed 14 credits to complete it, but I was determined to finish, regardless of how long it would take. So after I got out of jail, I decided the best option, would be to return to an alternative school, like the one I spent most of my time at before jail. The new school was even in the same building as the other program, but instead was for high school students over the age of 16. However, the important thing was that it had the exact same course structure, allowing a student to work at their own pace.

Within a couple of months after getting out of jail, I ended up getting my first real job, working at Burger King. Not only was I really excited to start the job, but I also very much enjoyed working there. I was always a hard worker, and would often go out of my way to do extra things, without even being asked. Unlike what I've been used to, during my time in jail and in school, I also seemed to get along with my colleagues quite well. At one point, I even became friends with one of the shift managers, who was around my age, but slightly older. He also sold weed, and initially, when I started buying weed from him, it was just small amounts for myself. But because of how often I was hanging out downtown during my free time, and frequently heard people asking if anybody had weed to sell, and no one ever said they did. I quickly realized there was an opportunity to make money, in that under-serviced market. I promptly started buying larger quantities from my shift manager, and opened up shop downtown. I'm sure I smoked as much as I sold, and at the very least, it paid for my own smoking habit, but more importantly, it was the start of my career as a drug dealer. Little did I know, that experience was really only the beginning.

One of the things I liked the most about it, was that it suddenly made it a lot easier to meet new people. Even though I realized most of the people I would meet were not really friends, and just wanted weed, it did still allow me to meet some people who I did feel were really friends; it was the first time in my life when I actually felt like I fit in somewhere. It was this feeling more than anything else that was addictive, and as we'll see later in my life, it would turn out to be a feeling that would continue to influence my decisions for years to come.

The coffee shop Nick and I would spend a lot of our time at, would only end up being open a few more months, after I first started going there. Although it was enough to be able to establish a healthy new social circle of friends, that I've never really had before. A lot of them would smoke weed, and some would do other drugs as well, and while technically illegal, drugs are definitely not something I consider to be morally wrong in anyway. In fact, I completely believe that drug laws are actually the morally wrong things, as well as judging people who use certain drugs over others, such as alcohol that so many judgmental hypocrites love to chugged back. Simply using drugs, is *not* a morally valid reason to question a person's character. If someone is addicted to drugs or alcohol, to the point where they start stealing to support their addiction, then that would obviously be wrong, but only the stealing would be wrong. What most people, who don't do or know anyone that does drugs, don't seem to realize is, just how many people they know, who *do* use drugs. Most people who do drugs, don't fit the ignorant stereotype of a drug user, and because they usually know which friends have such biases, they simply hide it from them; they will even lie, because they don't want to lose those friends.

When the coffee shop finally closed, most of us would still see each other at various other places downtown, but it was never quite the same after that. There never ended up being a single new place where everyone would hang out at regularly. The one large group of us ended up forming a number of smaller groups, and each ended up finding a new place to regularly hang out at. For the most part, Nick and I would spend the majority of our free time with each other, which would often include a few other people from the old coffee shop. Still, when the old coffee shop closed, it left a feeling of a void, when we'd find ourselves downtown, with no one else around, bored and looking for something fun to do.

One night, while hanging out downtown, we were trying to find some weed to buy, but no one we asked could get any. This led us to asking about other drugs as well, because we were bored, not tired, and we were open to having some Magic Mushrooms or LSD as well. While we were asking people we knew about drugs, one of them started talking about a new after-hours club in the east end, that played electronic music (which I liked, but had limited experience with, because it was not at all mainstream at the time.) He said he was going there when it opened at 2 am, and that we would definitely be able to find drugs there. Although buying weed was our preferred choice, but because we were asking about other things as well, I wanted to know more details, before we went all the way to the east end, and paid to get inside the club. When I asked if he thought we could find weed there, he said maybe, but probably not, because not that many people there smoked weed. Considering that weed was my drug of choice, and not having much experience with other drugs, I was surprised to hear that. When I asked what kind of drugs would likely be there, he said, "Mostly just Ecstasy." I'd never even heard of that before, and at first when he mentioned they were pills, I was not at all interested, due to my past experience taking random pills. But it was only around 12 A.M, so he wasn't ready to leave downtown yet, and because I'm a curious person, I decided to ask him what Ecstasy was like. He basically said, "it makes you feel happy and gives you a bunch of energy." He seemed certain that I would like it, and because I was still sad about the coffee shop recently closing, Nick and I ended up deciding to go check out this new club.

Initially, I was still hoping to just find weed, but like my friend predicted, the only thing we could find were Ecstasy pills. I was still hesitant about trying it, and was even more reluctant, when I found out a single pill was 30$, and back in 1999, making 6.25$/h, that was many hours of work. After being there for about an hour, and seeing how unusually happy and friendly everyone was, even towards complete strangers, I decided to give it a try.

AFTER ALL MY HOURS

At that point in my life, I was still very shy and insecure around people I didn't know, especially towards any girl I found attractive. I always wore a lot of dark clothes, had the same Mohawk hairstyle I had since I was 15, but was beyond the point of having any desire to spike it up. Instead, I would just comb it to one side and let it hang down to just below my ear. I also had the most ridiculous looking mustache that did not look good on me at all. I also never danced. It wasn't that I liked the way I dressed and styled my hair, or wasn't interested in dancing, quite the opposite actually. Those were all things I'd often think about, and were a big part of what I wasn't happy about, but was too anxious and afraid to change. When it came to how I dressed and cut my hair, I knew I understood a bit of the puzzle.

Part of the reason, relates to when I first started wearing dark clothes and dressing as a little punk rocker. Because my older sister was that way, when I was 15, all her friends were always nice towards me, so it felt nice to fit in with them. Most of her friends were a number of years older than her, so there was definitely an age gap, which always made me feel like I didn't fully fit in. At the time, I didn't have much self-confidence, and it was during this period when I started realizing that most of the people I thought were my friends, were never really friends, so suddenly feeling like I fit in a bit, and was accepted by others, was understandably very influential, and dressing the way I did, was essentially a security blanket I was still carrying around.

The other bigger piece of the puzzle, which I wasn't aware of yet, was caused by a couple negative comparisons, that were buried deep in my mind, and as a result of how traumatic these two events were, my mind hid them even from me. The moment when I found these two memories again, I immediately realized the first one that happened, was the single moment that traumatized me for all those years later.

One day at school, when I was in grade 2, a bunch of kids came in with a new binder that was a fad at the time, and was called a "Note Tote". It was a rather expensive binder for the late 80's, and considering I rarely ever did my school work, there was no way my parents were going to spend money on something I'd never use. They knew the only reason why I wanted the binder, was because of this little spring-loaded clip mechanism in the back, that utilized levers to clamp down papers. Kids quickly realized, if you put an eraser under the clamp, you could then use the arm of the clamp as a catapult to shoot other little pieces of eraser across the room. My parents knew that was the only reason why I wanted the binder, so I never ended up getting one. Of course this once again left me as an outsider of the group and made me feel further isolated from everyone else.

A few weeks or months later, after the fad had passed, and the market for those binders had been saturated, the company came out with a cheaper version that was all made of plastic, which was called the "Note Tote Too". More importantly, it still had the same mechanism that could be used as a catapult. When I first saw this much cheaper version, and realized how much less it cost, my mom saw how excited I was about it, but at the time, said we couldn't afford it. Obviously I was quite disappointed, but to my surprise, a few days later, she came home with one for me and my sister. I was so excited; I couldn't wait to go to school the next day! I finally felt that I was going to be part of the group, even if just a little bit. When I got to school, and proudly pulled out my new binder, I was shocked at how the other kids in my group responded. Immediately one of them turned and said, "Oh look at Adam, he's got a Note Tote Toooo. He's trying to be like us!" Because I was already so used to being picked on and teased, I didn't really think much of it, despite the fact that it obviously hurt; I had no idea the deep scar this moment would leave me with, and how it would ultimately affect my behavior and choices, for the next 11 years.

The other example of how this kind of teasing would go on to reinforce this fear, has to do with hair styles and happened in grade 5. Up until that point, I never really cared about what was popular. Thinking about it now, this is a good example of a mildly autistic thing; something most people understand the social merits of, well before grade 5, but I only started realizing how much of an influence such a thing as a haircut can have on how another person sees you. Normally, I'd cut my hair quite short, so when the new mushroom-cut style became popular, I started growing my hair long enough to cut it that way. So after a few months, when it was finally long enough, I went and got it cut. Once again, I was so excited to go to school. But just like before, this is what I heard, "Oh, look at Adam! He's trying to be cool like us Tooo!"

Eventually, I came to realize, these experiences became the source of the fear I ended up having, which discouraged me from changing how I dressed and cut my hair; it even made me afraid of dancing.

When I took that first Ecstasy pill, I was told it would take about 30 – 45 minutes to start feeling the effects. Initially after swallowing the pill, I walked around the whole club to check everything out, and eventually found a comfortable place to sit down, where I could wait for the effects of the pill to kick in. As I sat on the couch, a girl I knew, and had a crush on, walked by. After seeing me sitting on the couch, she sat down next to me and we started talking. It was mostly just small talk, such as asking me how I liked the club, because I had told her it was my first time going there, and was also the first time I had an Ecstasy pill. I thought the club was cool, but it had already been over an hour since I took the pill, and I was starting to feel like I got ripped off; I was even thinking about leaving before she sat down. She asked me who I got it from, and after pointing the person out, she told me he's trustworthy and just be patient, because sometimes it takes longer to kick in.

While I was sitting there waiting, not long after she said that, I casually scratched an itch I felt on my arm, and as I did that, I suddenly found myself, completely distracted by the intense sensation I felt, from such a simple thing as scratching my arm. As I sat there gently touching the hairs on my arm, in awe of how sensitive and amazing such a simple thing like touching my own arm felt, my friend turned and looked at what I was doing, chuckled then said, "Looks like you're starting to feel it now." Clearly still amused by watching someone start feeling these effects for the first time, she then told me to close my eyes. ...and stop touching my arm like I was still doing. After closing my eyes and sitting there for a moment, she then started touching my arm like I was, but in a random way. Each time she'd lift her hand off one spot, then start touching another spot, each time feeling more intense than the last. Eventually, she told me to turn a bit and started giving me a back massage, which at that point in my life, was the most amazing sensation I had ever felt, better even than sex. Unsurprisingly, I knew I'd be coming back! I started going as often as I could. But I only had the part time job at Burger King, which meant, I was usually only able to go Friday and Saturday every other weekend.

Over the next few months, I continued to go as often as I could, usually taking 2 or 3 pills a night. I still would never dance, but was enjoying how friendly and social everyone was. Most of the time I walked around, just kind of stepping with the beat of the music as I walked. I was always very good at timing myself to the beat, without even needing to think about it, but I was still too afraid to actually go on the dance floor and dance. Just like I was afraid to cut my hair differently, and buy new colorful clothes, in a completely different style than I normally wore. Clothes like most of the people at the club would wear, but I was still too afraid that someone would make fun of me, and comparing me to others. After the newness of the club wore off, I stopped going for a while, because after the pills wore off, my depression would often become much worse. When I started feeling depressed even at the club, while I was high on pills, I knew I needed to take a break.

The first night I went back after not going for weeks, I didn't have any money to buy pills, but Nick convinced me to go, by offering to give me half a pill for free. After going so often and taking many pills in a night, I didn't really expect much. I felt that I'd be my usual shy self, and be too afraid to talk to people, unlike the way I would usually be, when I went and was high on many pills. After the half-a-pill was in full effect, I was walking around like I usually would, but unlike every other time when I'd be high on one or more pills, because I had only taken a half a pill, I found myself feeling very reflective, due to the underwhelming intensity from taking only half. As a result, walking around like I usually did, stepping with the beat of the music, wasn't at all enjoyable like it normally was. Not only was I still depressed, but after I stopped going to the club for a while, and spending a lot of time alone, I was even more depressed over all.

As I was walking around, passing the dance floor, again and again, knowing how fun it looked, but still being faced with the same old fear that always got in the way, something happened that would forever change my life. As I stood there, looking at the dance floor, depressed and unhappy, I thought to myself, "What's the worst that could happen? I'm already so unhappy anyway, and can't image it could cause me to be unhappier, even if I do see someone laughing at me dancing." So I thought to myself, "Fuck it! I'll just keep my eyes closed and not look at anyone." And just like that, I went onto the dance floor and started dancing.

SUDDENLY DIFFERENT

It didn't take long for me to forget about my fear, and find myself completely engaged in what I was doing. I'm not sure how long I was dancing for, when I suddenly remembered the fear I had, and instantly I panicked! I quickly opened my eyes, looked around, but to my surprise, not a single person was looking at me. As I continued to look around, I realized that no one even knew me, and are so distracted by what they are doing, no one even cared about how anyone else was dancing. In that moment, all of the fear I had, instantly melted away, and I found myself filled with joy. I continued dancing until the music stopped. As I drove my bike home afterwards, I realized something fundamental inside of me, had forever changed, and I would never quite be the same again. By this point, it was during the summer, and I had recently started working full time, and the next cheque I got, was going to be the first big one; I knew exactly what I was going to do when I got paid at the end of the following week.

    After I got paid, I went to the mall, got my hair cut short like I had been too afraid to do, bought 600$ in new clothes, and shaved off my mustache; I even had a bit of a bounce to the way I walked, and I wasn't even sure when that started. That Friday night, I went downtown as usual to meet up with Nick, and as I approached the group of friends he was sitting with at a coffee shop, every one of them looked at me in complete shock. None of my friends had seen me during the week, not even Nick, but if any of them had seen me during the week before I cut my hair and got new clothes, they still would have been just as shocked. The change that happened inside of me, was so fundamentally profound, it affected just about everything about how I interacted with others, to such an extent I seemed, and felt, like a completely different person.

That night, Nick and I went to the after-hours club, and again the following night. Both nights, I still did some drugs, but even though I still had enough money, I only took a half a pill at a time. I also started dancing both nights as soon as I got there, even before the first half of the pill kicked in, and kept dancing until the music stopped.

During the Saturday night party, when I was walking around like I use to do, just to cool off from dancing so much. As I walked passed a friend, who was sitting down, I felt a slight tug on my pants. He was worried about a girl sitting near him, and asked if I could see if she was ok. So I sat down in between them, and leaned over to ask her how she was. She just kind of turned and smiled then said, "Oh ya, I'm just really high." After thanking me for checking on her, I sat for a moment just thinking about how surprisingly easy it was to talk to her, especially considering how beautiful she was. Before, I always would have been way too shy to talk with someone I found to be that attractive, even to simply ask if they were ok, but I didn't even hesitate now. A moment later, I leaned back over to ask her if she wanted a back massage, and again, to my surprise, she said yes.

We ended up spending most of that night together, and then exchanged phone numbers before we left. Initially, I was a bit disappointed when I found out she lived in the States, about an hour away, and was even more disappointed that she was going to school over 3 hours away.

When the Saturday night party ended (technically early Sunday morning), the owner told everyone there was going to be a free party Sunday night, because Monday was a holiday. Initially I wasn't going to go, because I had to work Monday evening. As I was getting ready for bed Sunday night, I got a call from the girl, Allison, asking me if I was planning to go to the free party, because she wanted to go if I was going to go. *Obviously,* I suddenly decided to go, despite knowing I had to work the next day.

When I got there, I was surprised at how few people were there, despite it being a free party. No one was dancing when we showed up, but that still didn't stop me from being the first one on the dance floor. Rather than feeling any kind of hesitation or fear, I was actually happy about having all that space just to myself. Initially I wasn't even going to take a pill, because I didn't have much money left, after spending most of my money on new clothes, but when Allison showed up with her friend, she offered to buy me a pill. While I was waiting for the pill to kick in, someone I didn't even know, came up to me on the dance floor, and offered me the rest of the joint they were smoking; this only further increased the high I was feeling, both literally and figuratively. Shortly after finishing the joint, I started wondering where Allison went.

After asking her friend, I found out she had an upset stomach from the pill she took, but that was normal for her, and she'd be out of the bathroom once it passed. I then offered to go to the store a few blocks away, to get her something for her stomach. After she accepted the offer, she gave me her keys. Because it was very close, and the pill hadn't even started to kick in yet, I knew I had time to go there and back, before the effects of the pill would cause any kind of impairment that would make it unsafe to drive. As for the weed I just had, I smoked weed all the time, so the little bit from the end of the joint I had, only gave me a small buzz similar to having one drink, and definitely not enough to make driving unsafe. When I got to the store a few blocks away, I was surprised it was closed, but not wanting to come back empty handed, I decided to go to the next closest store. Admittedly, it definitely wasn't the smartest thing to do, and I would soon realize why.

When I was almost at the next closest store, I started feeling the effects of the pill, but unlike any other time I've taken a pill, with in a couple of minutes, I went from feeling nothing, to suddenly being completely high. I'm sure it was related to the weed I smoked, because I had never smoked weed before taking a pill, and when that pill did kick in as I was driving, something else happened that had never happened before. In an instant, I found myself no longer driving the car, and instead found myself back in grade 2, pulling out my binder, and getting made fun of. Then an instant later, I was in grade 5, getting teased about the haircut. After that, I wasn't even sure where I was; it felt like I was seeing all sorts of different things at once, all related to being bullied and picked on, and in that moment I suddenly *saw*, without words, exactly how all of the bullying from my life affected me in ways I never realized, and all my fears about dancing, the haircut, plus the clothes, all made sense and became completely obvious.

I was finally jolted back to my existence in the car, by the sound of a loud horn from a big semi-truck!

During those moments when I wasn't driving any more, I had started drifting into the lane it was in, but thankfully, I knew which way to turn the wheel, and got out of the way just in time.

By the time I got back to the club, quite a bit of time had passed, and I was greeted by signs of relief. Everyone was afraid something had happened, and even though I was lucky to have not been hit by the truck, something did happen, and it was obvious to everyone. It affected me enough that I no longer had any interest in dancing that night. No one else felt like staying either, so we all ended up leaving and went to a nearby park. Over the next few hours, I explained to the three of them, in detail, exactly what had happened.

It was during this time, when I first thought about writing a book, and after thinking about it for a bit, I quickly realized that I definitely would. Because of how often my mom and I would watch movies together when I was younger, I knew enough interesting things had already happened in my life up to that point, to already make an interesting story, but little did I realize it would take another 20 years, before I would finally complete it.

A few weeks after this sudden change happened, I found myself lying in bed, thinking about everything that had happened and unable to sleep, unable to even put my thoughts to words; I picked up a notepad, and suddenly I found myself writing the first poem I had ever written:

Gist

Tears of happiness can it be
these sweet salty drops, they fall on me.

When the storm begun to soar
I took my mind and locked the door.

Throughout the storm I could not see
these tears of happiness were crushing me.

When the eye had passed on through
I said good-bye to the pain that grew.

From this storm, I did learn
that fright and pain will always burn.

For when that storm had finished with me
the pain inside was filled with glee.

MY FIRST LOVE AND A PAINFUL GOOD-LIE

Ultimately, Allison and I started dating for about 8 months, which was by far the longest relationship I had up until that point, and it was also the first time I ever felt truly in love with someone. Before that, I did have a fairly short relationship with someone not long before I went to jail, that I thought I was in love with, and for the longest time I was certain that was my first love, but up until that point in my life, I really hadn't had much dating experience. Over the years, I've come to realize that it was really just puppy love, rather than a true intimate kind of love like I would first experience towards Allison. She was beautiful, we had great chemistry and we never had a single argument. The only real issue was that her parents didn't really approve.

Part of their concerns, had to do with how much she was driving back and forth from school, which was three and a half hours each way. I knew it was definitely affecting her grades, to the point where I was not only expressing concerns, but even started telling her not to come see me as often. Her dad also didn't like that I didn't have my own car, which meant that she was putting a lot of miles on her new car they had bought for her. The other big issue, was that I worked at Burger King, and wasn't even going to college. Eventually, things got so bad between her and her dad, that I actually asked her if it would be ok for me to write her dad a polite, but blunt email, in response to an angry email he had written to her; with her permission that is what I did.

Initially, I was going to include what I wrote without hesitation, but it's been a long time since I read it, and after reading it now, I almost decided not to include it here, partly because I was a bit cocky with a few things I said, which was motivated by some of the rude things he had said about me. I also said something to him that wasn't actually true, as to why I broke up with his daughter. I wasn't sure if she would end up reading the email, but just in case she did, I decided to tell a white lie, because if she knew the main reason I broke up with her, there would be a good chance of it causing resentment towards her dad, and end up pushing them further apart, which would be the opposite of what I was hoping to achieve.

The main reason I broke up with her, was because of the problems our relationship was causing between her and her dad. I knew her and her dad were always very close, which is why she was so upset about the things her dad said in that angry email to her.

Something I want to say before sharing the email, relating to what caused me to hesitate about sharing it; basically it's a bit wordy, and has a bunch of tangents at times, much of which was also motivated by his rude comments towards me. But after reading it a few minutes ago, I remembered that I had the same hesitation, when I was reviewing the email before I sent it to him. I ended up deciding to include the random personal details about me, because he really didn't know much about me at all, and I felt it could help make the overall letter seem more personal and pleasant, instead of just some lecture from some "bum" he doesn't like. (I've also left the grammar and everything as it was. Obviously after 20 years, my writing skills have improved, and because I want this book to be as accurate and true as possible, so it just seemed like it would be a bit disingenuous for me to change it in any way.)

"Hello Matt.

This is Adam your daughter's ex-boyfriend. I understand you do not like me and personally I do not like you either, however, I have reason why I do not like you. You make judgments about me without knowing anything about me. Perhaps if you knew about my past you would still come to the same conclusion. I have been through a lot. I have made a lot of mistakes, including going to jail for 10 months. Now going to jail is among one of the best things that have happened. I learned so much ONLY because I chose to take as much good out of it as I could. Now one thing I can also say is that if my parents did not support me when i needed them the most, then I most likely would still be destroying my life. If you ask anyone who really knows me, they would most likely tell you I am one of the best friends a person could have. I do not go around thinking I am better than anyone else, but when someone pisses me off I will tell things as they are. I am probably one of the most intelligent people you will ever meet. I have tests from ever since I was a kid proving this. As a kid I had no friends. I got in to trouble every day at school (I really do mean every day) and I do not see how anyone, including my own parents, could have liked me. When I look at myself now, I do not even know who I am. I know I am not the same person I was when I was a kid. I have many friends now and they are very important to me. I have two loving parents who have supported me when I gave them no reason to. When I hear everything Allison has ever said about you and her mom I never hear anything good, she is always upset about something.

    You can take what I say keep your mind closed and just think that I am just some punk who has no respect for anything. Or you could open your mind and look at the advents in your life and think that maybe I am right. I am not spending and hour writing this letter at 1:44am when I have school tomorrow if I didn't care. I see Allison is very upset and it hurts me to see my friends upset. Because I have been there; however I didn't have anyone to talk to.

    I broke up with your daughter because I realized that I did not care her about her in the same way she cared about me. I do believe that she does love me. Maybe because I was the only boyfriend she has ever had who would listen to what was bothering her. And I didn't care if she was not dressed up just to go downtown to have some coffee. I liked her for who she is. Just from talking with Allison about her life I know that you and you wife have the least amount (or close to it) of money compared to the rest or your family. When I first met Allison she would put on so much make up. At times it was gross. So I asked her why she used so much and she told me she did not think she looked good without it. Could this be because you and you wife always nag on her about things that really do not matter? Only because you feel like you have to impress the rest of the family. It is sad what money does to people. I would say most of my family has just an average amount of money but I think they are much happier then you and your wife. I do not know how many times she came to me to talk about what was bothering her and it was always because of how you and her mom were yelling at her for such small insignificant things. It is sad, you put so much pressure on her to do well in school without asking her what she really, really wants. You compare her to Jake, Brook and her sister. Her grandparents give them money because they were doing well in school but did not give her any because you all think she is just fucking up school. How do you think this makes her feel? The whole time she was at Western and I knew her. I would always try to get her to go to classes, and to some extent I succeeded. Just from knowing her for about 9 months I have learned that she really wanted to be a doctor (and I am sure she still does. That is her dream!) But she seems to have a problem with reading. Not that she does not like it but that she will read something and then forget what she read the page before and only get discouraged. I know this because she said she was having problems with reading and so I tested her by giving her a few pages to read and then tell me what she read. Well what I found out was that she did not remember very much. But you do not see this. I think she is afraid to say anything to you and her mom. The thing you are disappointed about is a learning difficultly that is not her fault. We ALL have problems. I have chosen to face mine and work on them the best I can. But Allison hides hers from her own parents out of fear. Why do you think she would always come down here instead of going home? Maybe because I do not yell at her when she is already feeling like shit and one of the reasons being because she gave up hope of being a doctor. Then she goes home and only gets yelled at. (Do not deny it because I read that email from you to her, remember, and for the record. she asked me to check her email for her while she was in the shower getting ready to go out.) I almost cried just typing this letting and thinking how sad it is.

You know I never use to have an open mind but I changed that. I realized this because of music. I never use to like rap, why? Because so many people I did not like listened to rap. But now I like it, along with every other type of music. Classical, Rap, Jazz, Classic Rock, Rock, Heavy Metal, Ska, Techno, Trance, House.. Name a type of music and I am sure i will like it. Why? Well because I learn something from all of it. It is all different. But I chose to try and keep an open mind with everything. When I meet someone I chose to keep an open mind and learn as much as I can from them, from anything I come in contact with each day. For years I would always kill bees when they buzzed around me, but just yesterday I had one on my hand walking around. It realized that I was no threat to it and so it did not sting me. I knew I would not get stung. That was so interesting just having this bee walk around my hand. And so I became friends with my enemy.

When you go home today and see your daughter you have the choice of yelling at her, or talking (and listening with an open mind) to her, the choice is yours. But for the sake of you daughter, and any hope you may have of every being at peace with your daughter I would recommend the latter of the two. One day many years from now you will look back at this day. Do you want to regret it?

Post Script: I am always here if you daughter ever needs a friend to talk to; however I would rather see you being that friend. "

I sent her dad that email on a Wednesday, at 2:27am, and two days later when she forwarded me an email from him, I found out he emailed her about 5 hours later at 7:44am.

"Hi baby girl,
I never get time with you anymore. Our schedules are so busy now days
This is your old grumpy dad, I just wanted to say, Thanks for being Allison.
You turned out pretty good, I'm so proud of you. I don't say it enough. I just keep reminding you of things that need to be handled by you.
I love ya Al, Yelling or just being in the same room saying nothing.
Have fun at school, work hard for you, your sculpting your life right now.

ILOVEYOU
Dad"

Even though my email ended up having the type of positive result I had hoped for, I still continued to have very mixed feelings about the whole situation for many years afterwards. On one hand, I knew I was in love with her, yet on the other hand, I ended things because of the situation with her family. I've heard a lot of relationship advice over the years, mostly from others to others, but some towards me as well, especially lately with my most recent relationship ending. Over all, most of the advice has essentially been the same; saying that I should take care of myself first and do what I feel is best for me. Even after thinking about such advice, I still had mixed feelings about breaking up with her. Sure, the choice was mine to make, and clearly part of me wanted to do that, or else I wouldn't have made that choice, but the reason why I wanted to do that, wasn't really looking out for myself. If I had been looking out for myself, I would have not ended a relationship with someone I was in love with. Nevertheless, I still feel like it was the right thing to do, because I knew I wouldn't be able to make all the changes I felt were needed for her parents to feel differently about our relationship.

A MOMENT OF REFLECTION

Something I've come to realize over the years, is that just because most people think something is right, definitely doesn't mean that it is. Sometimes, after thoroughly thinking about something logically, objectively, and only caring about what is right, I'll find myself coming to a very different conclusion that most people will passionately disagree with, even after much debate. Usually such conversations are mostly just a theoretical exercise, but sometimes, when it relates to something I said or did, that the majority feels I was in the wrong for, it usually ends up causing at least some sort of social issue, ranging from something minor, like simply being upset with me for a bit, to something as big as never wanting to talk to me again.

   Most people who know me, even close friends and family, would probably tell you that I'm a very stubborn person, and that I always think I'm right about everything. But if any of them realized how much time I spend thinking about things before even discussing them with anyone else, they would understand that usually I have already, not only thought about the points they bring up, but have also spent a lot of time considering those ideas as well, which is why it seems like I sometimes dismiss things without knowing what they were going to say, simply because I interjected in the middle of it. I understand why people feel the way they do about this, and it is something I constantly keep an eye on, since it's not usually something that I'm bothered by someone doing that towards me, because if I feel the person was listing to the first part of what I said, then I would usually assume they knew where I was going with that, and understood the rest of what I was going to say. The odd time someone gets it wrong, I can usually tell before they finish what they were saying, and back and forth we go. I very much enjoy such conversations with that kind of trust and faith in each other. Fundamentally, I don't care about *who's* right, what matters to me is *what's* right.

TEENAGE TOILET TRAINING

I still continued to live in Windsor for about another year after breaking up with Allison, and during this time, I mainly focused on finishing high school. After having spent most of my high school years in an alternative setting, I decided to try going back to a normal high school. I still wasn't sure what I wanted to do after high school, but I knew I wanted to go to college or university and I felt it would be better to get my diploma from a normal school, instead of having a diploma that had "Alternative", in the name of what school I graduated from.

The school I ended up attending, happened to be in the richest area of the city. Initially I didn't think anything of that, and simply figured because no one knew me at that school, there shouldn't be anyone from my past causing issues with me. Overall, that assumption was correct, and most of the other kids were very polite and friendly, but there were a small minority that seemed to be extremely stuck up, as well as one kid who had some kind of serious psychological issue, and I would eventually end up having a *necessary* confrontation with him.

When I started attending that school in the fall, I was almost 20, and not only was the oldest student at the school, I also already had a lot of crazy life experiences, and as a result, I really had very little tolerance for bullshit. I was definitely a lot more confident with myself compared to even a couple years before that, but was still the type to keep mostly to myself and my mind my own business about things, but unlike when I was younger, if I was faced with something that was directly affecting me, I was definitely much more likely to stand up to it.

Almost from the beginning of the year, I started noticing that the bathroom closest to my locker, almost always smelled like someone peed all over the place. I can't even smell that well, but it was such a strong smell, I was still able to easily smell it. I knew if I could, then there was definitely something weird going on. Initially I thought maybe it was just a really lazy janitor, but then one day, a few months into the school year, I was in the bathroom peeing at one of the urinals just before afternoon classes started, when I finally found out why the bathroom smelled like piss.

Now, peeing at a urinal in a public washroom, is an interesting thing, but it's something that most guys do so often, from such a young age, it becomes so casual and the subtle awkwardness of the situation can easily be forgotten about. Essentially you're standing there holding yourself while peeing next to other guys who are often complete strangers, and they are holding themselves too. Usually, that subtle awkwardness can be seen by the way almost everyone will look straight at the wall in front of them, because most guys don't want to even accidentally look at another guy's private parts, and potentially make the very routine situation, into something that is noticeably awkward.

So there I was, standing there peeing, looking straight at the wall in front of me, as this other kid started peeing next to me. Initially I heard the very common sound of someone peeing into a urinal. Then suddenly, the sound changed to the distinctly different sound of pee hitting the wall and dripping to the floor. So I looked over, and confirm that is exactly what the kid was doing. So I said to him, "What the fuck are you doing?" (This was definitely something that affected me, because I had to smell it every day.) He turned around, looked at me, obviously stunned that someone would confront him about it, and said, "Ummm... Oh, it was an accident!" Obviously it wasn't, so I told him, "Bullshit! I just saw what you did. If it was an accident, you wouldn't have turned your whole body towards the wall!" By that point, I was standing at the sink next to the urinals washing my hands. The kid didn't really say much else, but because of how annoyed and disgusted I was from having to smell his piss every day, I continued to give him a lecture about it.

After washing my hands, I was using the hand dryer, which happened to be next to the door and mounted in such a way, that when someone was using it, they would be partly in the way of the door. Normally, when someone was using that dryer, they will stand slightly to the side of it so others can still get in or out of the washroom. In this case, I intentionally stood in front of it, and in the way of the door. I had no intentions of starting a fight, but I wasn't done saying what I had to say. I was also about

4 or 5 inches taller than the other kid, and even though I still looked young and innocent, with all my experience of getting into fights, I could tell I'd easily be able to deal with this kid if he decided to make it physical. Well, to my delight, that's exactly what ended up happening.

As I was standing there drying my hands, he walked by and pulled the door into me, even though I was clearly in the way. At that point, we were face to face, only inches apart, and instead of saying "excuse me", or something to that affect, he decided to try pushing me out of the way instead. So I had zero moral issues responding physically, but as soon as the fight started, I knew exactly what I wanted to do. I had no interest in trying to punch him or hurt him physically. My only goal, was to deal with the situation the same way most people would deal with a dog or cat that peed on the floor; by shoving their nose in it.

Over the next few minutes, I slowly started getting control of him, pulling him back towards the corner he pissed in, and positioning my grip on him in such a way, that would eventually allow me to be able to shove his face in his piss, without him being able to put his hands in the way. I'm pretty sure he realized what I was trying to do, because as I pulled him towards the corner, he quickly stopped trying to hit me, and was desperately holding onto the toilet stalls instead. Unfortunately, just as I got his arms held behind his back, and was about 5 seconds away from accomplishing such a wonderful thing, a teacher walked in to break up the fight. I actually would have been able to get his face into his piss, before the teacher could have physically stopped us, but I knew if I did, I'd likely get in more trouble, and then the true story that I didn't start the fight, would be less likely to be believed.

The moment I let go, the other kid ran out of the washroom faster than I'd ever ran from the cops, despite the teacher yelling at him to stop. As the teacher and I walked down the hall towards the office, I started explaining what had happened. The teacher mentioned me he knew about the issue with the smell in the washroom, and after I told him, "Sir, I wasn't trying to hurt him, I was only trying to shove his nose into his piss." I was surprised by his reaction when he said, "Ya, I saw that. I wish I would have waited a few more seconds before walking in." Definitely not a reaction I would ever expect to hear from a teacher, but it also wasn't at all a normal situation, and the disgusting smell of pee, was something that was negatively affecting everyone who used that washroom.

While I was in the office lobby waiting for the vice principal, an old science teacher of mine from the first month and a bit of grade nine, walked in. It was the first time I'd even seen him at this school, and even though I was only in his class for less than 2 months, 5 years or so before this, he still immediately recognized me. He turned and said, "Mr.

Unlisted! What brings you here?" I responded by saying, "Oh, I go here now." He nodded his head in acknowledgment, and then said, "I see. So how come you're waiting here in the office?" So I told him exactly what happened. Afterwards, he paused for a long moment, and then extended his arm out to shake my hand. Instinctually, I extended mine out as well, and as I shook his hand, he said, "I'm glad we have someone like you here at our school, keep up the good work!" Again, not at all the type of thing you would ever expect a teacher to say, but it definitely put a smile on my face.

While meeting with the V.P., we went through the security cameras and he was able to identify who the other kid was. We both ended up getting suspended, but the V.P. told me he didn't even want to suspend me, but had no choice because any time there is a physical fight, there is a mandatory suspension for everyone involved. So he only suspended me for the minimum, but the other kid got the maximum and also was required to see a psychiatrist! Also, normally if someone misses a test because of a suspension, they would be given a zero for the test and not be able to take it afterwards. The midterm tests were just starting that week, and the V.P. even went and talked to my teachers and allowed me to take any missed tests or assignments when I was back from the suspension.

After that incident, the washroom no longer smelled like piss, but I did ended up having some ongoing issues with that kid and his group of friends, which was surprising that he even had the guts to start another fight, despite how easily I was able to handle him in the washroom. By the end of that first semester, between the ongoing problems that kid was causing and me once again not doing very well with my school work, I ended up leaving that school and finishing my last few credits at an adult high school. However, the school was nice enough to arrange for me to get my diploma issued from that school, if I was able to finish my credits at the adult high school by the end of that year.

THE FINAL ALTERNATIVE

One of the last classes I took when I started the next semester, was a Law class. The teacher for the class, was another one of those rare teachers you'll never forget, and in this case, what she did during the very first day of class, was one of those things that has forever been etched in my memory. Every teacher and student knows how unproductive the first day of class is. Usually, the teacher will write their name on the board, and then once it looks like most of the kids are there, they will spend a few minutes trying to get everyone to stop talking to each other. Not only did it seem like the teacher was very aware of this common dynamic, but the unusual way she started the class, stood out so much to me, that I even asked her after class, if she did it on purpose. She smiled, and then admitted she had. Instead of the usual name written on the board, when we walked into the class, not only was there nothing on the board, but the teacher wasn't there either. She actually waited so long to come into the class, that there was actually talk about going to the office to see what's going on.

Just before someone was about to go to the office, the teacher walked in. Since she had waited so long, by the time she came in, the whole class was quiet and she had our complete attention, before she even said a single word. Instead of introducing herself, the very first thing she said to the class was, "So I'm assuming everyone here knows that ignorance of the law is not an excuse for committing a crime?" The whole class was a little perplexed at how she started off, but after everyone agreed, she then added, "…but did you know that an honest mistake is [an acceptable excuse]?" On the surface, those two statements could easily seem like they contradict each other, but they are actually two very different concepts, which she then explained. "In order for a crime to occur, two things need to exist, "*Actus Reus*", and "*Mens Rea*", or in English, a guilty act, and a guilty intent. Personally, I found that subtle distinction to be *quite* fascinating and it explained why something like insanity can, and does get people off charges as serious as murder. More importantly, it gave me a new respect towards law in general, knowing that such an important distinction, is one of the fundamental principles of law, and that someone is not actually guilty of something, if they truly didn't know what they did was wrong.

The rest of that school year was relatively uneventful, and even though I was 20 years old at that point, I was still quite proud that I had actually managed to get my high school diploma by the end of that school year; I often worried that I would get frustrated and give up before.

Now that I was done school, I needed to figure out what I wanted to do next. I was still living with my dad, but he had recently gotten married and was waiting for me to finish school, before he moved to the states. It's not that he was pressuring me to make a decision quickly, but I was aware of the situation. I knew I needed to figure out what my next step in life was going to be, and figure out a way to support myself, which was no easy task for a person like me. Not only did I already have a lot of diverse interests at that point, but because of how much I had struggled with school my whole life, I had a lot of anxiety and hesitation about going right into college or university.

ATTEMPTING THE START UP

At some point during the last school year, Nick started working with some friends that we met shortly after we started going to the after-hours club. A lot of them were DJs, which was pretty cool, because we'd often get in the places for free, or at a reduced cost. I also had the opportunity to start learning how to properly DJ and mix records. A few of them also did web development stuff which Nick got involved with as well. By the time I finished school, they were doing well enough to have an office downtown, because of a down payment for a big project they were currently working on. Because the company was essentially a startup, no one was really getting paid yet. Most of the money that they did get, went towards expenses, and the little bit that was left over, was divided based on the amount of work each person contributed to a project.

Even though I was really good with computers, I had zero experience with any kind of web development programming, but they needed somebody to develop a database, for one of the large car dealerships in the city, for the new website there were building. They realized I didn't know anything about databases at the time, but Nick was confident in my ability to quickly learn, and had convinced the others to give me a chance. Since it was costing them nothing to give me that opportunity, I quickly moved my computer into the office, and started learning everything I could about databases.

I had a lot of hopes that I could get really good with databases, which could turn into a long-term job, and make enough money to support myself with. I did a little research on the Internet to find out what books were good to learn databases from, and I came across two that were highly recommended. After getting both of those books, I wasted no time, and started reading them right away. Initially, I was doing quite well, but as I got further into the books, I started realizing that databases are actually a lot more complicated than I first thought. This started causing me a lot of anxiety, because I was afraid if I couldn't learn the database stuff quickly enough, that I'd be kicked off the team. Anytime I get anxious about feeling the pressure of needing to get something done, it often causes a negative feedback loop in my head. Basically, the more anxious I become, the harder it is to say focused on what I need to do, which in turn causes me more anxiety. In moments like these, I usually stop doing that thing altogether, at least for a period of time, since I know it's only going to make things worse. It's not that I'll give up completely, but I recognize the importance of taking an immediate break. But a "break" might not quite convey things accurately, because those kinds of breaks often last for days or weeks and sometimes longer.

Ultimately, the amount of stress that this caused, resulted in me completely avoiding learning anything more about databases, and when other people were there, I just made it look like I was working on something. Adding to the anxiety and stress I was feeling, was how often I was thinking about not being able to hang out there anymore, with all these other people who I had a lot of fun with, and considered my friends. For a person like me, who grew up with very few friends, and was often picked on by so many random strangers, the fear I felt about losing those connections, was so intense that I became completely overwhelmed by it. Like usual, I did my best to hide all of the stress I felt, and the depression that accompanied it. One thing I couldn't do, was stopping the stress and depression from affecting my perception, judgment, and ultimately the decisions and choices that I made. This state of mind ultimately led to an unforgettable moment, that still continues to influence me almost 20 years later.

OH K; NOT OKAY

At that point in my life, the only drugs that I'd done included: weed, ecstasy, LSD twice, mushrooms once or twice, cigarettes, alcohol, morphine while was in the hospital for shoulder operation (but didn't continue taking afterwards), and who knows what else I took that night I put the box cutter though my wrist.

The first person I ever saw on Ketamine was my buddy Nick, which happened while I was still dating Allison from the states. We went across the border to Detroit for a rave party, in a very sketchy part of the city, which really says a lot, when you realize that the least sketchy parts of Detroit, are still sketchy by most people's standards. However, in this case the party was so sketchy, we all decided we wanted to leave, not long after we got there. When we got back into the car, Nick mentioned that he wanted to do some Ketamine, that he was given from a buddy in Windsor, before we start driving. Initially, I got upset when I found out that he brought drugs across the border, because from all my years of crossing the border with my family, I knew that was a serious no-no that you *never* do. But the deed had been done, and so the focus went to this new substance, that I'd never seen before.

I was driving, so I didn't want any, especially anything that I've never done before, and have no idea what it's going to do to me. As we watched Nick pull out the bag, and dump the entire contents onto a CD case, he began attempting to crush it up into a finer powder. I asked him,

"How much are you supposed to take?" He replied by saying he didn't know, but he thinks he's supposed to take all of it, because it was just a small amount that was given to him. Allison and I looked at each other thinking, that doesn't quite seem like a good idea, but we were pretty certain, the little bit that was there wasn't going to kill him, so we just sat back and watched. Once Nick busted up the crystals, as well as he could on the plastic CD case, he rolled up a bill and snorted back the whole lot. As he did so, he let out a sound that it made us realize it was obviously quite painful, so of course we laughed, but with that out-of-the-way, we started driving and heading back to the bridge to go back home to Windsor.

As we drove towards the bridge, Nick went from very chatty, to slowly making less and less sense with each word he spoke, and I became increasingly concerned about crossing the border. By the time we got to the exit to the bridge, it was very clear that there was no way we were crossing the bridge while Nick was in the state that he was currently in. We were not worried at all about his safety because he seemed to be enjoying whatever this stuff was doing to him. Left with no other choice, we stayed on the highway and just kept driving towards the Ohio border, until he was sober enough to go across the bridge. We had no idea how long he was going to be like that, and because there were no smart phones back in those days, there was no way we could check the Internet quickly, to find out more information about Ketamine. Once he seemed sober enough, we turned around and headed back to the border.

As we were driving back, and Nick became coherent enough to talk to again, one of the things that really stood out, was how surprised he was when he asked how long he was like that for. When we told him it had been about 45 minutes, he was so shocked, that he was sure we were playing a joke on him. He believed this no matter what we said, and even thought we changed the time on the car radio just to mess with him. It was only when we stopped at a store and he asked somebody else what time it was, when he finally realized we were telling the truth. Apparently to him, the whole experience felt like many, many, hours.

After that experience, I swore Ketamine was a drug that I would never touch, because it didn't seem very fun to essentially tranquilize myself, the way Nick had done in the backseat of the car. Then a few weeks later, while at a bar one night, the friend who had given Nick the Ketamine, offered a bunch of people a small amount while we were outside having a cigarette. At first I was going to say no, but then when I saw how much he was giving to everybody, I suddenly realized that the amount he gave Nick, was enough for the three of us to enjoy all evening. Of course, before I accepted any, I first asked what it was like. They said it was kind of hard to explain, but the closest comparison would be kind of like an alcohol buzz, that made you feel like dancing a lot. All of that seemed very safe and reasonable, so I accepted the free drugs, snorted it, and went back inside to dance.

As the drug kicked in, I found that the little aches and pains that I had went away, I also felt very light on my feet, very connected with the music, and very fluid with my movements as I was dancing; I was immediately a fan of this new substance. I had no way to know at the time, but Ketamine would go on to become one of my most favorite recreational substances to use. I also had no way to know at that point that eventually I'd realize, Ketamine does not impair me in the same way it impairs most other people. Essentially, what I ended learning much later, is that Ketamine impacts semantic memory, which explains why Nick was speaking gibberish in the car that one night. The reason why it doesn't affect me so much that way, is because of that really high aptitude score; besides being good with law, another way to interpret the details of that test, is being really good with semantics. It's not that my semantical abilities are not impacted, but I've since learned that I could have done as much as Nick did, but you would still be able to understand me quite well, and it's usually quite funny, because I basically end up talking like Yoda, "Funny, my talk, maybe, understand what I say still."

Over the next few months, I started doing Ketamine a little bit more often, but at first only when it was offered to me. Eventually I bought a little bit of my own for the first time, and because it's usually more enjoyable to get high with friends, I would share what I got with others as well. After that first party of having my own supply of Ketamine, and being in control of when we would do more, I quickly realized something that's very unique about Ketamine that's unlike any other drug I've ever tried.

Normally with every other drug, you start off by doing a little bit. When that starts wearing off, and you start feeling almost sober again, if you still plan to party, you would take another dose, that's about as much as you did the first time, so that's exactly what we did. With other drugs when you take your second, approximately equal dose, you expect to get, at most as high as you were last time, but usually a little less, because your body tends to get a little desensitized to the substance. Well this was very different, because rather than getting almost as high, or just as high as the first bump, it actually made us noticeably more high, than we were after taking the first equal amount. At first I just thought I was imagining that, because no other substance I have ever taken, has that kind of effect. When that second equal bump wore off, and we felt about sober again, we then took a third approximately equal size bump. Once again, we became even higher than we were the second time, and went much further down that rabbit hole. Now even though Ketamine is a tranquilizer, even once you tranquilize yourself, or go into what party people refer to as a "K-hole", you still have very lucid thoughts the whole time. I also noticed what Nick mentioned in the car, about the way time slows down. That is definitely a universal sensation that everyone experiences, and personally I find that to be one of the most fascinating aspects of it.

IT'S OH K, IT'S A GOOD FRIDAY

During Easter weekend, before I finished high school, on Good Friday, I spent almost my entire paycheck on an eight ball of Ketamine, with the intent to start selling it, because I knew a lot of people were interested in this substance. Well that Good Friday night, Nick and I went to the office, and like usual there were other people there as well, and the four of us proceeded to play some networked video games.

The top surface of all our desks were glass, so before we started playing, I went to everybody's desk and gave everyone a little pile of their own Ketamine, to do at their own pace, as we were playing games all night. We were playing a game called unreal tournament, which is one of those 3D first person shooter games. The object of the game mode we were playing, is to capture the other team's flag; two of us were on one team and the other two were on the other team. At one point, while we were playing this one particular board, which is basically of two towers on an asteroid floating in space. Given the state of mind that I was in at the time, at one point after doing a bunch of Ketamine, I found myself staring off somewhere else, very disconnected from where I actually was.

I got up from my desk, went to the washroom, and dumped the rather large amount of Ketamine I had on the counter in the washroom. I remember looking at this very sparkly, crystal substance, intrigued that has the ability to do what it does to the mind. After a few minutes, I got bored of that and decided to put the Ketamine back into the bag. As I put the bag next to the counter and attempted to slide all of the Ketamine back in, I suddenly had a moment of complete horror, as I saw most of the Ketamine miss the bag and fall straight down onto the floor.

The floor in that bathroom was less-than-perfect, and the linoleum was not installed correctly. Normally the linoleum floor is placed on the floor first, and then the floor molding between the floor and the walls is installed afterwards, so that it sits on top of the linoleum floor to stop it from curling up on the sides. This is exactly where the Ketamine fell; directly into this crack, where the linoleum was curled up away from the side of the vanity counter. Knowing I just spent my whole check on that, and realizing there was really no other easy way to get it out of there, in the state of mind that I was in, it seemed perfectly reasonable for me to get down on my knees, roll up a bill, shove the bill into that crack, and snort up what I could.

Because what was in the bag, hadn't been chopped up at all, the crystals were rather large, and the larger the crystals are, the more painful it is in the nose. As I was kneeling on the floor, bent over with my face almost touching the floor, the moment I snorted however much I did, the pain in my nose was so intense, my upper body immediately shot straight up in the air, and my head extended as high as it could, while still staying kneeled on the floor. For a moment, I was almost motionless. Because I wasn't holding up my body any more, slowly, my body began to lean back further, and as I started to feel my limp body fall backward, my mind suddenly fell into a different place. My memory of those last moments, are clear and very distinct; there's no reason for me not to assume, that my body did not fall over onto the floor the moment my mind fell into that different place.

Not only was I conscious the whole time, but I was very lucid and very aware as well. I have absolutely no memory of the physical world around me, from the moment my body started falling, until a moment when I was in the hospital, and the reality that I was experiencing, very slowly, began to merge with the reality of the people who were in the emergency room around me. But unlike the moment in the bathroom, when I instantly went from one place to another, the transition of going from that place, back into this reality, was such a slow and gradual transition, by the time I realized I was in the hospital, with a catheter in my penis, nothing about it seemed strange at all. Because it wasn't any kind of suicide attempt, I was released from the hospital as soon as I was sober enough, but in both realities, I wouldn't be completely sober again for another few days. During that time when I went somewhere else that night, because of the way Ketamine affects your perception of time, the entire experience, felt like I lived an entire lifetime in that other place.

Over the next few weeks, as I talked with all my friends who were there that night in the office, I learned that I was mumbling and saying some things the whole time, and although it was organized in some sort of structured sentences, they had no idea what I was saying, because it seemed like I was speaking some entirely different language. So of course they realize that I was still conscious on some level, but as much as I tried to explain to them what I had experienced that night, eventually I gave up, because I realized it was impossible describe with words, that strange place I went to that night. The only thing I could explain, was that I suddenly found myself feeling as though I was much older.

I'm not exactly sure when I realized this, it wasn't right away. Eventually, I noticed that the depression I was feeling before that experience, was completely gone, and I found myself having a new appreciation, not just for life, but I also felt I had touched some other realm of existence, and for the first time, I suddenly had a feeling like there's some other life after this one, which is a feeling I still have today.

ANOTHER BEGINNING

Eventually things got back to normal around the office, and because I was still struggling in my efforts to learn how to build and operate databases, I knew I needed to figure out something else I was going to do. Around the middle the summer, I met somebody new through some mutual friends around the office, who I started hanging out with fairly regularly. He was actually from Ottawa, but was just going to school in Windsor.

One random summer day, him and I were casually talking, when he mentioned that he was going to Ottawa in about a month, to visit his mom and his brother, before school starts in the fall. When I asked him what Ottawa is like, he mentioned that there are a lot of high-tech companies, a lot of mountain biking trails and biking paths throughout the city, all of which were things I was very interested in. The more he told me about Ottawa, the more I found it interesting, so when he suggested that I come up to visit at the end of the summer while he was there, I quickly accepted his offer.

During that week while visiting Ottawa, I immediately fell in love with the city. I found a job at Second Cup while I was there, and arranged to stay with his brother until I was able to find a place of my own. At the end of the week I went back home to Windsor, told my dad that I wanted to move to Ottawa, started packing my things, and then a week later, barely a month after I first considered the idea, I was living in Ottawa, and it was a decision I have never regretted.

OTTAWA; A NEW CITY, A NEW LIFE

By the time I moved to Ottawa, I had already been through so many things that very few people would experience in their lives. At the time, I had no idea of the extent to which my past experiences had influenced my attitude, and behavior towards others overall, but I was aware of a few things. I learned at a very young age, the best way to deal with a bully was to be direct, assertive, and always be willing to stand up for yourself; showing fear is not an option, as that will only encourage them further. Although my dad always taught me never to start a fight, walk away if possible and to never hit first, however, my experience with jail in particular, had taught me a very different lesson. It taught me that if somebody is acting towards me in an aggressive or threatening way, inches away from my face, I'll usually take a step back initially, and very sternly tell them to get the fuck out of my face, more often than not, that's the only warning they get. At that point, if they step towards me again, in that same aggressive manner, I'll usually end up hitting them first, rather than waiting for them to hit me, because I don't want to get hurt, and I wasn't the one that started the fight. The history I had in Windsor with such things, combined with how many people knew me from all over the city, is one of the big influential factors in why I decided to move to Ottawa.

Moving to a new city and not knowing anyone, would likely be a lot harder for most people, than it was for me. I was used to spending a lot of time alone most of my life, so it really wasn't a very hard transition for me.

When I wasn't working, I spent most of my free time riding my mountain bike around the city. The mountain bike that I had at the time was a fairly nice bike, and unlike all the bikes that I had stolen in the past, this bike I actually saved up and paid for myself, a few months before I moved to Ottawa. Fortunately-Unfortunately, within a few weeks after moving to Ottawa, I came out from work, and to my horror and disbelief, I saw that my bike had been stolen. Initially, I just wanted to cry and collapse on the ground, but the first thought that came to my mind, considering all the bicycles that I've stolen when I was younger, was that this was just simple karma, and surprisingly, that somehow made me feel a little better, and I just started walking home.

Now that I found myself without a bicycle, with no easy and efficient way to explore this new city, and without the distraction of biking, I found myself feeling very alone. This actually had an unexpected, positive affect and effect, since it caused me to be more motivated to make new friends.

Unsurprisingly, the first few new friends that I made after moving to Ottawa, were all people who I worked with at The Second Cup. Three of them, two girls and a guy, like myself, were all looking for an apartment, so we decided to find one together. Eventually we did find one, but almost from the beginning, it was obvious things were not going to be as expected. First of all, the other guy never actually moved in, although he did spend the night there a few times and paid the rent for two months, but for all practical purposes, it was more like he was just a friend who would often hang out and sometimes sleepover. What this meant, was that I was now living with two girls and one of their boyfriends, but this didn't cause me any kind of concern initially. I'd already been used to living with my mom, my sister, and one of her female friends when I was younger, but it didn't take long for me to realize just how wrong I was to believe things would be fine.

When we first made plans to find a place to live together, I'd only known them for about a month, but they all seemed pretty cool, and we all got along very well, but more importantly, because of all my experience being around thieves, I was definitely certain that none of them were sketchy like that at all. For the first month or so, everything was completely fine and we all got along great, but then I started noticing something a little odd about the single female roommate, Nikki. Initially, it wasn't very noticeable, and at first she just seemed rather hyper and full of energy, but as more time passed, I started seeing her become disproportionally stressed out about random things. At the time, I didn't understand what I was seeing. So when she wasn't home, I decided to ask the other female roommate, Jen, about what I was noticing, since I knew they had been friends for a long time. Jen quickly explained, that Nikki had a really serious anxiety issue. The whole concept of anxiety was unknown to me; I actually had to ask her what anxiety meant. Satisfied with the answer she gave me, I went back upstairs to my computer and continued what I was previously doing. Because I was also somebody that grew up having a lot of social issues, I always tried to be as accommodating and understanding as I could, but ultimately, everybody has their limits, and my limit came one evening in December on Christmas Eve.

It all started, when a bunch of us were upstairs playing some networked computer games with each other, because I brought more than one computer with me from Windsor. On that particular night, there was my buddy Heider, Nikki, Jen, and Jen's boyfriend at our place. At one point, we took a break from the video game for a few minutes to smoke a joint. Considering that all of us worked at the coffee shop together, clearly none of us had very much money, so a luxury such as weed, was not exactly cheap for us, and was definitely something to be treated with care. As Jen was rolling the joint in her lap on a piece of paper, I turned and said to her in a completely playful tone, "Heeey! Be careful you're going to spill it!" Jen and I would often playfully razz each other this way. I knew she was actually very good at rolling joints, and the way Jen looked up at me, it was clear she knew I was joking around. I'd also known her for quite a few months now, and we actually got along very well. We would often playfully tease each other, and keep each other on our toes, and if she hadn't had a boyfriend, it could have easily been seen as flirting. Everybody else in the room, clearly knew I was just joking around, everyone that is, except Nikki. Then suddenly, without warning, Nikki yelled: "Please! It's Christmas, no fighting!!" Then before anybody could say another word, she stormed off downstairs.

Stunned, I looked around the room for a moment to see everybody else's stunned face, and because I know I sometimes have a habit of putting my foot in my mouth, I asked Jen if I was correct to assume that she understood I was just joking around. She looked at me, surprised that I even asked, and said "Obviously you were joking!" Then I quipped back by saying, "Well it sure didn't seem so obvious to her."

After we smoked the joint, Jen and her boyfriend went downstairs to be with Nikki; Heider and I continued to play the game on the computer. About 30 minutes later, Nikki came stomping upstairs, as if to announce her presence before we could even see her. She got to the top the stairs, turned a full 90° towards us, and told me in the most authoritative voice she could muster up, "Turn The Music Down!" She then turned another full 90°, walked down a couple steps; again stomping her feet as she walked, then turned her head towards me, and said "I *don't* want to hear it again!"

Here's the thing about that situation, I fully understand the importance of compromise when you're living with other people, and I even try to keep my music or computer games, at a volume I don't think anybody's going to complain about in the first place, because I really don't like doing things that disturb others unnecessarily. If it ever was too loud, all of those roommates knew by then, that all they have to do is ask, and I'd gladly turn it down. If Nikki had simply done that, I would've gladly done just that, and that would've been the end of it, at least from my point of view. But obviously that's not what she did, and instead, she decided to come up and bark an order at me by demanding I do something, and that is a type of thing I will always have an issue with. Not only was it rude, but having a roommate give me an order, was not something I was going to tolerate, especially considering I know I'm a reasonable person.

As I paused for a moment, to process what had just happened, and thought about how I was going to address the situation, my other buddy turned and simply said "Wow!" I echoed his statement and said, "Yes, Wow indeed!" I paused for a bit longer, because I didn't want to go down there and get into a fight with her, but at the same time, it was one of those moments when I felt something needed to be said. Once I formulated an idea in my head, I turned to my friend and casually said, "Excuse me for a moment." and then I calmly walked downstairs.

Once downstairs, without ever raising my voice, I proceeded to try to explain to her the issue I had, with what she had just done. I explained to her, "First of all, that comment you freaked out about that I said to Jen when she was rolling the joint, was between me and Jen. Second, it was a fucking joke! If you had come up stairs and asked me to turn the music down, I would've turned it down like I always do. But if you come up and give me an order to do something, like you just did, you will quickly find, that will never work with me, and if anything, there's a good chance I might just do the opposite and turn the music up." At that point she started getting really upset and started yelling and shouting, calling me an asshole and saying how rude I was, how nobody has ever spoken to her so horribly before, and all sorts of other ridiculous things. If she hadn't started freaking out after I calmly said what I came down stairs to say, I would've been done and went back upstairs, but since she decided to escalate the situation, I decided to address those new issues as well, so I continued. "I understand you have some kind of anxiety issue, but that doesn't give you the right to go around giving people orders, and call them an asshole when they stand up to your bullshit. Have you ever thought about the reason why nobody has ever stood up to you like this? It's because everybody's afraid that you'll freak out, and have some anxiety fit just like you are right now."

At that point, she turned and looked at Jen and Jen's boyfriend, and said to them, "Tell him how much of an asshole he's being!" But before Jen and her boyfriend could say anything, I said, "I don't know what you're looking at them for. I'm not the only one that thinks this. I've had conversations with Jen, her boyfriend, Heider…. Everyone thinks the same thing, they're all just afraid to say anything to upset you, because you can get like you're being right now." At that point her jaw dropped so much, you may have thought it was as unhinged as her attitude. As she turned to look at Jen again, with a look on her face that said, 'Please tell me it's not true', instead of the reassurance she was looking for, she was horrified when Jen and her boyfriend just looked at each other, both with shocked looks on their faces, and without saying a word, they both turned and went into Jen's room. At that point the conversation was pretty much over, and so I went back upstairs.

When I got upstairs, Heider turned and asked me, "What the heck did you say to her?" I was a little surprised he asked, because of all the yelling, so I replied, "You didn't hear?" "No", he said, "All I heard was her yelling as loud as she could." So I explained, "I just told her the truth!"

Not long after that conversation, she called her dad to come pick her up. About 30 minutes later, while she was waiting for her dad, she ended up walking up the stairs, very calmly, and in a very thoughtful tone, said to me, "I've never said this to anyone ever before, but I've thought about it for a while, and then waited until I was calm, and thought about it a little bit more, just to make sure, but… I really hate you…. I truly… and honestly hate you."

Unsurprisingly, she ended up moving out a few days later, but after she left that night, the four of us that were still there talked about what happened, and I found out from Jen, that Nikki had a very sheltered life, was extremely spoiled, and quite literally nobody had ever stood up to her, anywhere remotely close to how I did that night; suddenly, it made sense why she was like that.

I definitely had some mixed feelings for a while about that incident, wondering if maybe I went a little far by implicating other people, but ultimately none of them were upset with me about it, and even felt that it was something that she needed to hear. The way my dad would say it, it's tough love, and tough love is usually tough for the person that loves you to say, but also tough to hear somebody you love say it to you. Eventually I came to believe that, although harsh, I think it was the right thing to say, and I think she needed to hear the truth of what people think, if she had any hope of getting better control of it. But I'm sure it's one of those things, not everyone would agree with.

After Nikki moved out a few days later, it was just Jen, Heider and I, left living at that place. As I mentioned, Heider only slept there a few times, and he had already informed us that he was going to stop paying rent at the end of December. Shortly before the new year, Jen broke up with her boyfriend, and not long after that, Jen and I started dating. I also enrolled in college for the winter semester, taking computer engineering, and considering the difficulty I've always had with school in a normal setting, I was definitely more than a little nervous. Ironically, not long after I had started the winter semester, I was faced with yet another situation, almost identical to what happened with Nikki, but this time, the issue involved Jen's mom.

A MOTHER CONFRONTATION

Jen had been "preparing" me to meet her mom for quite some time, and even though she totally loves her mom, she was still dreading that she was going to be coming to stay with us for a week or so. Her mom had struggled with drug and alcohol addiction most of Jen's life, and rarely ever had custody of Jen and her brother. It was obvious that Jen was becoming more and more stressed, the closer the day came to when her mom was coming. One of the big things that Jen forewarned me about, was to expect that her mom would spend hours, going on and on about her problems, how the government is screwing her over, and will talk endlessly about some lawsuit, but isn't actually something that is happening.

Because I've spent quite a bit of time living with people that had a variety of mental issues, I find it makes it easier to empathize with people who have such profoundly difficult problems, that most people are fortunate not to experience. I also felt I had a really good idea of what to expect, based on Jen's descriptions, and ultimately the perception I had was pretty accurate, compared to how she was when I finally met her. Since I was anticipating such a thing, I mentioned to Jen ahead of time, that I'll likely have homework every night, now that I was back in school, I have to stay on top of it, or I'll end up getting overwhelmed, will almost certainly not be able to recover, and end up failing.

When I got home from school, I walked in the apartment to see that Jen's mom finally came. After all the pleasantries and introductions,

I waited for a moment when her mom wasn't paying attention, looked at Jen, pointed to my textbook and then pointed upstairs to let her know that I have homework to do.

At the time, I had electronics, programming, and calculus homework to do, all of which requires a lot of concentration. The small kitchen table we had, was essentially right at the bottom of the stairs, and my computer desk was directly at the top of the stairs, so even if they were whispering, I could hear every single word they were saying. But Jen's mom was so loud, I wasn't even sure if she knew how to whisper. I came down a few times and poked my head around the edge of the stairs, so only Jen could see me, as a subtle way to hint at how loud her mom was. Each time Jen would ask her mom to be a little quieter, because I was upstairs trying to do homework. This worked for a little while, but eventually I started getting more frustrated, because of how distracting it was.

At one point, my indirectness stopped working altogether, when her mom started noticing that I was coming down. After her mom noticed, she was initially very polite and apologized, but then the moment I'd go back upstairs, I'd hear her very clearly, start complaining to Jen about how she is visiting her daughter, and she should be able to talk how she wants to talk, and blah blah blah. When she started becoming disrespectful behind my back, assuming I couldn't hear what she was saying. I came back down again, and not at all quietly, gave Jen this look and said, "Jen you know how I can get."

Jen immediately knew, I was referring to what happened with Nikki. My comment caused her mom to start being very dismissive, by saying, "How you can get? You don't know how I can get, boy!" She then continued trying to play the age card with me, but Jen knew exactly how her mom's approach was going cause me to react, if she kept pushing me further. As soon as I mention that commented to Jen, about how I can get, the look on Jen's face instantly turned, to that of complete urgency, topped with a big pile of "Oh shit". Jen started pleading with her mom, begging her to please stop. I was also trying to politely convince her to stop, and even suggested moving the table and the chairs into the living room, so they could sit in there, but even that wasn't acceptable to Jen's mom. Eventually her mom ended that conversation by saying, "The only way I'm moving out of this chair, is if you make me! And I don't think that's happening anytime soon." I was still very reluctant to do the same thing to Jen's mom, that I did to Nikki, because I was dating Jen at the time. But after her mom said that, I turned and looked at Jen, in a way that made her realize, I finally had enough. Jen looked at her mom and simply said, "Don't say I didn't warn you", then got up off the chair, and went into the living room. Then just like with Nikki, I simply started telling her mom the truth, about what people think.

Since I had heard everything they'd talked about that night, I used certain parts as starting points. One common thing that her mom said countless times, were complaints about why Jen doesn't invite her over more often, or why she doesn't want to see her much. So I helped her out with that and explained, "The reason why Jen doesn't want to see you so often is because of how you are right now. It's been hours since I got home from school, and I don't know how many times I've heard you say the same things over and over and over and over and over again. It's like you're stuck in a loop. Even before you came, Jen was explaining to me how you are, and was preparing me before you even came, so I knew what to expect. You are exactly as she described you to be. You won't stop talking about how you been wronged by the government, and that you are going to sue them. How many years have you been going on about these things? Do you think your daughter, who I know loves you, wants to keep hearing these same things, when you come visit?

Of course, her mom starts trying to tell me how disrespectful I am, and how I should respect my elders and all those common sayings, to which I replied, "I was taught to respect people from the start. All people, regardless of age. I've also been taught to show respect when you're in somebody's home, and right now you're in my home accusing me of being disrespectful, but the only reason why I am down here, is because *you* were being disrespectful, by talking so loudly, despite multiple polite comments. I've been upstairs trying to do my homework, which I can't do because all you're doing is going on about all your problems and talking really loudly. How do you think your daughter feels right now? I don't think I've heard you complain about a single thing that Jen didn't already tell me. I know she loves you, but how do you think it makes her feel not wanting to see her mom, because it's just the same loop conversation every time?"

By that point, her mom had already been sitting there silently in shock for a few minutes, but I felt it was important to really drive home the point, because of how stuck in her head she was about those things, for who knows how many years. I felt by continuing a while longer, she might realize for a moment how her daughter feels. I even told her mom that most of the things that I said, were things that Jen actually thinks as well, but had long given up trying to tell her, because every time she's tried to say similar things in the past, her mom just dismissed it and didn't really listen. At that point her mom said, "If Jen really thought those things about me, she'd tell me herself, because we're honest and open with each other." I then replied by telling her "Jen has tried to tell you those things many times, you just don't listen and dismissed them." Jen even shouted from the other room, "That's true!", and that was about the point when it all seemed to sink in and I could tell her mom finally understood something important.

With that last example, despite how much harsher I was with Jen's mom, than I was with Nikki, I never once felt that I might've went too far. If anything, I sometimes think I should of went further, and continued a bit longer. Between how long her mom was talking that night, before the confrontation started, and how much Jen had told me before I even met her mom, there was still plenty of ammunition I could've fired at her.

As far as the moral view of doing something like this goes, if you were to look at it assuming I was doing it only for myself, so that I can work on my school work, then I think I'd even agree I didn't need to go as far or continue as long as I did, and most definitely there would be no need to go further. But this wasn't something I was doing out of anger or malice. Just like with Nikki, I was very calm, focused, and thoughtful with the things I was saying. Because I knew I was going to implicate Jen into it, I realized there may also be an opportunity to create a positive change in the dynamic between Jen and her mother, and I was happy to see it did have that effect at least for a period of time.

Thankfully, not only did it have a positive effect on their relationship, but by the time her mom left a few days later, it was quite clear that her mom also developed some respect and fondness towards me as well; she even went so far as to let us know that she approved of our relationship.

Before Jen and I moved, there is one more interesting thing that happened, which I want to share.

A TRIP OFF THE BUS

This incident involved an altercation I got into, with a city bus driver on my way home one night. It was in the middle of the winter and quite cold out. Because of how late I often got off of work, it wasn't uncommon for me to catch the last bus that went the full route. I always tried and rush to catch that last bus, instead of the following buses, which followed a modified route, and stopped a lot further from my apartment. Well one particular night, I caught the last bus that took the full route, which I was quite happy about, because the winter coat that I brought from Windsor, was not exactly ideal for the much colder winters in Ottawa, compared to Windsor.

I wasn't the only one on the bus at this point, and there was also an older lady sitting near the front. When the bus stopped where the modified route would normally end, I was surprised when the bus driver told me that it's the end of the line. The old lady seemed a bit confused, but didn't say anything and got off the bus when asked to do so. I was also confused because I was certain of the bus number on the side of the bus, and after mentioning it to him, he even agreed I was on the last bus for the full route. So I politely mentioned that the stop I wanted to get off at was still a couple of stops away. But instead of continuing on his assigned route as he should have, instead he started arguing with me and demanding that I get off the bus. The lady saw this, and instead of walking away, actually stood outside the bus watching what was taking place.

Most people I know, would've probably just gotten off the bus, like the old lady did, to avoid any kind of conflict or confrontation, and even though I generally don't like confrontations, I was particularly annoyed by this situation, especially considering the old lady, clearly wanted to get off at a later stop as well. Some of the people I later told about this situation, even went as far to say that they thought I was in the wrong for insisting he do his job, that my bus fare is paying for. But just because most people might feel a certain way or do a certain thing, it doesn't mean that it's the right thing to do. In a case like this, I definitely don't think walking away was the best thing to do. All it would do is encourage him, to slack off even more in the future, if he knows nobody will ever make an issue out of it. If he would have been nice, and explained that he needed to get somewhere, and was running late, it's quite possible I might've been willing to do him a favor, and walked the rest of the way. Not only did he not have any kind of reason at all, for not finishing his assigned route, but he was quite rude and had an attitude right from the beginning. Why should I have sympathy for him, and do something for him, when he is acting that way towards others?

So I insisted, and refused to get off the bus before my stop. He then replied by crossing his arms, and said he's not going any further. I then demanded that he call his supervisor, which he refused to do. After a minute or two of the stalemate, and thinking about it for a moment, I decided to pick up the bus phone, and call the supervisor myself. As soon as I grabbed the phone, the bus driver suddenly grabbed me and tried physically throwing me off the bus. At that point, almost everybody would have just given up and walked away. But in this case, that actually felt like the morally wrong thing to do, because at that point, he's not acting like a bus driver, he's acting exactly like a bully, and bullies always need to be stood up to.

After this first happened, and I was telling my friends about the incident, it's interesting how many different people told me the exact same thing even though they weren't around each other when I told them the story. The things I heard the most from people, were comments about how I should take into consideration what kind of bad day this bus driver was probably having, or other similar types of comments that were all trying to defend the bus driver. I do usually consider those types of things, I did in this case as well, because it was obvious from the beginning that he was having a bad day, however we all have bad days, but having a bad day is never an excuse for physically assaulting someone for simply picking up a phone. It doesn't matter that it was the bus phone; it still does not justify him touching me physically. If I was trying to damage the phone, then he would have a legal right to use force against me, but it was quite clear I was picking up the phone to call his supervisor because he was most certainly in the wrong and didn't want to get in trouble. Eventually when he was unable to get me off the bus, he gave up and finally decided to drive to the last bus stop, and the old lady got back on the bus as well, and even thanked me.

After I got home a few minutes later, I spent some time deciding whether or not I wanted to file a complaint, knowing the trouble it could cause him, especially realizing everybody has bad days. After thinking about it for a while, I started feeling like it would actually be the wrong thing, not to make a complaint, because there's absolutely no way to justify his decision to physically grab me, and try to force me off the bus. When the supervisor came over to my house to take my statement, I made a point to stress to him, that I don't want to press charges, because I wasn't hurt, and if he has no history of doing anything like this, I definitely don't want to see him get fired, but I still felt it was important that there be a written record of what happened. If he had never done something like this before, then ideally, this would be a wake-up call to him, and hopefully would prevent a similar incident or worse, from happening to anybody else in the future. If he does have a history of doing stuff like this, then clearly he'll almost certainly do something like this again, and a person like that, clearly can't handle the stresses of being a bus driver, and it's in the public's best interest that he doesn't continue to be.

A NEW APARTMENT;
A NEW KIND OF ENDING

Not long after this, Jen and I finally moved in to a new place not too far away. We hadn't been living at the new place for very long, before things started getting weird with our relationship. For the most part, we never really fought, or had any big fights or anything like that. The biggest issue I can remember, had to do with her feeling like I was embarrassed to bring her around my friends, because I never really invited her out with us. I tried explaining to her, that I wasn't embarrassed at all about anything like that (which was the complete truth, and in fact I thought she was really attractive, and supercool), I just didn't think she was interested in hanging out with my nerdy friends, because she hadn't expressed any kind of interest before.

In retrospect, after she told me, it seemed like one of those things, that would probably be obvious to most people, but is a type of thing that isn't obvious to me. It's definitely obvious to me now, after she mentioned it, and it's something that I've never forgotten, because I wouldn't want to ever make a mistake like that again. I really hadn't had much experience being in a relationship up until that point in my life, at least not a long-term relationship, I had hopes could actually last. In situations like that, when I have strong emotions that make me feel a bit vulnerable, I can sometimes feel a bit overwhelmed; it's not at all uncommon for me to miss very obvious things, that most people would naturally understand without even thinking about. I know sometimes this makes people think I don't really care enough to consider those things about other people, but that couldn't be further from the truth. The reason I will often miss things that are obvious to others, is really just a consequence of how many things my mind is always thinking about, regardless of if I want to think about them or not. I don't think even my own parents realize, how much time in a day I spend thinking about things to say in hypothetical social circumstances, because of social anxieties. By the time anyone finishes this book, hopefully, such things as that will be better understood.

Even after I told Jen it wasn't intentional, it didn't seem to help the situation between her and I, because she just ended up feeling like I was just saying that to make her feel better. Despite how much I was insisting that wasn't true, I could tell it still continued to bother her, and it's my best guess I have as to why the relationship ended not long after. Besides that, the only other issues I remember us having, were just a few little trivial things, that wouldn't make sense to end a relationship about. One issue was related to the dishes, but I've always felt she misunderstood the nature of my comments.

When we first moved in to this new place, we made agreements about chores, responsibilities, and stuff like that. It was her that mentioned always doing the dishes right after using them, which isn't something I normally do if I'm living alone, but I grew up like that while living with my dad, so I had no problem agreeing to it. At one point, she started slacking off and not doing the dishes like she suggested, and I started making the occasional comment about it, which was intended to be playful, like with many other things we would say to each other in the past. Due to a note she left when she moved out, it always made me feel like she misunderstood that, and thought I was being serious and actually complaining.

One last issue, which was definitely something I was serious about, had to do with some really cheap computer speakers that were hooked up to my second computer downstairs that she would use. They were cheap $10 speakers, and had no meaning to me at all and I wouldn't have cared if they got destroyed. She often turned them up so loud that, the distortion was horrible to listen to, and I'd often complain that they were way too loud and sounded like crap. I also added, that eventually it'll damage the speakers and destroy them. I only added that second part, because then she wouldn't have had speakers to listen to, and felt that maybe she could relate to that point, more than the distortion, since she obviously didn't mind listening to distorted music.

So then one day, I came home from work, and walked into the apartment to hear the speakers on full blast, louder than she'd ever played them, only to discover that she had moved out while I was at work. The only note that she left, was one on her closet door in her bedroom, that said "Let people come, and let people go." And another note that was on the fridge, which read, "It's easier to complain about the dishes not being done, than it is to admit that you're a misogynist." At the time I actually had to go look up what the word misogynist meant, and I was shocked to find out that it has to do with somebody that hates women in particular. This is even more shocking for someone like me, who had so much womanly influences growing up around my mom and my sister's friends, and all of my close friends have definitely heard me say more than once, that I feel equally in touch with both sexes.

Because of how unexpectedly surprised I was, to come home to find that she left, as well as the fact that we'd only been dating a few months, it was fairly easy to dismiss how I felt, and I just kind of laughed it off, but I knew right away how much it hurt, because I did really like her a lot. Thankfully we hadn't been together long enough to really fall in love, or else clearly it would've hurt a lot more.

After finishing the book, and now just editing, I can't help but wonder if this had some kind of long-term effect on me. It's really hard to say, even after thinking about it a lot. I'm not sure if I just feel that way because of what happened with my ex recently, or if it really did have some kind of long-term effect. It's definitely a question that will be on my mind for a long time, but something I do know, is that I wouldn't have any kind of long-term relationship for another eight years or so….

Either way, I don't want to ramble on about that. Obviously there's no moral principle with the story, I only included it as an interesting example of the effect misunderstandings can have. As with a lot of things in this book, writing about it definitely caused me to look at some things differently, but with this story, I'm not sure what I think about it at this point. Since there was no intense trauma associated with this, I won't start obsessively thinking about it, but it's definitely going to be a reoccurring thought; I can't help but feel there's something to learn from this still.

ROOM FOR A NEW MATE

After that relationship ended and she moved out, I quickly got a new roommate, who was somebody I went to school with. He was also in the computer program like I was, and was pretty laid back, so we got along quite well. Besides school interests, we had a lot of other similar interests like physics, science, and other subjects like that. We'd often share random new facts, and research papers with each other, but there's really only one that truly stands out. In order to understand why, I need to jump back a little bit, and onto a slightly different topic, but it still seems like it fits with the book, because it definitely has to do with the whole issue of morality, at least to some.

The issue I'm referring to has to do with the concept of "God". I was baptized and raised as a Catholic, and a fair bit of my family on my dad side is quite religious, but personally I don't identify as a Catholic. As I started learning about Catholic doctrine when I was younger, because of the way my mind works and will pick ideas apart, in an attempt to find contradictions or logical flaws, it caused me to develop an active interest in religions overall, not just Catholicism. I definitely never studied any, to the point where I would consider myself even close to being an expert, but I definitely feel I know more than the average nonbeliever, and possibly even the average believer. I don't just limit myself to religions, but any sort of doctrine that attempts to make sense of everything around us, the meaning and purpose of life, and all such things like that. So this definitely includes things like Buddhism, as well as science, physics and biology, or even things like L.S.D, Ketamine, Magic Mushrooms and D.M.T.. Even concepts like the simulation theory, falls within that broader category.

Starting in my late teens, up until my early to mid-20's, I'd often have religious discussions, with all sorts of different people, especially with highly religious people. Because I have spent time reading Bibles, and learning about religions, it allowed me to have fairly decent conversations on the subject. Sometimes you'd often hear me say, that I had the best anti-God arguments, but in actuality, nobody would've ever heard me say, there is no God, back when I was frequently having those debates, even though most people likely felt that I was saying that. The reason it was often misunderstood that way, had to do with the way I would go about debating religion with people, who were firm believers.

Instead, I would simply just ask a lot of questions. Since I knew a fair amount about religions and have read most of the bible, I was good at asking very pointed questions, that would quickly create so much doubt in the validity of what they're saying, that it would make it seem like I was disagreeing with them, even though I didn't disagree or agree. Eventually, on one particular day, two different people who didn't even know each other, very quickly reacted in the exact same way.

The first person was a girl I worked with, who was taking astrophysics in University, and I had a huge crush on. The reaction that I got, when they finally had no other response to support their argument, was "well that's just what I believe, I have faith." The interesting thing about a statement like that, is you can never say anything else that disproves it, because after all, that is the nature of faith. Anytime someone would say that, it would essentially be the end of the conversation. Well when I left work that day, I had a new bike by then, and just took a cruise around the market on a nice afternoon. I came across somebody that most would consider to be crazy (and they likely were), since he was holding up some signs saying the end is near, preaching the Bible, kind of thing. But from my experience, such people are often fascinating to chat with, so I decided to stop by and start a conversation with him. Like the conversation at work earlier, within 10 minutes at most, I heard those exact same words come out of his mouth, "well that's just what I believe, I have faith." And likewise that essentially ended the conversation. This definitely frustrated me a bit, because it seemed like a copout that they said, simply because they had nothing else to counter with. So I had enough of that for the day, and also I don't think I really had much religious debates again since that day, because of what happened when I finally got home later.

Once I got home, my roommate was home and as I passed his room I stopped to chat a little bit, like I usually would, and often exchange new things that we learned recently, that we are both interested in. So when he asked, "what's new?" I shared some new thing about quantum physics I recently read about. I knew he would find interesting, so I was really surprised at his unusual reaction when he said "Well how do you know that's true?" This made me feel like I didn't explain it well enough, because he's never said something like that before, so I reworded it but again he says "But how do you know, that's true?" So then I paused for a moment, knowing I was already frustrated by the lack of progress with the two religious conversations that day, and after I realized I couldn't think of a way to say it that he couldn't respond to that same way. I told him I'll think about it and get back to him later.

I'm not sure how long all of that rattled around in my mind, but eventually I came to realize something quite profound. Ultimately what I realized is that it doesn't matter if you believe in God, science, or anything else for that matter, at some point faith becomes a necessity to validate your belief in anything.

Morals are a good example of the necessity of faith.

The questionable stories I'm sharing in this book for example, regardless of if it's something I felt was morally justified or morally wrong, it would be impossible for me to feel one way or the other without faith.

ANXIOUSLY DISTRACTED

Shortly after this new roommate moved in, I was chatting with him one time about A.D.D. and the difficulty I often had focusing on homework for extended periods of time. He suggested that I go see someone, in the Center for Students with Disabilities at the college, because I might qualify for getting extra time on my exams, and able to take them in a room by myself. Given my past experience in school, particularly with how well I did while I was attending alternative high schools, I knew this was something that would certainly help me, so I made an appointment the next day.

I had only recently discovered that I have A.D.D. while I was randomly researching different things on the internet one day. I wasn't diagnosed as having A.D.D. as a kid, but when I found a diagnosis checklist, I essentially checked every box on that list, and given my school history and past, once I saw that checklist, I knew for certain that I was. When I discovered this checklist, I actually found it extremely surprising that nobody ever noticed when I was younger considering all of the psychiatrists, psychologists, social workers, and counselors that I'd seen when I was younger for the problems I was having in school.

Back in the 80's, when A.D.D. first started to be officially recognized as a legitimate condition, most of the focus was on A.D.H.D. Because I was not hyperactive, I think that's why nobody ever noticed it about me. Shortly after I self-diagnosed myself, I was talking to some friends about it, when one of them stated that he also has A.D.D. and actually has a prescription for Ritalin that he never takes.

Even though at that point in my life I'd never taken any kind of chemical stimulant, I was still very interested in trying Ritalin in the hopes that it would actually help me with my schoolwork because I knew I was going to end up failing based on how things were going with school at the time. So I decided to ask my friend if he would be willing to get the prescription so that I can try it, and because he wasn't using it anyway, he agreed.

I'll never forget that very first time I tried it, and the effect that it had on my ability to focus on schoolwork. When my buddy got his prescription, he only gave me about six pills or so because he decided he was going to keep the rest and start taking it again to see if it helped him with things he was struggling with. After I got those few pills from him, I was so excited that I went home right away to try working on some school work. Because I didn't have that many, the first thing I did when I got home was to research a bunch of things about Ritalin, just as I've always researched any drug I've ever taken. I was especially curious about the most efficient way to take Ritalin because I wanted to make the most of the little bit that I had. Based on what I read, it seemed very clear that the most efficient method of using Ritalin was to crush it up and snort it, because if the opinions that I read online were correct, I'd only need to do ¼ as much to get the same effect versus if I were to swallow it. After reading this, the choice seemed obvious.

Even though I wasn't quite sure what to expect or how effective it would be actually in helping me with my homework. I still wanted to make the most of it, so I got all my homework set up in front of me and loaded all the software I needed on the computer before I crushed up that first pill. Once everything was ready and I snorted the first bit, I begin working on my school work right away. The amount of Ritalin I did was relatively small and the effect was so subtle that it wouldn't have even been noticeable if it wasn't for the fact that suddenly I had no difficulty at all sitting there and doing the work. I kept working as long as I could until I noticed I started getting distracted with other things. So I snorted a little bit more, and not long after, concentrating on my school work became effortless again. This pattern continued all evening and late into the morning, until I finally finished all of the work that I had to do. I was completely astonished at how effective just a small amount of the substance was in helping me with my work, and I couldn't help but wonder how much better I would've done in school as a kid, if somebody had noticed I was A.D.D. when I was younger.

When I made the appointment, to see somebody in the Center for Students with Disabilities, talking to them about getting a prescription for Ritalin, was also one of the things that I wanted to discuss. When I finally was able to see somebody, I brought in the psychological assessment that was done of me while I was in jail, and after she read it, she decided to have me take a few more detailed aptitude tests, that related to my lowest score from the tests that I took in jail. The report from jail says. "Adam's lowest subtests scores are all well within the average range and, interestingly, were earned in three subtests which make up the working memory index. These tests include a range of activities which require the examinee to orally attend to information, hold it briefly and process it in memory, and then to formulate a response. While these tests are Adam's lowest scores, they are still within the average range and, even relative to his highest scores, do not constitute a significant area of weakness." Even though the report itself says that, something that I've noticed on my own over the years since this report has been done, is that most of the time it's true, it is not an area of weakness, but just like the paragraph about becoming obsessive and when I'm overwhelmed emotionally, I have noticed that my memory is also one of those things that seem to be significantly impacted negatively during times of overwhelming stress.

The results of the tests from college, mainly focused on more specific memory subtests, which were not part of the assessment done while I was in jail. I found the results of the tests to be very enlightening, and has helped give me more insight into areas of weakness I could focus on and try to improve. The test report from college indicates. "A memory test assessed different aspects of recall (Immediate Memory, Delayed Memory and Active Working Memory) using different sensory modalities (visual and aural content)". Before I share the test results, I just want to explain something for those, who might not have ever heard of percentile ranking (which I didn't even understand when I first saw this report). Basically if you score in the 2nd percentile, what that means is based out of 100 people 98 people, would score that high or higher than you). Obviously this is a very simple concept, but could easily be confusing if you've never heard anything listed in terms of percentiles. So, the results from these tests are as follows:

General Memory Index: 13th percentile
Verbal Short-Term recall: 23rd percentile
Visual Short-Term recall: 14th percentile
Visual Long-Term recall: 42nd percentile
Verbal Long-Term recall" 2nd percentile
Working Memory Index: 63rd percentile

Additionally, they also administered an A.D.D. test, and as I expected, it does support my self-diagnosis that I do have A.D.D.

The reason I wanted to share the test results in this book, is because of how they relate to ways people often misunderstand me. The test scores also help illustrate, how much stress can impact my intellectual functioning, and when I took those tests that day, I was definitely stressed. Not only was I late for the appointment, which caused me to feel rushed while taking the tests. But also, because of how high I scored on some of the other tests I took while I was in jail; I felt a lot of pressure to do well on these tests too. When the tests for verbal recall started, it was explained to me that she was going to read a paragraph, and then immediately afterwards I had to repeat that paragraph as accurately as I remember.

As the testing started, all I was thinking was, "Okay I have to remember what she is going to say." I kept repeating this to myself, until she started reading the first paragraph. When she started reading the paragraph, I was still repeating that for a moment, and when I realized I'd completely missed the first part of what she said. Instead of immediately focusing on what she was saying, the next thought that went through my head was "Oh shit, I just missed what she said." For the rest of all of those paragraphs, I was distracted the entire time knowing that I just screwed up, and that continued to affect me for the rest of all those tests. Normally I actually do really well with repeating exactly what somebody says right after they say it, normally I'm sure I'd score well above average with something like that, but the test results that day, showed I only scored in the 23rd percentile. And then one of the last tests, were a series of yes or no questions, based on those first paragraphs that were read to me, which was then testing my long-term verbal recall, which again I normally am very good at, but because I was so stressed and distracted when I first heard the paragraphs, by the time I was asked yes or no questions about those paragraphs an hour later, unsurprisingly, I only scored in the 2nd percentile.

Another way I find I'm often misunderstood, also relates to both my highest and lowest scores with memory. Because of how noticeably intelligent I often seem to people just from talking with me for a few minutes, at other times when I forget important things, a lot of people seem to think I'm selfish, self-centered, lack empathy, or other similar things I've heard too many times in my life, simply because I forgot some relatively important thing. Interestingly, and quite hypocritically, most of the people who have ever said such things to me, have also forgot about things that I consider to be important, but I have rarely ever even pointed such things out to any of them. Also, I definitely don't think it means they lack empathy or other similar things, because it's very clear it is just a simple issue of different people having different interests and everyone places varying degrees of importance on things. Most often though, when I forget about something that's important to someone else, it's also important to me too, even if it's not something I find interesting. Such important things would almost certainly relate to friends and family, and even if I didn't find a thing to be interesting, it would still be very important to me, because doing things that make others happy, not only makes me happy as well, but it's a type of happiness that is far more enjoyable than simply doing something only for myself. If we stop to think about this for a moment, we notice that when I forget about things that are important to others, quite literally, I'm also forgetting about doing something that would make me very happy.

The issues I have with certain types of memory also directly add to my difficulty in remembering important things. As I mentioned, I've spent a lot of time over the years thinking about those lowest scores and ways to improve upon them. Not only have I been able to do just that and not forget important things nearly as often as I did before, but it's even quite simple to explain; hopefully by sharing it, some of you may find the technique helpful in your life as well.

The two most important types of memory related to forgetting such things, are short term recall and long term recall. It could be visual memory, if you saw the important thing written down, or verbal memory if someone said it to you, but it doesn't matter as far as this technique goes. The basis for this technique is already well known, I just adapted it for this specific issue.

Essentially, when you first find out the details of the important thing, the idea goes into your short term memory. Short term memory typically lasts between 15-30 seconds. If the important thing is something you find interesting, then the mind usually ends up performing these next steps automatically, which is why it's usually quite easy to remember something important that you also find interesting too. If the important thing is about an upcoming event you want to attend, usually it's actually quite hard not to keep thinking about it, especially the closer it becomes. Because it is something interesting, as soon as it first entered your short term memory, thoughts of the future when that interesting and fun day would take place entered your mind without even trying. When that happens, the thoughts in short term memory are automatically being transferred into long term memory. The more you think about those thoughts, the more reinforced those long term memories become.

After I first understood this way that memory works, it was just a simple matter of actively doing those same things, when presented with an important, but uninteresting thing. Usually, when something does not interest us, we don't spend any more time thinking about it after, so the idea never really gets imprinted into long term memory. Instead, if you want to remember the uninteresting, yet important thing, the moment it first enters your short term memory, start thinking about the day in the future just like you would if it were something interesting. Think about as many different details as you can, including thoughts of the specific day. Also think about some specific dates before, not only will this help reinforce the whole long term memory, but as those days before the important day approach, it can help act as an advanced reminder as well. The more details you can think of, the clearer the long term memory will be, and you will be more likely to remember it. If you do this for only 2 minutes, you'll be surprised at how much less you forget about such uninteresting things.

Another small part of why I sometimes forget important things like that, is in fact because it's important, and since I know that I have issues with my memory sometimes, I feel a little bit of stress, and I'll consciously try to commit it to memory, because I hate how I feel when I miss something that's important to one of my friends. This whole issue right here, is a big part of why I hate hearing compliments about my intelligence, since I know my overall intelligence isn't that high; I just actually seem a lot smarter than I am because my highest score is something that relates to communicating with people. So that's what people base their impression of me on, but they don't realize all of the other things I struggle with daily. Additionally, because of how often people will make a comment about my intelligence, for as long as I can remember, any time somebody makes a comment about how smart I am, it makes me feel very uncomfortable due to the pressure and expectations such comments cause me to feel. And because of all the bullying I've experienced as a kid, people don't usually see the anxiety or stress, since I learned at a really young age from being bullied to hide any kind of emotion that would show any kind of vulnerability.

Getting back to college, when I met with the psychiatrist to hear the results of those most recent tests, even though my A.D.D. tests showed that I do have it. But the psychiatrist refused to give me Ritalin because in her words, "Due to your history of drug abuse." Yes, I have experimented with and used drugs in the past. I even done some rather large, and irresponsible amounts a few times, but I didn't mention those specific moments, so I knew I never had a history of abusing drugs. But if she actually listened to how frequently or rather infrequently I used drugs, it would have been obvious that the amount that I've ever done was nowhere close to an amount that would indicate abuse. All this made me feel is that I should not have been honest with her about those details, and so when she asked if I'd be willing to come back on a regular basis I lied and said yes, knowing I would never want to talk to her again. So instead of giving me a prescription for Ritalin, which I knew would've helped me with school, she prescribed me an antidepressant, even though I wasn't depressed at all. She also gave me a seven-day sample pack, and then a little booklet about anxiety because she thought I had an anxiety disorder. I was so upset and irritated when I left her office, that I actually threw the sample pack and booklet on anxiety into the garbage just outside the office. But because of how curious I am, I ended up turning around and taking them back out of the garbage because I wanted to go home and learn more things about the pills she had given me and about anxiety.

When I got home that day, my roommate asked me how the appointment went as soon as I walked in. He knew I went in to get the results from the test, and even asked if I got the Ritalin. I quickly explained to him what happened, and when I mentioned the antidepressants that she gave me, he asked if I was planning to take them. At first I said no because I wasn't depressed, so why would I take them? Afterwards, I went upstairs to my room. I'm not sure how long the pamphlet on anxiety sat on my desk, but I did start researching more about those pills right away, and ended up changing my mind and figured I would at least try them. Shortly after I took one, I told my roommate that I changed my mind.

Then later on that night, I came downstairs and went into my buddy's room. He turned and looked at me and asked, "So how are you feeling?" And I told him, "I feel like I took some ecstasy!" I then vented a bit about how absurd the whole thing was that she wouldn't give me Ritalin, because she felt I had a drug abuse problem, but then gave me something that makes me feel like I took a club drug, which only made it a lot harder to actually focus on my school work, instead of something that I knew actually did help me.

All of my prior experiences as a kid, seeing all those countless doctors, social workers, and such, were almost all completely positive experiences. I already realized this one bad experience with the doctor at the college, completely discouraged me from wanting to see any kind of psychiatrist again. I knew I would hesitate about being honest and open about things, and then what's the point of going to talk to somebody about anything like that?

The only real positive thing, that came from meeting with that Doctor and taking those tests, was what I ended up learning, when I finally started researching anxiety in great detail. Up until that point in my life, I never thought I had anything that would qualify as a panic attack, which is why I was so dismissive when she gave me that little booklet. But when I finally started researching more about anxiety, I started realizing that panic attacks were just an extreme example of anxiety, and that most of the time, the ways anxiety affects your life is sometimes barely noticeable to others, or not noticeable at all. One of the things that caught my attention about anxiety, that I knew applied to me, was about how it'll cause people to avoid certain situations that cause them anxiety. I knew right away when I read, that how often I do avoid certain situations, because of how uncomfortable they make me feel. Remember, I only learned what the word anxiety meant a few months prior to this, and before learning this new word, I would always refer to these feelings I had, simply as stress, or just feeling uncomfortable. Now that I was spending so much time researching anxiety, I started realizing more and more, that the doctor was definitely right in thinking that about me.

I'm very grateful I turned around, and took that booklet out of the garbage that one day. If I hadn't, I'm sure my life would be a bit different in certain ways, and most likely I would be worse off. Over the years, as I would eventually see, I'm definitely capable of having full blown panic attacks, but it would usually come out as frustration, hidden from even me. Within in a year or two after learning about anxiety, I started realizing some of the things I was doing that hid it, and quickly started realizing it has always been a big problem. Thinking about it now, no doubt, it relates to being bullied and teased. Also, once I was only working for myself selling drugs, I was able to remove most anxiety inducing stresses from my life, which is another example of avoiding vulnerable emotions.

Since I have spent a lot of time learning and thinking about anxiety, it's given me insights and I came to my own fundamental conclusion as to what it actually is, which has given me a "trick" that often helps managing anxiety. After spending countless hours researching anxiety, and watching people looking for signs of it, I started noticing a pattern, it seemed like everyone that seem to have anxiety issues, were also noticeably intelligent. When I first noticed that, I immediately tried to start finding people that didn't seem very intelligent, who also showed signs of anxiety, but I was never able to find any clear examples of that. This led me to the dictionary definition of anxiety, which shows the word does not just have a negative meaning, and the positive example from the dictionary, says, "Eagerly desirous". Eventually I put all those pieces together, and realize something quite profound: "Fundamentally, anxiety is simply a type of functional awareness." This explains why essentially everyone you know who has an obvious anxiety issue, is also very intelligent in at least some ways, because of the direct relationship between awareness and intelligence. If you weren't aware of anything, intelligence would essentially be meaningless, because you wouldn't have any things that you're aware of for your intellect to think about. As interesting as all that is, the thing I considered to be most profound about those simple realizations, is that it actually offers a tool to help deal with anxiety in a healthy way.

First, I want to illustrate a point that relates to why anxiety often feels impossible to control. As I'm writing this sentence, I want you to not think about a purple dinosaur. Of course, as soon as I said purple dinosaur, you keep thinking about it. So clearly, trying to not think about something, is an impossible task. That's exactly what happens when people are having an anxiety issue; trying not to think about anxiety, as a way of stopping anxiety, is just as effective as trying not to think about a purple dinosaur when being asked not to think about a purple dinosaur. However, to continue with the dinosaur analogy, now think about the purple dinosaur for a moment, and continue to try to think about it, as I start trying to tell you not to think about a pink dinosaur, whatever you do don't think about the pink dinosaur, pink, pink, pink. Stepping away further, do you have a car, if so, what kind? Do you live in a house or an apartment? Do you have kids? What kind of things do you like doing for fun?... As you read those things, you probably stopped thinking about that purple dinosaur, until now at least.

Because anxiety is simply awareness, the only way to effectively take control of it, is indirectly, and instead of trying not to think about it, which usually just makes the anxiety worse knowing that you can't stop it, the better thing to do, is just fill your mind with other things. Go do something fun, or distract yourself with anything other than what's making you feel anxious. Anytime any of those anxious thoughts come into your mind, don't feed them in any way. Getting frustrated that they keep coming back to your mind at first, only further feeds the negative anxiety.

Sometimes it's definitely harder than other times, even for me, and I've been doing this for over fifteen years. If you're anxious about something that you're putting off doing, then either get it done right away, or understand that you're going to continue feeling that way until it is done, and it will likely get worse as a deadline approaches, before gets better. Obviously those are just a few examples, but just by understanding an issue on its most fundamental level, almost always offers a practical answer, and a way of dealing with the problem; in this case, it's simply a matter of practice, persistence and determination.

Once I realized what anxiety actually is, of course I first noticed it was both a blessing and a curse. But after realizing it is simply awareness, I was especially motivated to master the trick I discovered which I just shared, I realized it could be possible to turn that into a controllable asset, similar to A.D.D. and the ability to hyper-focus. A recent example, similar to the futility of trying to control anxiety by trying to not think about it, I've always failed to control the intensity of my emotions in the same way. After I recently discovered that I'm slightly autistic, because emotional sensitivity and intensity, are core parts of autism, I realized I was attempting the impossible by trying to control that. Simply being aware of the autism link to my emotions, has already caused me to look at things more carefully, and I'm sure that will never change, in the same way that I'd never forget what I look like in a mirror.

The only "trick" I've learned so far, when it comes to dealing with the intensity of my emotions, is something I've recently stopped doing all together, that I would often do intentionally. In the past, any time my emotions became really intense, and I felt nervous or anxious, I'd often tap my foot or hand quite quickly. I always felt it was a good way to dissipate excessive energy, and I had been doing that for years. After I found out I was slightly autistic, and noticed I started doing that, while feeling very emotional thinking about how much I miss Karo; I suddenly saw that habit in a very different way, and immediately stopped doing it. Clearly it was never effective at dissipating any kind of significant emotional energy, and likely none. What I noticed was, by allowing myself to do that with my foot or hand, it was actually very similar to trying not to think about anxiety, and was only causing me to think about the whole issue, and get that much more consumed by it; not only was my mind thinking about it, but my body was involved as well. It only took three or four times, noticing I was doing that, for me to finally stop it for good. It's not that I still don't miss her, and I'm sure I'll continue to have really sad days for a long time, but just by stopping that one physical reaction, I realized right away that simple little thing I was doing with my body, had a surprisingly big effect on how much worse things would progress, once I started thinking about her a lot. It's truly interesting how such a little thing as that, could have such a huge effect.

Besides the tapping issue, I have other ideas in my head too. They seem to be working so far, but I don't like giving out questionable advice, and because I don't know how to explain the other things just yet, I wouldn't even attempt to try to write them down at this point. Simply put, the emotional link to autism is ever present in my mind, and anytime I start feeling any type of emotion at all, I'm much more mindful of it, since the intensity of my emotions, were directly related to me losing, likely forever, the most precious person I ever loved. This is definitely one of those things I will continue to think about, just like the dancing moment, no doubt for the rest of my life.

On the topic of A.D.D., I feel it's worth mentioning a few things about the way I research things, that others may find practical and useful. Normally when it comes to somebody who has A.D.D., the main problem it causes, is mostly the difficulty concentrating, and staying focused on a task. Very few people who don't have A.D.D. or know somebody that does, are aware of another interesting aspect of the condition, since it's not really a negative thing, and instead can be quite a useful thing. Pretty much everyone I've ever talked to who has A.D.D., is very aware of this and also enjoys this ability. While most the time it is hard to concentrate and stay focused, at other times, when they are really interested in something, not only is it easy to concentrate and focus on the thing of interest, but they can focus on it so much, it's actually referred to as hyper-focusing. When somebody is in the state of hyper-focusing, a person can become so concentrated on what they're doing, that almost nothing can distract them from it. They become so focused, it could almost qualify as an obsession. Even things like, needing to eat, going to the bathroom, or even sleeping, all become completely unimportant to the person whose hyper-focusing. I realized this about myself from a very young age, but after researching and learning that I have A.D.D., and learning about this hyper-focusing trait, I've been able to learn how to use it as a tool. Over the years it's often helped me learn how to focus on something that I otherwise would've had difficulty concentrating on.

Take for example, the difference between reading something long like a book vs reading a short scientific paper or article. Most the time somebody with A.D.D., would find it difficult to stay focused on the book, even if it's a topic that interests them. However, using the Internet to learn about the same thing, is often a lot easier because there are so many different websites with the same essential information, and while reading, I'll also highlight certain words or terms that I want to know more about, and right click the mouse, and in the menu, select "Search Google for…". Personally, if I start finding it hard to concentrate after reading one source for too long, as soon as I start noticing that my attention is starting to wonder, I'll just open one of the tabs of things I searched for, and I'm completely interested in it again.

I've developed a lot of little tricks like this, that help me focus on things for long periods of time. So when I start researching something of interest, it's usually very easy to induce states of hyper-focus, and so when I research something that really interests me, I can easily do it for countless hours over many different days, and quickly develop a good understanding of the topic. After taking advantage of the resources on the Internet for over 20 years, and researching so many different things on so many different topics, it's not surprising that I have a lot of knowledge about a lot of different things. Even though I don't think anybody would ever see this as anything but a good thing, interestingly, even this passion that I have for learning things can often contribute to misunderstandings that people have of me.

As an example of a misunderstanding I've notice people often have of me, is a belief that I think I know everything, or that I always think I'm right, or that I'm full of myself, and other similar things. First of all, if I really did think I know everything, then I really wouldn't know very much at all, because if I really did think that, and was so full of myself that way, then I wouldn't think I was going to learn anything new by researching something, and I obviously wouldn't waste my time doing that, because I would think I already know it. But it is precisely the fact that I know that I don't know everything, which is the reason I continue to research things as often as I do.

INAPPROPRIATELY; "INAPPROPRIATE AND SERIOUS"

Getting back to my time at college, during a time when I confronted some other students, relates to an incident that occurred in a computer lab. There was no class taking place at the time, it was just a computer room that was open for anyone, to work on their homework between classes. There were lots of signs posted all over the place that said, "no talking in the computer lab." The reason for this should be pretty obvious to anyone, since it could be very distracting for somebody who was trying to do work. There were only about five or six people in the lab, only three of which were sitting together, and were obviously friends. Despite all the signs that said no talking, the three friends were not only talking, but were talking quite loudly, about things that had nothing to do with school or computers. For someone with A.D.D. like me, this was completely preventing me from being able to get any work done at all. Once again, I'm faced with a choice that causes anxiety, regardless of what I decide to do. If I do nothing, I know I'll keep anxiously thinking about it for hours, or if decide to do something, then I'll be anxious about the whole confrontation. This type of no-win situation, when caused by selfishness of others, is especially irritating, which is often what ends up leading to me to decide to pick the option that directly deals with the situation, because if I'm distracted by their loud talking, then others would be too at some point.

Rather than confronting them directly, which would cause the most anxiety, I took advantage of what I know about computers. The computers in the lab were networked together, which means every computer has a unique address, which is called an IP address. I also knew that the addresses in those labs were assigned in a sequential order. So the first computer closest to the door, had an IP address that ended with the number 2 (1 is for the router that connects the class to the rest of the school), and then the computer next, ending in 3, then 4, and so on. I also knew that the computers have a built-in function, that allows you to send messages between the computers, and all Windows computers have this as part of the operating system.

Starting from the computer closest to the door, I simply started counting from 2, up until the computers that they were sitting at. After I figured out which three IP addresses their computers were assigned, I thought about the message for a few minutes, then sent it to the three computers. Because I was sitting further back in the room, I was able to see that the three messages, did indeed, pop up on their computers. I basically just said that they weren't supposed to be talking, and were disturbing other people in the room. I saw that they all looked at the messages, read them, but then continued to talk. What started as ignorant selfishness, was now willful disrespect, so I decided to send them an email to their college email addresses, since the network messages are limited to not that many characters. The computers also have tools, that allow you to find out the username of the person logged into a computer, and that user name is also the first part of the college email address we all had. So I sent them each an email, basically saying "Clearly I know who they are (because I could identify them by their email address)..." and, "If they don't stop talking, I won't be so considerate in the future." Then I sent them another network message, telling them to check their emails. At that point they stopped talking and I continued trying to work on my school work.

A few days later, at the beginning of one of our classes, our professor said she had something important to talk to the class about, and wanted everybody's undivided attention. She then explained that there was a serious incident, in one of the computer labs, and some threats were made to some other students, that were very inappropriate. She explained that the security was taking this matter very seriously, they are investigating the incident, and when they find out who sent the messages, the person will probably be expelled from school. As soon as I heard this, I obviously knew they were looking for me; I also knew I didn't make any threat at all. When I sent the emails, I logged into my home computer, over a secure and encrypted connection, and sent the emails from a random Hotmail account I had, just in case something like this happened. This is a good example of why I think about all sorts of hypothetical, "what ifs" ahead of time, exactly because of the way people make incorrect assumptions, that cause them to misunderstand things. Because I had sent an email, the security department had a way to contact me, even though they weren't able to identify who I was.

But because of the message the professor shared with the class, about how serious they were taking it, and how the person would likely be expelled, it would really take a special kind of idiot to actually agree to go meet with the security, after being told they would likely be expelled. Needless to say, there was no way I was going to meet with them, like they asked me in the email they sent me. Instead, I replied with the following email, which I've had on my computer since then:

> "It is good to see that you were thankful for my response. Unfortunately, however, I have a prior engagement; as a result, I will be unable to attend the meeting.
>
> Given the amount of attention and dedication, as well as, the required time, needed to maintain my Honor Roll status while taking a heavy course load, I have little time left for other activities. Also considering that my presence is required at other, non-educational related endeavors, I am left with even less free time in a day.
>
> After reviewing my schedule, I see that the earliest possible date that I would be available for a meeting would be May 2 at 7:15pm. If this time is inconvenient for you, please inform me so we can arrange a time at a later date.
>
> Considering that I have not yet inquired directly about what you found to be "inappropriate" and "serious" about the email in question, I will do so now.
>
> Since you have not mentioned what it is that you found to be "inappropriate" and "serious", I can only assume that you see this as a form of harassment. If this is the case, I would like to point out your error. There is one key ingredient that must be present for harassment to exist that does not exist in this situation; the unwanted criticism must be persistent, i.e. it must occur more than once. Considering that my condescension took place only once, harassment did not occur.
>
> If your concern is in relation to my comment of "Not being so considerate in the future" and then my listing the offending, riotous, individual student's account names, well that too is unwarranted. I can understand if a person who is generally suspicious would see this comment as a threat, however, if a person were to have such thoughts, then they would be a victim of their own misunderstanding. Since I was not too clear in my choice of expression, and seeing your obvious concern, I would like to correct your misunderstanding by stating this: The lack of consideration that I was intending to exert in the event that I were to encounter any of those same disruptive students again, would be to report their disturbance to the proper authorities.
>
> I would now like to turn our attention to one last issue. I agree with what you said in your previous email; an investigation would, indeed, be an inadequate use of resources. Considering that any investigation would most likely be based on the assumptions that:

1) I was in the class room when I sent the email.
2) I was the only other person in the class room at the time.
3) And I sent it from within the college network.

Since you can never know for certain if any of these conditions are true, your investigation, in the best possible outcome, could result in one or two suspects. With whom you could tell what you already told me via email; if you sent an "inappropriate" and "serious" email to another student, well, I think it was ""inappropriate" and "serious"". However, the best possible outcome, most likely, will not occur. Considering the assumptions that any investigation would be based on, I would like to note that usually the computer labs have more than one person in them.

I would also like to add that if, by some miracle, your computers happen to log, just the right information that could identify me, for certain, there is still nothing you could do about the email that I sent.

I have already spent time writing this correspondence to you while enjoying my supper, time I otherwise would have spent relaxing my mind and enjoying the simpler things in life. In fact, I would, myself, consider any more time spent on this issue to be wasted and unwanted. Since each email from you, up until now, has been unwanted by me, and since I am now telling you this, any more conversations I incur that relate to this issue, would in fact be harassment. I will, however, permit one more email from you, confirming your understanding on this matter, and possibly even apologizing for your misunderstanding.

Good Day!

"To be curious about that which is not one's concern, while still in ignorance of oneself, is ridiculous."

-Plato"

Since there were no threats made, what I said definitely didn't violate any kind of law or warrant expelling someone from school. On top of that, the teacher and security department, clearly didn't realize the hypocritical irony of their actions, by turning a simple statement about not being so considerate in the future, into a serious threat, to kick someone out of school, for politely asking three kids who were not following the rules to be quiet. Because of all that, yes, I was a little bit cocky when I sent this email, and it was intended as a politically correct and polite, "Fuck you", because nothing I had said, came even close to warranting the type of response and investigation, which obviously caused me some anxiety, when all I did was confront three students who were doing something they weren't supposed to be doing.

From a moral point of view, it should be obvious, that I don't see any issue with this at all, but based on their reaction, obviously not everybody would agree.

THE CANADIAN TIRE INCIDENT

About a year or so later, I had a different roommate who I was friends with before he moved in. By this point, I'd already bought a new bike, and also had another much crappier bike, that had put together with random parts I had been collecting, because it's much more fun to go biking with somebody else. On one particular afternoon, my roommate and I set off for a bike ride, both wearing crappy shorts and shirts, that we didn't care about getting dirty or ripping while biking. We also both had backpacks on, to carry some drinks and snacks that we would need along the way. As we drove towards the biking trails, one of the bolts on the crappy bike started getting loose. Instead of going all the way back home to tighten it up, we went to Canadian Tire to buy a tool, because it was much closer to where we were.

After finding the tool we needed, we headed towards the cashier to pay for it. When we got to the cashier, the girl asked to check our bags. Seeing no reason for this, I asked her why she wanted to check our bags. She said that it was just store policy to check *everyone's* bags. So I looked around at the other cashiers, and noticed that there were many ladies in line with fairly big purses, and they were not being asked to open their bags. So I asked our cashier, "How come those girl's bags are not being checked?" She responded by saying, "Well, those are 'different' kind of bags". Slightly confused, I asked "Different? How are they different? They could still steal something with those bags." So the cashier said that it is just store policy, and that if I didn't let her look in my bag, she was going to have to call security. I told her that was fine, and went about my business.

As my roommate and I walked outside, the security (some older lady in her mid-40's), came up to me and told me, "I *had* to go back in the store so they could check my bag." I politely explained to her, they had no right to demand that because of Section 8 of the Charter of Rights (Everyone has the right to be secure against unreasonable search or seizure.), and Section 9 (Everyone has the right not to be arbitrarily detained or imprisoned.) Since they were not checking everyone's bags, it was clearly quite arbitrary to check our bags, and not theirs. But she wasn't really listening, and was still trying to get me back in the store. Well she was getting really close and almost touching me, so I said to her, "Please don't touch me!"

Just then, the manager came out. He started telling me the same thing the security told me, so I told him what I told her. He too wasn't listening, and was quite determined to get me back in the store. When he told me that the police had been called, I told him that was fine, and that I would be over there fixing my bike, and that I wouldn't even unlock the bikes until the police got there. So rather than understanding that they were breaking the law, he now stood in the way towards my bike. I tried going around him, but he moved in my way again. So I tried quickly dashing around him, but this time he grabbed my arm. Right then, the security grabbed my other arm, and they threw me up against the wall.

So now, let me point something out; it was a beautiful Friday afternoon, around 4pm, in the middle of the summer, and there were a LOT of people walking in and out of the store. Well, I proceeded to make the biggest scene ever, because witnesses are important. I started shouting things like "My Rights Were Being Violated", and that, "These People Are Assaulting Me". Just then, a couple walked out the door. The lady had a purse, so I asked her if they checked her purse on the way out. She stated that they did not check her purse.

The manager appeared to be about my age, but quite a bit shorter and very skinny, and the security guard, well, she was about an average older lady. I knew I could have easily broken free from them, and at one point between my shouts, I looked the manager in the eyes and calmly said, "You know, I could hit you right now to defend myself, but I'm not going to do that because I'm a nice person." Needless to say, the expression this caused on his face was rather interesting.

Moments later the cops showed up. As soon as they got out, I also told them that my rights were being violated and that I was being assaulted, and that I wanted to press charges on these people, but they cuffed me anyway, just to get control of the situation. One cop went to talk to the manager and security, and one talked to me. Well before I had finished telling him what happened, the other cop was telling him to let me go, because I hadn't done anything wrong.

The two cops said that they had no right doing what they did, and that I was totally in the right. The one also said that he had been coming there for years, and he didn't even know they had a sign saying, to leave your bags at the sales desk. He said that, although they can ask people to leave their bags at the sales desk, but they can't expect everyone to see the sign. He also said it doesn't give them the right to search people, just because they didn't see the sign. He even said that if they asked him to search his bag, that he would also refuse. The couple that I got involved by asking about the woman's purse, said they saw the whole thing, and they would be willing to testify, if I needed them to; they left their information with the police.

After, the police also asked me if I still wanted to press charges, but I had only said that at first as a way to quickly point out to them that I wasn't in the wrong, so of course I told them that I didn't.

During the ordeal, the strap on my CD case snapped off, and it fell to the ground. When I got home, I realized that my cd player didn't work. The next day, my shoulder that had been operated on a few years ago, was hurting from being pulled each way by my arms, and as I was stretching to help my shoulders feel better, I ended up dislocating it, which was the first time that happened since I had the operation. So I called Canadian Tire's head office the next day, too see what they had to say about the situation. They told me they are going to call the owner of that store and that he should call me sometime that week.

Eventually, I met with an insurance representative for Canadian Tire, and ultimately got $2000 because of what happened. When I asked for the $2000, I knew right away that I could've gotten a lot more, based on the way the insurance guy looked up at me, and said "You want two thousand dollars?"

Thinking about it afterwards, I'm sure I probably could've gotten at least five digits, because it would've cost them at least that much in lawyer fees to go to court. Either way, $2000 is still nothing to complain about. More importantly I feel pretty confident that the store policy will change because of what happened, and hopefully nobody else will have to experience something like that either.

THE SECOND CUP SCENARIO

Of all the jobs that I've had over the years, working at The Second Cup was probably one of the most enjoyable. Two main reasons why I loved that job so much, was partly because it was such a low stress job that I found quite relaxing. The other reason I enjoyed it so much, was because I've always been an avid people watcher, and since the coffee shop was located inside of a mall, that provided lots of opportunity to watch people all day long. I worked there about 2.5 - 3 years, and I likely would've continued working there longer if it wasn't for what ended up happening one day.

    The old lady that owned the coffee shop, in general seemed like she was very polite. I'm sure she always intended to be, but she was a bit stingy and greedy, and she would often say things to the staff, which I don't think she realized were the cause for her going through so many employees. She was also a very big micromanager, and anybody who worked shifts with her, knew that she'd already be telling people what to do, before they were even finished what they were currently doing. But it's not like anything about that job was complicated at all, and during the evenings when she wasn't working, things always ran much smoother, than during the day. During the time I worked there, I can't even remember how often we went through new employees, that couldn't stand working for her. Often people were given a key to the store after only working there for a few days, only to end up quitting a week later. The owner's daughter also worked there and managed the day-to-day aspects of the business. The granddaughter worked there as well as one of the shift supervisors. Even the daughter and the granddaughter often couldn't stand working with their mother/grandmother. Even they found it quite surprising that I didn't mind working with the owner.

The reason why I wasn't bothered by the old lady's personality, was because she was polite and friendly, and never acted towards me in a way that I found to be offensive or rude, and anytime she was trying to micromanage, I would simply nod my head and do what she wanted me to do, rather than taking her micromanaging style personally. I actually found it rather amusing to playfully act as though I was a robot, and sometimes, if she wasn't specific enough about a task, or she got distracted and stopped sending new commands, the robot would sometimes get stuck in a loop, doing the last command over and over again until instructed to do something differently. :D Because she was never aggressive or raised her voice or anything like that, it was very easy for me to just dismiss and ignore her short comings, because after all, no one is perfect; everyone can still be polite though.

At one point, I booked some time off of work, to go back to Windsor to visit my family. When I got back from Windsor, and went back to work for my next shift, I found out that somebody had stolen the float and money, the night I was last at work, before my trip. I was informed that the detectives had already talked all the other employees, and they were waiting to speak with me. I knew I still had a criminal record, so understandably, I was a little bit anxious about seeing them, but I still called them right away, and made arrangements to go speak with them.

I stopped stealing after I went to jail for the computers, and normally all of the things on a criminal record, which happened as a young offender, would disappear when you turn 18, as long as you don't commit any other crimes as an adult, within 12 months after you turn 18. Due to an incident shortly before I moved to Ottawa, when I got arrested with over 70 rolled joints, that meant my entire young offender record carried over and stayed on my adult record. Eventually, I did get a pardon for everything, and at this point, I no longer have a criminal record. But I knew when I went in to see the Detectives, they were probably already going to be suspicious of me. Knowing how anxious it made me feel, they were also going to notice that I was anxious, which would only make them more suspicious.

When I finally went into see them, as I expected, they were basically accusing me right from the beginning, and because of that, I was clearly very nervous while talking with them, to the point where I was even stuttering a bit with my words. All of which they pointed out, and tried to use that to justify their belief that, "I'm their guy." Because I knew I was innocent, I definitely found it quite offensive and rude, the way they started off accusing me right from the beginning, before I even said anything. I can only speak for myself, but I still imagine that most other people would find it offensive as well. When I got home, after the interview, I ended up writing them an email, since during the interview, there were many things that I said, they took out of context, and even a few things that they claimed I said, but I didn't actually say. I also told them to consider this email as my formal statement:

To Det. Kevin Wilcox.
After your accusation near the end of the interview that, "I'm your guy", as well as some choice comments from your female friend who was also there, I feel the need to clear up some of the confusion and false ideas that the two of you may have.

First of all, I would like to say that while some of the comments in this letter are going to be quite direct and bold, none of it is intended in any kind of negative way towards you or your friend. Another thing that I would like to mention is that I recorded the conversation that took place between the three of us. My reasons for recording it stem from the fact that people often misunderstand what is said when the idea is closely related to some other, similar, idea that one already has. I would also like you to take note of the difference between how I express my thoughts in this letter, vs. how I attempted to express them during the interview.

The clarity of thought that I attempt in this letter, is ideally, how I wish to express them in person. However, as I mentioned during the interview, I have been diagnosed as being an anxious person. Your response of asking if I was having a panic attack reflects the general misunderstanding that exists about anxiety. As I said in the interview, panic attacks are cause by anxiety, but anxiety itself is much more complicated than that. To state it simply, anxiety is more akin to a level of mental activity rather than some people's reactions to it. (i.e. panic attacks) Anxiety is a biological function that is seen in many other animals. It is what causes a person to be aware of their surroundings to look out for possible danger; it is a survival adaptation.

My decision to not take the polygraph is, as I mentioned, related to time, but more importantly, related to my anxiety. But it also has to do with my understanding of the science that goes into it. I am by no means an expert, but I know enough to understand why they are not accepted in court. A polygrapher determines a baseline for questions by measuring, at a minimum, three things, those are: the cardiovascular system (heart rate and blood volume), the respiratory system (abdominal and thoracic breathing), and the skin (sweat gland and electro-dermal activity). All three of those things relate to the Autonomic Nervous System. The Autonomic Nervous System is one of the body's functions that are being investigated with respect to possible causes of anxiety disorders. Since a polygraph is testing the Autonomic Nervous System, then there is a large probability that intense anxiety will skew the results. If I were to take a polygraph, I would understand what questions that the test was trying to see if I was lying about. When asked such a question, I would, with no doubt, begin to worry and become anxious about how the answers would be interpreted. This anxiety would also cause a change in the Autonomic Nervous System; the very thing that the tests measures for. I hope now, you fully understand my reasons for refusing a polygraph.

To get one more thing out of the way before I move on to something else, I feel the need to express a major concern. When we were talking about the polygraph, I mentioned that part of my reason was because "…they have been known not to be entirely accurate." Immediately after my comment about the accuracy of polygraphs, your friend snickers. At the end of the interview, she indirectly explains her snicker by saying that polygraphs only pass or come back as inclusive. She then attempted to quote me by saying that I said, "Sometimes the polygraphs come back false", but when in fact I never said that.

I find her snickering to be quite affronting and unprofessional. I also feel that it expresses some pre-judgment on her part. I was never questioning how the results are perceived; I was only questioning the accuracy of them.

The fact that Krysti misunderstood me saying "nothing looked out of the ordinary" for "I observed that the money was still there" is similar to the misunderstanding that your friend made during the interview.

Another important aspect of the investigation that I feel has been overlooked is the fact that you seem to be assuming that the robbery was conducted by someone who was a current employee at the time. You might have asked Sue how many people working there had a key, but did you ask her how many keys she has given to past employees? Personally, I was given a key about a week after I started working there. In the two years that I have worked there, I have seen many employees come and go; many who were also given a key after only being employed a short while.

That brings up another equally as good of a point, the number of employees that I have witnessed come and go in my short two years there. Sue's attitude is, on average, just about the worst attitude out of any bosses I have ever had. I find her to be rude, self-centered, and inconsiderate of her employees (generally that is….but of course, everyone has their moments). But, before you go making assumptions again, that comment doesn't give you any more reason to suspect me as having motive. If you feel it gives me more motives, then you have to consider that since my view of her has been shared by other employees, that fact gives each of us equal motive. In fact, I don't remember an employee that came though, during the years I worked there, that didn't share those same feelings. (most likely the cause of Sue going through so many employees). Even her own granddaughter would join the staff discussions of her grandmother's short comings as a manager. I even remember one comment in particular when Krysti mentioned how cheap her grandmother was for not wanting to help out with her tuition. Actually, come to think of it, this was shortly before this all happened.

Have you ever questioned Krysti about this? The way I am starting to see things, is that she has even more motive than anyone else. I know she was angry with me about the end of our "relationship", since she seemed so delighted to call me an asshole on more than one occasion. She has made the comment to me (and most likely to other employees) about her thinking her grandmother was cheap for not helping with tuition. She also knew that I have a criminal record. But most importantly, we also have the discrepancy between what she said that I said, and what I actually said. Since you most likely still don't trust me on this, check the mall camera's and find out what time I actually went back to get my bike. I KNOW it was not 2, since the Hull buses stop running between 12 – 1am. The last interesting thing is that Rica told me she thought it was weird that Krysti happened to be in quite early to work that morning.

But just for the record, I personally would be surprised if it was actually her. Then again, Krysti telling me (before we ever got involved with each other) that her mom said she should break up with her (then present) boyfriend, to go out with me, because I was cute, I was smart, and that "…I was going to be rich one day." Now I am also reminded of the fact that Sue's own son owes Sue money that she lent him, but he refuses to pay her back now and that has caused some family legal problems. Given the rampant greed in their family, I suppose I might not be that surprised if Krysti actually did do this.

Realistically though, I think the most likely suspect would be someone who didn't even work there anymore when this happened. Since Sue gives out keys to her store more often than I go 'Partying it up with my friends', then realistically, the number of suspects dramatically increases.

The fact that I happened to go in and fill up my water bottle was nothing new for me to do. I would often leave my bike locked up in the stairwell after work, go out with some friends down town, and then pick my bike up later on (including going back into the store to fill up my water bottle if needed.) I would often lock my bike in the stairwell even when I wasn't working that day, since I feel it is safer than locking it on Rideau with all the street kids hanging out doing noting with their life.… Something I can relate to from my past before I took control of my life and learned to have more respect in myself and my abilities. And while I am on my past, I remember you and *your friend being a little surprise that I stole 100 000$ worth of computers. Well like I said in the interview, I got ratted out by someone involved (which I am thankful for due to the things I have realized) , after the first time, but I left no evidence. In fact, we didn't even know we got ratted on. We never even would have been caught if we never did it a second time. The relevance of this is related to your accusations towards me. IF, and I wish to stress the IF, so there is no misunderstanding.*

IF I were to take a risk with my life by stealing things again, I would have made sure there was no way for anyone to know I was there. Second of all, IF I were to do it on a night when I was working, I would have waited until it was a busier night when there would have been about twice the 800$ you say was taken. But even 1600$, I feel insulted for being accused of taking. Given my record, IF I was going to take a risk, I wouldn't go from doing a single 70 000$ job, to some petty theft of 1600$.

So I feel I have said enough here…

Just for the record, if you still wish to continue investigating me, please, feel free to accept this as an official statement. Lawyers often recommend that their client say as little as possible with them not present, well given that, I hope the length and detail of this letter will help to convince you of the truth.

As a final note, I would like to mention one more thing. Since I didn't steal the money, there will be no evidence against me. Telling me in the interview that "I am your man" when it is only based on circumstantial evidence isn't very proper. That I happened to be there that night is only a coincidence.

P.S. If you have any further, non-accusatorial questions, please feel free to contact me.

Thankfully, I never heard from them again, and even though the owner had no grounds to fire me, I still decided to quit, because I felt quite uncomfortable after being accused of taking the money. I was also no longer in college, due to the same kind of difficulties I always had in a normal school environment, and because I had a second job at a fairly high-end restaurant, where I made a lot more money, I could easily quit from the Second Cup right away. The only reason why I kept the job at Second Cup was because of how much I enjoyed working there.

RE-DEALING

After I quit working at The Second Cup, and started working more at the restaurant, I started noticing how many servers were asking if anyone had a gram or two of weed to sell. I recently met a new drug dealer that I bought my weed from, who had high-quality weed and cheap prices. So I decided to start selling weed again.

Regarding the stigmas and misconceptions surrounding the drug industry: because of my personal moral principles and beliefs, I've always taken the same, customer service based, approach to selling drugs, as I would with any other job that I've ever had. I always made sure things were weighed accurately, never miss represented the quality of anything that I would sell, always charged a fair price, and just like you would expect from any kind of store that you'd buy something else from, I would have always gladly either refunded someone's money, or exchange the product if they were not happy with it; just as the people I bought things from would have as well.

It was sometimes during 2003, when I started selling weed by the gram at the restaurant, and I continued to do so, until recently when I finally retired from that industry.

A HARD THING TO SLEEP ON

One of the problems I've often had my whole life, has to do with sleeping. Like most people with autism, I've often had difficulties getting enough quality sleep. It usually takes a long time for me to fall asleep, because my mind is just thinking about so many countless things, as I'm lying in bed. Even when I do finally fall asleep, my REM cycle is often interrupted by waking up frequently. Often, I don't even notice that I wake up, which is caused by simple things like twitching, and the frequent disruption it causes, usually makes it very difficult for me to wake up when I need to.

I've known since I was pretty young, that I rarely ever remember dreaming. People often think, just because you don't remember your dreams, doesn't mean that you weren't actually dreaming. That may be true for most people, but it's not true for everybody. I first learned that I had some kind of neurological issue with sleeping, while I was in jail. One time, while I was sleeping, a guard noticed that I was twitching quite a bit. It concerned him enough, thinking I may be having a seizure, for him to come check on me. After one of the doctors heard of this, they ended up booking an appointment at the hospital to go have some tests done.

At first, they did a simple E.E.G. while awake, which basically involves hooking up a bunch of little wires to someone's head, and measuring brain wave activity. After they noticed some weird anomalies, they decided to investigate further and a sleep deprived E.E.G. was scheduled. The main difference with that kind of test, is needing to be awake for a whole night before the test, to ensure the person would be able to doze off. This time, the testing showed even more anomalies in certain regions of my brain, some of which were in my motor cortex, and the results showed that there was random firing taking place while I was sleeping, which was disrupting my sleep cycle and preventing me from achieving REM sleep.

This is exactly why I often don't remember dreaming, since I often don't actually dream a lot of the time, and as a result, I'll wake up feeling exhausted, like I hadn't slept at all. Sometimes I'm so exhausted when the alarm goes off, I'll actually shut the alarm off, without even realizing it. Unsurprisingly, this has often caused a lot of issues with school and work, and is the primary reason why I was known for being late regularly and often falling asleep in class. I've also lost quite a few jobs due to this health issue, and eventually, was a big reason why I started selling drugs full-time.

Knowing that I have this unusual brain activity, when I recently found out that I'm slightly autistic, I immediately started researching the issue, and the unusual brain activity that the tests showed when I was younger, which none of the doctors knew what it was, but recent research has shown, that it's the exact type of unusual activity shown in people who are autistic.

Eventually, my sleep issues caused me to get fired from the restaurant. I had already been written up a few times for being late, and then when I finally missed a shift completely, during one of those times where I shut the alarm off, and fell right back asleep without even realizing it. Because I knew I sometimes did that, I learned a long time ago, that the alarm needs to be far away from me. But this one time, while working at the restaurant, despite the alarm actually being in the other room; I have absolutely no memory of getting up, turning it off, and going back to bed. Having to deal with a problem like that your whole life, would be stressful for anyone, but for someone like me who is constantly trying to make self-improvements, being fired from so many jobs, for something that you realize is outside of your own control, is a very disheartening and discouraging thing to have to deal with. I've always been a very hard worker, and can usually excel at any task I put my mind to. At least that has always helped me keep jobs longer, because all of my bosses have always been very happy with my work ethic. But eventually, my sleep issues which cause me to be late or miss work, become too numerous for them to ignore.

AN OILY LANDSCAPE

After I got fired from the restaurant, I quickly found a job at a very prestigious landscaping company in the city. Like most jobs I've had, I very much enjoyed this one too and quickly learned the proper way to do all things landscaping related. Despite needing to wake up at about five in the morning each day to be able to bike to the job site on time, surprisingly, I actually managed to keep that job for almost a whole season, but as usual, I was late one too many times and ended up being fired from that job as well.

Thankfully, I've never had difficulties finding a job, and within a few days I started working for an oil and fuel company. It wasn't a very big company, just the secretary, the owner, and myself. I wasn't a licensed oil technician, so most the time I always worked directly with the owner, but he was actually a really cool guy and we got along great. He had been working in the oil business his whole life, because his dad had started the company before he was even born. He basically knew everything there was about the oil business, and because he quickly realized I would absorb information like a sponge, he went out of his way to teach me all sorts of things and it didn't take long for me to become very proficient at that job either. He even let me take home the extra company work van after only a few days of working for him.

I also didn't live very far from the shop, and because he understood the problems I had with sleeping, whenever I wasn't there on time for my shift, he'd give me a call, and I could be there in less than 10 minutes. He also knew that I had no problem working as late as we needed to, so I was actually able to keep that job for a couple years or so. When business started picking up, he ended up hiring a kid fresh out of college, who had his oil and gas technician license, which meant the owner didn't need to be on the job site, and could spend time setting up other jobs. By this point, I knew everything about the oil and gas work that we would do, and could have easily passed the exam to become licensed, so when he hired this new kid from college, he put me in charge. I was able to teach the kid a lot of things, because he didn't really have any hands on experience.

Eventually, I ended up getting laid off from that job, only because business started slowing down again, and he could only afford to keep one of us; it was only logical for him to keep the other guy that had his license. Even though it was by far the dirtiest job I've ever had, and it wasn't uncommon to go home covered in black soot and smelling like fuel oil, I still very much loved that job, and the friendship I had with the owner. It was definitely very emotional when he had to lay me off. Even writing about this, and thinking about it now, almost 15 years later, I still am a bit emotional about it, enough that it brought some tears to my eyes. He wasn't just my boss, but a friend as well. He was the only boss I've ever had, who realized the genuine problem I had with waking up on time, but instead of firing me for being late, he was very understanding and cared enough to put in the effort, and simply call me to wake me up.

When I started the job, and he let me start taking the van home, he made a deal with me that I could drive it as much as I want, when I'm not at work, as long as I pay for all the oil changes and the gas. He was also a weed smoker, and knew I sold and delivered weed on the side, when I wasn't working. When he laid me off, he knew I was also going to lose money from not being able to do the deliveries, since I didn't have a vehicle my own.

During one of the last days I worked with him, he surprised me in a way that I'm forever grateful for, and I'm sure my life would be very different if he hadn't done this for me. He knew how much I loved driving, and during those years I had the work van, he knew I drove all over the place when I wasn't working. He also knew, that even though I could get another job, and make enough money to afford a car payment, I wasn't able to, because my credit was so bad from unpaid student loans. He also knew that I had nobody who could cosign for me, since my dad lived in the states, and my mom's credit was even worse than mine. During that last day working for him, when we unexpectedly stopped at a car dealership, I was initially confused when he told me to go check out the cars, and find one that I like. I just kind of looked at him and said, "You know my credit sucks, and I couldn't get a car even when I had a job. There's no way I'd get approved now that I'm being laid off." But he just kind of smirked, and said, "I'm sure we can figure something out." I was still a bit confused, and didn't think I'd end up getting a car, but I went and looked around anyway, and found something that I liked that I knew I could afford the payments for. A few minutes later he came out of the office, asked me if I found something that I liked, and then told me, the owner of the dealership was waiting to talk to me inside. I was still a bit stunned, and in disbelief about what was going on, but I went inside and did the paperwork. Since I wasn't technically laid off yet, and with him willing to cosign, I was able to get my first car! I knew having a car, would open up so many more job opportunities, and that would also allow me to continue making my weed deliveries as well.

It's interesting and surprising, how emotional I got just now writing this story (and again while editing). I don't know how many times, I had the wipe off my face just writing that last paragraph. At the time when that happened, I was obviously happy, excited and grateful, but my face never got wet at all. I suppose it's because I had no idea, how much his kind act that I didn't even ask for, would end up changing my life in a very positive way. The fact that he thought of helping me this way, and that he trusted me enough to put his own credit on the line, without even asking him to, or even talking about it at all, was one of the nicest things anybody has ever done for me.

I haven't talked to him in many years, but I do think about him often whenever I drive by his shop. I always found our friendship to be fairly unique, and like me, I find a lot of people often misunderstand him too. He's definitely a very unusual and polarizing character, that most people either love or hate. You never quite knew what to expect would come out of his mouth, and sometimes he'd say the most inappropriate things at the most inappropriate time, and other times the most inappropriate things at the most *appropriate* time, but anybody that really knows him, knows he has a heart of gold. At the time when he helped me get my first car, it was impossible for me to realize just how grateful I would ultimately become.

When I finish this book, I'm going to get in touch with him and give him a copy, and tell him what I'm saying here now: "Angelo, I know of no words, that can adequately express just how grateful I am for how much you helped me. Not just with the car, but also with how understanding you were about me being late, and simply calling me instead of firing me. I never told anyone this before writing it here now, but after losing two other jobs in a row for a sleep problem caused by an issue in my brain, and not just simply me being irresponsible, I was already fairly depressed and anxious, knowing that it was probably going to happen again. If you hadn't been so understanding, and simply fired me, like most other employers would do, I might've decided to give up on life. As I've mentioned in this book many times, I've always been really good at hiding the true extent of how anxious or stressed I am, so I'm sure you didn't realize, how much I was actually bothered every time I was late, each time feeling like I was going to get fired from yet another job. I learned a lot from you, and I don't think you realize how much you helped me become more confident with myself, and not worry so much about what other people think. Thank you, for everything."

A DIFFERENT KIND OF JOB, FROM A DIFFERENT KIND OF LOAN

During the initial few months after I got my first car, I took advantage of the fact that I was on E.I. and laid off of work, so I didn't get a job right away. Because I lived on the Québec side, just across the river from Ottawa, my rent was fairly cheap, and the amount I got from unemployment insurance, was just enough for my car payment and rent. The little bit of extra money I made from selling weed, covered food and such things like that. Now that I had a car, there were a lot more possible jobs I could get, and I really took my time looking at different ones. Since I knew I had issues with sleeping, I wanted to find a job that had a bit more flexibility with the hours, or at the very least started a little bit later than typical jobs do. Something else I know about my sleep pattern, is how I seem to not have problems getting up, when I allow my body to follow its own kind of schedule. For me, this usually meant I'd naturally fall asleep around three or four in the morning, and then I can usually easily get up around ten or eleven. Most important of all, I wanted a job where I wouldn't get in trouble if I'm five minutes late.

After taking my time looking at different jobs, I eventually found a job opportunity selling alarm systems. The job was purely based on commission, and because of that I wouldn't have anybody getting mad at me for not being able to conform to a specific 9-to-5 kind of schedule, or if I was a few minutes late; it was perfect that way! I would only ever need to go in the office to submit paperwork, if I made any sales. Even then, there was a lot of flexibility about when I went in to submit the paperwork. So I wrote up a cover letter, for that job specifically, and I successfully got hired. I had to go to Kingston for a week to train with the regional manager. This was in May of 2006, and online banking was relatively new, at least to me.

As I was preparing for the trip to Kingston, I logged into my bank online, to figure out what my budget was for the trip. I knew I didn't have a lot of money, but I was shocked to see that I only had about 40$. There should've been closer to 400$, which would've easily been enough for gas to go to Kingston and back as well as food for the week. I hadn't checked my bank account in a long time, because I rarely used my debit card. I'm also pretty good with numbers and math, so I had a decent idea in my head about how much money should have been in my account. I knew my unemployment cheque was automatically getting deposited and the payments for my insurance and car, were a little less than how much I was getting from E.I. As I started investigating the transactions in my account, I saw that the missing money, was due to my car payment getting bounced. The financing company charged me 75$, and then the bank charged me 35$. As I investigated even further, I noticed a number of other 35$ fees from the bank, going back to November of 2005, and started shortly after I opened the account with the Bank of Montréal.

When I opened the account, I specifically asked for overdraft protection, and after the account manager behind the desk nodded his head, I assumed I would. But obviously after seeing all these fees in my account, I knew a mistake had been made. I called up the bank, and after explaining the problem, I was told I'd have to go into the branch where I made the account, and talk to them about it. After going into the branch, I was politely told that I didn't have overdraft protection, and there was nothing they could do about the fees that I'd been charged.

This would upset anybody at any point, but because of their mistake, I didn't have the money to go to Kingston to get training for the new job. I was quite pissed off, and because of the way my mind works, I couldn't stop thinking about how to address this issue. Part of the reason why was really pissed off, was because my E.I. payment was automatically deposited on a Saturday, just after midnight, since I knew from experience, that I could go to an A.T.M. and take money out, directly after the E.I. was automatically deposited. Yet when my car payment tried to go through Saturday evening, it was declined, since the EI payment wouldn't be officially authorized until the next business day. Clearly this is absolutely absurd, considering I could take the money out from an A.T.M. right away! In fact, my account actually allowed me to withdraw up to a thousand dollars a day from an A.T.M., directly after depositing a cheque, before it was even cleared. I had done that many times since I opened the account, and would regularly take out money from an ATM, directly after depositing a cheque from work, so I was very aware of the way the system worked that way. After thinking about this for a while, an idea eventually popped into my mind; which was quite beautiful in its simplicity.

The first thing I did, was to look up the banking laws, and find the section relating to fraud and bank transfers. I wanted to make sure I wasn't going to do anything illegal, and knew that I was going to be getting a call from the bank at some point, because of what I was planning to do. Essentially fraud is defined as "Filing some kind of false claim". So that means if you were to take an empty envelope, deposit it into the ATM, and enter a certain amount that you're depositing, clearly that would be fraud, because it's only an empty envelope. What I decided to do, was to write up a bill, both explaining the purpose of the bill, along with itemized charges that I was billing the Bank of Montréal for. Starting from when I opened the account, I itemized every day and the amount I was charged, either an overdraft fee from the bank, or the 75$ from my financing company. In total, the amount came to 325$. I indicated that I was billing them for that amount, because I was supposed to have overdraft protection on my account, and never should've been charged those fees in the first place. I also added an additional charge, just like banks *love* to do, and this additional charge was also 325$. I even stated the reason for this charge, which was "…because that's exactly what they had done to me."

After I wrote up this bill, I went to the A.T.M., put it in an envelope, and deposited it into my account. After that transaction went through, I then transferred 30$ from one account, into the other account that I deposited the bill for 650$ into. I was going to take out all of the money and I didn't want to leave ten dollars in each account. As I was trying to transfer money from one account into the other account, I swear, it was like an act of God, when the machine had a power outage for a moment, reset itself and kept my card. Obviously this was followed by an, "Oh Shit!", moment inside my head. But I quickly thought, "Not a problem, I'll just go to the bank first thing when they open and get a new card before anyone notices." Well I learned that banks don't just open up late because they're lazy or whatever, but actually they get there early enough to do all those deposits before they actually open.

By the time the bank opened, and I went to get a new card, I was told there was an issue with my account, and I had to go to my home branch and talk to them about it. So I went over to my branch, and ended up speaking again with the same manager who previously told me, there is nothing they could do about the fees I had been charged. I explained to her that I was just trying to make a point, and "Notice I didn't actually try to take the money out?" That convinced her to at least give me a new card, and she also agreed to look into the matter further. This was definitely more promising then the initial dismissive response I got the first time I went into talk to her.

A few days later, I got a call from her, telling me she had spoken with the banking manager who opened my account, and because he's been working at the bank for a long time, she doesn't believe that he would make such a mistake. Of course I wasn't surprised to get a response like that, so while I was waiting to hear back from her, I had already formulated another, better plan, just in case.

Instead of going to the A.T.M. closest to my house, which would cause a headache for the banking manager at that branch and be a bit unfair, since that manager had nothing to do with this issue, I intentionally went to my main branch, knowing that this lady would have to deal with this issue now; that just seemed like the morally right thing to do. But this time, I didn't give them a bill, but rather something much more appropriate, which related to the initial problem. Since I knew I could withdraw money directly after depositing a cheque, that's exactly what I decided to do.

I waited until Friday, just after the bank closed, at 6 p.m. I was actually waiting in the parking lot, and was at the A.T.M. at 6:01pm, because it felt like beautiful, poetic justice to be standing at the A,T.M. while looking at the manager inside, who basically told me to politely "Fuck off", twice. What I did, was took one of my own cheques, from my own chequing account, and made myself out a cheque for one thousand dollars, but I post-dated the cheque for exactly one year later. I made sure to write the last digit of the year, very dark, by writing over it a few times, to ensure it was *clearly* understood that it was post-dated for next year. I deposited this post-dated cheque into my savings account, and immediately took out a thousand dollars. I then deposited another post-dated cheque, for another thousand dollars, into my chequing account, and immediately took out another thousand dollars. So effectively, I just gave, and approved, my own personal loan for two thousand dollars, with a low interest rate 0.5%; the interest rate on an overdrawn account. No false claims, therefore I committed no fraud; all perfectly legal. However, just because something is legal, doesn't necessarily mean it's morally right. Personally though, I have no moral issue over what I did, especially considering how much the banks love to nickel and dime people out of their hard earned money.

A couple of days later, on Sunday afternoon, I headed to Kingston, because the training began on Monday. Before I left, I decided to reward myself for my exceptional legal work, and bought a nice little sound system for my car; I thoroughly enjoyed the drive to Kingston.

Come Monday, as I was driving around with my new manager, going to different appointments and seeing how she sold alarm systems, I got a call on my cell phone from a number I didn't recognize, and assumed it was the bank. Because I wasn't driving the car, I answered the call. With a tone in my voice, that could be best described as being part surprised, part confused (as though I don't understand why there's a problem), with a tad bit of smugness thrown in, and the conversation went like this:

Me: *"Hello"*
Bank: *"Yes, is Adam there?"*
Me: *"This is Adam, who am I speaking to?"*
Bank: *"I'm calling from the Bank of Montreal regarding a problem with your account."*
Me: *"Oh? What's the problem?"*
Bank: *"Well, it appears that you've deposited some personal cheques, took the money out, but there's no money in the accounts to cover the cheques."*
Me: *"Yes, I know, that's why I postdated the cheques for next year, because the money will be in there by then."*
Bank: *"Well, ummm, you can't do that."*
Me: *"Oh? Why not?"*
Bank: *"Because that's fraud!"*
Me: *"No ma'am, that isn't fraud. If you look up section 390 subsection (a) of the criminal code, you'll see that fraud is defined as 'knowingly makes a false statement in any receipt, certificate or acknowledgment for anything that may be used for a purpose mentioned in the Bank Act;', and because the cheques that I deposited were clearly marked as postdated for next year, I made no kind of false statement, and therefore I did not commit fraud."*
Bank: *"Well, umm, you can't do that. What's going to happen when we cash these cheques and there's no money in your account to cover it?"*
Me: *"Well ma'am, because those cheques are clearly marked as postdated for next year, if you cash those cheques, before the date clearly marked on them, then you yourself will be committing fraud."*
Bank: *"Umm… well.. ummm, someone is going to have to call you back."*

After I got off the phone with the bank, I kind of turned to my new manager, who obviously overheard that conversation, and I quickly explained what I had done, and why I did it. Of course for a brief moment, I had no idea how she was going to feel about that, and so I was relieved when she laughed and said, "You realize what's going to happen now? I bet the banks are going to change their policies because of this." I kind of laughed as well, and agreed she was probably right."

About twenty minutes later, I got another call from the bank. This time, it was the Vice President of the Bank of Montréal! That obviously put a smile on my face, knowing that I got somebody's attention, for something that shouldn't have happened in the first place. We basically had the same conversation as I had with the first person from the bank who called, and the conversation ended with him basically saying the same thing: they are going to look into it and somebody will get back to me.

No one ever did call again from the bank. A few weeks later, I got a letter in the mail from the bank, saying that I owed them 1675$, with the payment date being one year later; they gave me my 325$ back! By the following year, I never did pay any of it back. I never heard from them again about it and it never went on my credit record. From a moral point of view, I don't feel at all bad for that, because the way I look at it, the other 1675$ was just bullshit tax, and at the end of the day no one got hurt, the bank definitely didn't miss such a small amount of money, and it feels like the bank just got a healthy lesson in Karma. I also don't know if it's just a coincidence, but shortly after that, policies in all banks did change, and now all new accounts don't automatically have that ability to take out money the way I did. So if you've noticed that and you were affected by it, please accept my sincere apology for any inconvenience this may have caused you, just don't expect a percentage, that account has been overdrawn.

A HIGHWAY HARD-KNOCK

After the week of the sales training in Kingston, I got back to Ottawa and started my new job right away. Each night I would get an email, with a list of appointments of people who said yes to the company's telemarketers, who would explain the alarm system offer. Initially, I was doing really well, and was obviously very excited and enthusiastic about my new job. But Ottawa is actually a very tough market to sell alarm systems in, and most of my initial successes, were all from small towns just outside the city. I also knew which telemarketer booked the appointment, based on a four-digit employee number that was next to the appointment details. Eventually, I started to notice that appointments booked by certain telemarketers, were almost always impossible to close. I often heard the same kind of things, when I'd show up at people's houses for the appointment, such as, "We're not really interested in an alarm system, but the telemarketer wouldn't really accept no for an answer, so we just said yes to get them off the phone." Because I'm not a pushy type, I'd always apologize and leave right away.

After a while, this started happening more and more, especially as the appointments started being in Ottawa itself. Not only was this very discouraging, but it became increasingly stressful, knowing I was paying for gas, and not making any money. We didn't just have to rely on the appointments, in fact any sales that we made that we found on our own, we actually made more money for, and it was something the company very much wanted us to do. Because of this, I would often keep an eye out for new subdivisions that were recently built, and were much less likely to have alarm systems already installed. I tried going door-to-door a few times, but the social anxieties that I've always struggled with, made me feel really uncomfortable, bothering people in their homes and trying to sell them something. I realize this is both reasonable and unreasonable, because some people definitely get annoyed when sales people randomly knock on their doors, but I also know that some people very much like it. I kind of fought with myself about this issue, and had many internal debates over how I felt about it morally. Ultimately, I gave up going door-to-door, because it was impossible to know, who was going to like it and who was not. Because of that, I felt it was selfish, knowing that I would definitely be bothering some people.

As my sales started getting worse, the amount of stress and anxiety that I was feeling increased a lot as well. After a particular incident that happened on the highway, I decided to quit that job and find something else.

This particular event happened after I just got back to Ottawa from Brockville, which is about an hour drive away. The appointment in Brockville didn't result in a sale, which obviously stressed me out further, and I had to go to the other end of Ottawa for another appointment an hour later, so I barely had enough time. As I got to the far end of Ottawa, part of the highway was closed, because of a head-on collision that happened earlier in the morning, and resulted in someone's death. The traffic was backed up, unbelievably far down the highway, as everything merged into one lane, and traffic was diverted onto a side-road. This was right in the middle of evening rush-hour. At that point I knew I wasn't going to make the appointment on time, so I called the appointment to let them know that I was running late, only to find out that they changed their mind, and weren't interested anymore; this only further increased how stressed I was.

As I was waiting in traffic, ever so slowly getting to the exit, so I could turn around and go back home, I suddenly got a call from the appointment I had just been at in Brockville an hour before. They told me that they changed their mind and wanted the alarm system, but I needed to get there by a certain time, because they're going away for the weekend. Now not only was I stressed for needing to drive back to Brockville, but was also rushed, because if I didn't get there in time, I would be driving there for nothing and spending more money on gas; I was still completely stuck in traffic, with nowhere to go but wait.

When I got a hundred meters or so away, from where the construction cones started merging everything down into one lane, I became increasingly annoyed, from all the people who were selfishly racing right to the point where the cones force you into the one lane. When I got pretty close to the construction cones, I started blocking people from cutting in front of everyone who were patiently waiting. As I moved over to do a community service, and stop people from selfishly cutting in front, I suddenly realized that the person behind me was also a selfish asshole, and was trying to get in front of me, even though I was clearly just stopping other people from cutting in front of us. So I started slowly weaving back and forth, to stop both of them, and then the guy who I was initially stopping from cutting in front, went around one of the traffic cones, only to slam on his brakes a car length in front of me. It's really astonishing, how much effort people will put into doing things like that, when they're really not getting anywhere faster. Given how stressed and annoyed I was at that point, and considering the traffic was not going anywhere, I decided to get out of my car, to give this guy a lecture regarding the stupidity of his actions.

Just as I got up to his car, the traffic started moving a little bit and he started pulling away. Initially, I was only going to knock on the window and give him shit for being so selfish, but as the car unexpectedly started driving away, I just instinctually grabbed the door handle. At that point, he was completely startled and obviously scared, because he suddenly got out of his car swinging.

I had no desire to have a physical fight with this guy, and initially all I did was back up and block his attempts to hit me, but he still kept trying to hurt me. When he still kept coming at me even though I was backing away towards my car, eventually I didn't have much of a choice but to defend myself. Even at that point, I still didn't want to hurt the guy, because I could tell he was obviously just scared. Given my experience with fighting, I know how to regulate the amount of force I put into a punch or kick, and because I didn't want to hurt him, I didn't hit him that hard at all, but just the one mild punch I hit him with, still knocked him out and he fell to the ground. Not only was I shocked about what happened, but scared as well. I didn't want to get in trouble, because I knew how the cops would see this, even though I was only intending to give him a lecture. I got back in my car really quick, and drove passed everyone on the shoulder, which was obviously kind of hypocritical, considering I was trying to stop other people from doing the same kind of thing.

I've thought about that incident countless times over the years, almost every time I drive by that area, and have always had very mixed feelings about it, even to this day. Although, I didn't start the fight, and even kept attempting to back away from it, I still feel bad about it. My intentions were good when I got out of the car, and I know from experience; how much of an affect the right words can have on a person, leading to a change in their behavior. But even though I feel bad about it, when I think about the situation as a whole, it always seems like it's one of those moments where, from a moral point of view, it's definitely very grey.

After that incident, I realized the job was causing me too much stress; I couldn't, in good conscience, continue working at that job, especially considering how many telemarketers were pushy to the point, where people were saying yes, just to get them off the phone.

NICK, A PEACH, & A ROCKSTAR PUNCH

For the most part, I have attempted to keep the stories in a chronological order, because of how I've changed over the years as a result of the events that happened in these stories. I'm not sure how much it would be noticeable, to anyone except me, but I hope the details that I've included do show some kind of evolution over time. There are definitely moments when I've been stressed, which cause me to react more aggressively, in a way I'm much more likely to regret later, so there's definitely some ups and downs over time, from a moral point of view that is. This next incident happened before I quit the alarm system job, but I'm only including it now, because it is really unrelated to work, and is a separate issue all on its own.

After finishing my appointments one evening, I went directly over to a friend's house who was having a barbecue, and there were a bunch of other friends there as well. Since I was coming directly from work, I was wearing khakis, and a really nice shirt that was meant to be tucked in. I normally hate wearing a shirt that needs to be tucked in, since it feels very restrictive, but I still kept it tucked in because it was very long, and if it wasn't tucked in, having a shirt that's hanging down to the bottom of my ass, would be even more annoying.

As I walked into the backyard, one of my friends, Peach, immediately says to me, "Adam dear, you've got to un-tuck that shirt!" She was definitely being playful and said it in a jokingly kind of way, but I knew she was also being serious. I just kind of dismissed it, and playfully replied by saying,

"What are you talking about? This shirt looks damn good tucked in! And it shows off my ass nicely too!" Pretty much everybody at the party was right there on the back patio, and we all had a good laugh about it. I then went about the usual pleasantries and said hello to everybody. Then a few minutes later, Peach made another comment about my shirt, which I just kind of ignored, because that's just the way she is. Then another ten minutes goes by, and she made yet another comment about the shirt, but this time, I replied by saying, "If you keep going on about the shirt, I'm going to say something you're not going to like."

At that point, every single one of my friends there, knew me well enough to realize how harsh my words can be, when someone pushes me to that point. The reason why my words can be so harsh is because they would be based on something that's true, just like the situations with Nikki and Jen's mom. After I said that, I walked through the patio door into the kitchen, where Nick, the host of the party, was preparing shish-kebabs for the barbecue. After I walked inside, I casually said to him, "What's with peach and the fucking shirt?" To which he replied, "Well at least you're not loose!" This was a comment that was both funny and true, at least in a proverbial sense; it was no secret that Peach had slept with a lot of guys within that group of friends, but I'm not saying this as any sort of judgement, nor do I look down upon anyone just because they openly like something that is obviously enjoyable.

A few minutes later, I walked back outside, and once again, Peach made yet another comment about the shirt. So as promised, and with the ammunition just spoken to me by Nick, I replied, "Well at least I'm not loose!" Of course everybody was shocked at that point, but there was also a bunch of giggles as well. Peach's jaw dropped to the floor, and for whatever reason, I added, "Well... Nick said it." That of course got some more gasps and giggles, but overall, considering the way people in that group always talk to each other and joke around, I didn't think it was really a big deal, especially considering that Peach seemed to be very comfortable about her sexual activities.

A few days later, I ended up getting a message on my voicemail from Nick, saying that I owed him an apology, and Peach too, because Peach is really upset with *him*. Personally, I didn't feel I owed anyone an apology, because Nick did say that, and if he had a problem about what he said, it was his responsibility; he shouldn't have said it in the first place. I also didn't feel I owed Peach an apology, because I did tell her if she kept going on about the shirt, I was going to say something she wouldn't like. Also, the thing I said, from a proverbial sense, was absolutely true. So if she had a problem with that truth, then she should really be taking better look at her own choices, instead of getting mad at others, for saying something that's true; unsurprisingly, I ignored the voicemail.

Then a week or so later, I stopped by a different house, that's part of the same group of friends, for a poker party. As soon as I got to the party, I walked into the kitchen where the poker game was taking place. Nick was standing on the opposite side of the table, on the other side of the room, from the entrance I came in. Initially, I walked right up to the table, and stood around watching the game like everybody else. Almost immediately, Nick started going on about how I owed him an apology. I quickly explained why I didn't feel I owed anyone an apology, but still he wouldn't let it go. Even after I said, I didn't come here to argue and he wasn't going to change my opinion. He still kept going on, and was even getting a little bit aggressive in his tone. We were almost within reach of each other, so I decided to take a step back away from the table, since I felt he was going to say something that crossed a line, because I knew how he could run his mouth off at times.

The whole group of friends, had known each other since they were kids, so they were used to the way he could be mouthy at times, but nobody ever stood up to him. At that point, I'd known that group of friends for 5 years or so. That was more than enough time for Nick and I, to have had many heated debates, that were often interesting enough, we'd end up acquiring spectators, sometimes, quietly literally with popcorn. This was another reason why I backed up, because if he did say the wrong thing, I probably would've reached out and grabbed him, and I didn't want to do that in somebody else's home. I wouldn't have hurt him, just rough him up a bit, which for a person like him, I was pretty sure that would be enough of a point. But I stepped back anyway, leaned against the stove, and opened a Fruit-Punch flavored, Rockstar energy drink, that I brought with me, then simply ignored him.

Well he still kept going on and on, and eventually he got so frustrated because I was ignoring him, as expected, he crossed a line when he said, "Oh, don't be such a Bitch!" When he said that, one of the other guys standing there even let out a little gasp, and said, "Oooh!" knowing that Nick crossed the line. Where I grew up, when one guy calls another guy a Bitch, those are fighting words. I'm not sure if Nick realized that, but from the tone in his voice, I'm pretty sure he did.

At that point, no one in that group had ever seen me fight, or even be aggressive towards anyone, and because that group of friends, was initially the only group of friends that I had when I first moved to Ottawa, I'd usually just ignore a lot of the attitudes, and slightly rude things some of them would often say or do, because I didn't want to do something, that would make me not welcomed at any of the fun parties. But in that moment, when Nick called me a Bitch, I finally had enough of his collective attitude over the years; I made the choice to do what I did next.

The moment when he called me a bitch, I had the Rockstar energy drink in my hand and close to my mouth. Then in a very intentional way, like Bruce Lee's three-inch-punch, I quickly extended my arm straight out, directly towards Nick's face. This caused the Rockstar can to float through the air, as though it were standing still, not rotating on any axis at all, and contacted Nick's face perfectly centered. It actually left an imprint of the shape of his face in the can. I only found out about that detail, because one of my friends kept the can and showed it to me afterwards. Immediately after serving the sweet punch to Nick's face, I apologized to those who lived there, put forty bucks on the table, as another apology for the mess that I made, because the punch splashed all over the place as it contacted his stunned face. Rather appropriately, as the punch was both literally and figuratively, dripping off Nicks face, I turned, and walked out the door.

Interestingly, most of the people that were there, at one point or another, pretty much all agreed that Nick had it coming to him. But even if nobody would've agreed with how I reacted, I still don't feel bad about that. I intentionally threw the can in such a way so that it hit him with the side of the can, which was soft, rather than randomly throwing it, and one of the hard edges possibly hitting him, which could have easily hurt. The only point was hurting his pride, and throwing the can the way I did, was basically a slap rather than a punch, but in this case, it would be more accurate to call it a punchy-slap. It wasn't the first time he said things that I thought were out of line, which is why I was kind of anticipating him saying something like that, but there becomes a certain point, when enough is enough. I'm sure a lot of people will have the opinion that words are words and I shouldn't have made it into a physical thing. But words can hurt, often more than a punch in the face, and in this case, even though I wasn't necessarily hurt by being called a bitch, it was still disrespectful, and as I mentioned, he is known for being that way with other people as well. The very thing that he said about Peach is a great example, and she was obviously hurt by that, if she felt he owed her an apology. Peach is a tough girl, can take care of herself, and if she felt I owed her an apology, I'm sure she would've said something to me. This was later confirmed when I talked to Peach, and although she felt that me repeating it was a bit much, at least I had a reason for throwing a jab like that. The reason she was so upset with Nick, was because, what exactly was *his* motivation for saying that to me?

RICO SAUVE

This next situation I found myself having to deal with one day, is one of the few examples from my life, when I've gone out of my way after the initial incident and continued to confront the person about what they've done, not just once, but in this case, twice after the initial incident. And it wasn't just words, but rather physical in nature. That's because this time, I felt it was in the best interest of society, that this kid got a properly humbling lesson. For the longest time, I actually thought his name was Rico Sauve, because that's how my friend referred to him, I had no idea, until some years later, that it was a pop culture reference, but to me that will always be his name.

One night, I went and picked up a buddy of mine, Itai, so that we could go to a party together. When I got to his apartment, he asked me if somebody he met in his building could come along too. Because we're a friendly group of people, of course he knew I would say yes, but out of respect, he's going to ask anyway. I also knew the house we were going to the party at, was always welcoming of new people as well. Shortly after I picked the two of them up, I had to stop to get gas on the way to the party.

At the time, I kept my wallet in the center console of my car, because I knew I'd often forget it at home, and never wanted to be without my debit card, in case I needed gas. I never keep any money in my wallet, because money is the first thing people think of when they see one, which is why they often go missing and is precisely the reason I keep my money in my pocket. Besides my bank card, the only other things in my wallet was my health card, my driver's license, and a bunch of discount/points cards.

When we got to the gas station, I grabbed my wallet to use my debit card to pay for the gas, not thinking anything about this new person in the car. So we got the gas, and off to the party we went.

After the party was over, my buddy Itai, said that he's going over to a girl's house, but asked if I'd be willing to drive the new kid home. I was also driving my buddy Issa and Heider, and they live close to each other, so I didn't mind at all driving the other kid home as well. But even if I wasn't driving anybody else home, I'm still the type of person who would've drove this kid home, even though I just met him; simply because it just feels nice to do nice things for people.

During the party, I hadn't really interacted with or even seen the kid much at all, and even though I call him a kid, he was definitely an adult, it's just that he was obviously at least ten years younger than me. Since I hadn't been around him at all during the party, I had no idea that there was some kind of issue, between him and some other people that were there, but I quickly found out about that, as I was driving him and my other buddies home.

As soon as we left the party, this kid immediately started running his mouth, talking about how tough he is, and how "those" people at the party that he had a problem with, are all bitches, and how he's not afraid of them because he's got his "gats" (guns). Really it was quite ridiculous, and I just turned the music up; I've heard enough idiots like that, talk shit my whole life as a kid growing up in the Windsor and Detroit area, and nothing new would be understood from listening to more.

On the way back to drive them all home, I wanted to stop at the store to grab something to drink. When we got to the store, I wasn't expecting my friends to get out too, and after hearing the way this kid was talking, I immediately knew he wasn't trustworthy. I didn't want to create an awkward situation, by asking one of my friends to stay in the car, or anything like that. So instead, I quickly grabbed what I wanted, and then asked the person in line, if I could jump in front of them. Before the person even responded, I went to the counter anyway, quickly put 10$ on the counter, and told the cashier to give the change to the person I just cut in front of. In total, I was in and out of the store in under a minute!

My intuition was correct, and I walked out just in time, to see this kid going through my center console from the back seat. It was just a momentary flash, and as soon as he saw me coming, he already immediately pulled his hands away, but I'd seen enough to be sure of what I saw.

As soon as I got in the car, I didn't immediately confront him, because I wanted some extra confirmation, by looking into the center console first.

As soon as I opened the lid, I noticed that a little box that I kept gas receipts in, was not in there, and at that point I looked directly at him, and in a very firm and aggressive tone, I told him, "Get.The.Fuck.Out Of My Car!" He just looked at me, pretending to be all confused, as though he didn't do anything at all, but I knew one hundred percent he did. I just cleaned my car that night, before picking people up for the party, and when I looked at him, I saw that box of receipts scattered all over the backseat.

I immediately got out of my car, went around to the back passenger side, opened the door, and without hesitating, I grabbed him, and quite literally, threw him out of my car; tossing him about 8 feet away; his feet didn't touch the ground until he almost hit the building. He was still playing dumb like he didn't do anything, but I know from experience, the best way to deal with a person like this, is to maintain the initiative. You want to keep them on the defensive by being aggressive and firm right from the start, and then always stay 2-3 steps ahead. This is especially important for somebody who looks as innocent and harmless as I do, because the last thing you want, is for a person like that, to get it in their head that they might try standing up to you. As he continued to play dumb and denying everything, I was right up in his face, not just telling him exactly what he did, but I also kept using my hand to turn his head towards the open car door directly at the obvious truth.

Repeatedly turning his head, was actually the first time I had ever done anything quite like that, because it would clearly make a fight much more likely to happen, and if I'm expecting to have to fight, I'd always back up and keep my distance to let the other person come towards me. However, after hearing all his big-tough-guy-talk involving guns, and considering he was only around 20, I felt a harsh and humbling lesson could be very humane. Seeing the contrast between his big talk in the car and then not even having the guts to admit he went through my stuff, even though it couldn't have been more evident, is when I decided to provoke him the way I did; the tough-guy is the one who needed to be humbled, not some coward in denial.

After I turned his face towards the backseat the 4th time, I saw on his face a brief glimpse of his inner hulk-ette, before the alert coward managed to put him back to sleep. Upon seeing the intensity during that brief moment, I knew one more quick and firm forced head turning would fully awaken his little hulk, and this kid would finally try to stand up to me. Seeing that he was ready to react, when I grabbed the lower half of his face the last time, I added an extra dash of annoyance by using my thumb and index finger to squeeze his cheeks also. Just as I anticipated, he finally had enough.

I already knew what I was going to do next, and the moment I saw his body tense up and his right arm start moving to take a swing at me, I started moving as well.

In one fluid motion, I grabbed his neck with my right hand, reached around him and grabbed his lower back with my left hand, put my right foot behind his legs, and lifted him off his feet with the hand that was around his throat. The force from lifting him by his neck, also caused a pushing force as well; I knew that would happen, which is why I put a foot behind his legs, and as a result, he was unable to instinctually step back to prevent falling backwards. As he began falling, with my left hand, I pulled his lower-back up, and towards me, and used the momentum of his tilting body to lift him completely into the air; for a moment, his entire body was in level flight with a cruising altitude of approximately 4 feet. Like most flights, that was definitely one of those moments when time seems to slow down, and on final approach, I diligently reviewed the landing procedure. Upon descent, I engaged the landing gear, by holding the back of his head with my left hand to protect it from the rough landing a-head, I verified the flaps were in their correct positions by observing the movement of his arms, and then I braced for landing, once I ensured my seat was in its full upright position.

Standing over him now, pinning him to the ground by the neck, I yelled at him in a crazy tone, that even scared my friends a bit: "DON'T FucKING LiE too MEE! You'LL InSult me if You Lie to Me, and you don't want to FUCKING DO THAT!" At first, he was trying to resist and get up, but I kept telling him to submit, but he wouldn't at first. So I picked him up again and got him on his short connecting flight to his final destination a few more feet away. Like any good friend, I was there when he landed and made sure to stay on top of all the remaining details. When he finally did submit, and I no longer felt that he was going be a threat, I finally let him go and told him to "Get The Fuck Out of My Sight!"

As he started walking away, I turned, looked at my friends and smiled, but I'll never forget the looks on their faces; almost like they were worried I might hurt them too; I was fully in control of myself though. They heard me tell stories about crazy fights, but that's the first time they've ever seen me do something like that, and they never have since. From a moral point of view, that was definitely the right thing to do toward somebody who was talking about guns. If he had pulled one out, he had better pull the trigger and hope he hits me, because I would go straight for the gun, the moment I saw it.

After my friends and I got back in my car, I continued driving them home. Just before I dropped my last friend off, it occurred to me that my wallet was in the center console too. When I looked in there, I noticed that my wallet was gone, and it wasn't in the backseat either. Even though there was nothing of value to him in the wallet, it was still a big inconvenience for me, needing to replace all my I.D.'s, and everything else. More importantly, the reason why I wasn't done with this kid, was because society doesn't need somebody like him walking around, thinking he's going to get a gun, if he doesn't already, and I've got no problem being shot, while standing up for the greater good. I knew even though he got a bit humbled that night, but from my experience, he wasn't humbled enough.

The kid lived on the first floor, in the first apartment next to the elevator. A week or so later, as I was leaving my buddy Itai's place, fate seemed to be hard at work. Just as I stepped off the elevator, and looked towards his apartment, there he was, sticking his head out his door, simply because of two older ladies having a fairly loud conversation in the lobby.

We made eye contact right away, and without any kind of expression at all on my face, I just kind of nodded at him like we were buddies, and casually walked towards him. With an uncertain look on his face, he slowly started walking towards me too. When we got about two feet away from each other, I suddenly lunged towards him in the most explosive way I could. I head-butted him in his lips so hard, it sent him flying back fifteen feet, and the only thing that stopped him from falling onto the ground, was him grabbing onto his door frame. He just kind of looked at me with this fear in his eyes, and asked, "What the fuck?" And I simply pointed at him, and in a very quiet, but aggressive tone (because I didn't want to disturb the old ladies having their friendly conversation in the lobby), I said to him, "That's for my fucking wallet!"

The entire incident was so subtle, neither of the old ladies even noticed what happened right in front of them. But I've known enough people like him, too many in fact, so I wasn't done with him yet.

I actually knew some other friends that lived in that same building as well, and after they heard what happened, not only did they know who I was talking about, but the kid would actually come over sometimes and try to mooch free drugs off of them. They told me next time he comes over, they will give me a call, and tell me some subtle thing that will give me a hint that he's there, without actually saying anything that would make him suspicious and leave.

One night, as I was getting ready for bed, I got the call. So I put on some sport shorts, a T-shirt and my running shoes, because I knew what I was going to do. When I got to the apartment building, fate was smiling once again, and somebody just happened to be walking out the door as I was coming in, so I didn't even need to buzz their apartment, and I just walked inside. They also told me that they're going to leave the door unlocked, and to just walk in.

As I opened the door and walked into their apartment, initially everybody was all smiles and laughing, I just calmly smiled, but looked only at my friends. I went over to the table, set my keys down, and then casually turned, looked Rico directly in the eyes, and calmly said to him, "Now we need to talk about compensation for my wallet." This time, from the moment he saw me walk in, there was nothing but panic and fear in his eyes, and that is exactly the point of why went after him so many times, because now he is definitely regretting what he had done. As I calmly walked towards him, he was sitting in a big lazy boy chair, and slid back as far as he could, putting his feet up in the air in a desperate attempt to keep me away from him, but that was exactly what I'd hoped for, because I wanted one of his shoes. He tried to plead with my friends, asking them to talk me out of it, but I just smiled at him and said, "Who do you think called me over here?" And at that point you could see how alone he felt.

Unfortunately, I gave up trying to get his shoe off, because of how tightly it was laced up, and he started completely panicking, and losing control of himself. Although I knew it would be even easier to have control of him, if he was not in control of himself, I also knew, we would likely end up breaking something in my friend's apartment, if I continued trying to take his shoe off, because he was out-of-control, in the same way prey would act locked in a cage with something it knows is about to eat it. As he desperately pleaded with me not to take his shoe, even asking please. I even told him, since he was polite and said please, I would accept some other form of compensation, and so reluctantly, he brought me down to his apartment. Once inside, I saw a stack of DVDs sitting on the floor in front of the TV, and since this was well before Netflix, I picked them up, and said this will do, then calmly walked away.

Personally, I didn't care about the DVDs, that wasn't the point; it was just a matter of principle. I would've preferred the shoe, but to have him walk me down and let me take something out of his apartment, was actually much more humbling for him, and was probably a better lesson overall.

When I got home and looked at the DVDs, I was saddened to see that there were some cartoons in the mix, and I knew that I had taken some child's enjoyment away. After talking with my buddies the next day, I found out that he actually lived with a girl and her kid, and it was neither his kid nor his apartment. After she found out what happened in the morning, she ended up kicking him out. After I heard of this, I wrote an apology note on my computer, printed it out, brought the stack of DVDs with the note, and left it in front of her apartment door. But it made me even happier knowing an idiot kid like that, was no longer in this girl's life. What's even more fitting, is that he actually had to go back to Toronto to live with his parents, since he had nowhere else to stay.

Like with most of the stories in this book, I hadn't really thought about this one in a long time, at least not in any kind of significant detail. Even as I wrote this, the emotions that I felt were the same emotions and intensity as when it happened. I feel that this one in particular, could easily be misunderstood, with respect to my character. I pointed out a few times, when I calmly smiled, directly before or after a very violent moment, but really, there's nothing that I find smile worthy about any of this. As I mentioned, I don't think there's any other stories or even times I can think about, when I've repeatedly went back on different occasions, knowing I was going to be aggressive and violent with somebody. Holding a grudge or seeking revenge, is not something I really do, because I really don't like being that way, in fact I rather dislike it to the point of hate. But this particular situation, especially because of his talk about guns, and also his fairly young age, made me feel that there's a small possibility at least, my actions towards him might actually result in some kind of positive change in his life. I realize there's one way of looking at it which is basically that violence will generally only cause more violence, and for the most part, I do agree with that. I also know from witnessing similar situations like the way I was with this kid, that sometimes violence, if done in a controlled and specific way, can actually be very effective in making the other person realize that they're not really that tough at all.

For the lack of a better example, let's take the example of training a dog. As I mentioned previously, my mom helped run a wildlife group for thirteen years, and that's taught me a lot about how to really connect with animals of all sorts. From watching the animals over so many years, in a very close environment, I have learned that by mimicking the motions and movements of a particular animal, they will often start looking at you differently and become very curious. Most of my friends and family who know me, realize how good I am with animals, and even pets that normally don't like other people, often really like me. I don't know how many times I've trained somebody else's adult dog or cat, in a very short period of time. People say that you should never hit a dog, and mostly, I agree with that, but not completely, and it definitely depends on the dog. People often forget that dogs are pack animals, and they establish order and dominance through aggression, but once a dog submits to another dog, the fight is usually over. You should definitely never beat a dog, ever, because that's just senseless cruelty, and will only cause the dog to fear you; Alpha is about respect, not fear. If you have a dog, who thinks it's the boss of the house, and is Alpha, the only way to change that, is to show it that you are actually Alpha; with some dogs, that can mean a bit of aggression is required. The only way to achieve that change is by having the dog submit to you. With most dogs, this can be done relatively easily, without ever needing to smack the dog, at least if the training starts as a puppy.

Take for example a dog that likes to bite, a little bit too hard, in a playful, dominant kind of way. That kind of behavior, can usually be changed quite easily, by shoving your fingers further into its mouth when it tries to bite, and then pinching under its tongue with one finger, and up from under its jaw with the other finger. This usually requires very little force, because of how sensitive that area is. Most the time, the dog will end up letting go really quick, and then it's usually just a simple matter of repeating this, each time they do the same thing again. However, a small percentage of dogs I have done this with, become more aggressive, to the point where I've been bitten quite hard, almost to the point of needing stitches. In those situations, instinct would make you think of pulling your hand out, but all that does is encourage the dog and reinforces the idea that it is the boss. From my experience, I would do the opposite, and shove my hand deeper into its mouth, which prevents the dog from being able to bite as hard, and I'd completely wrap my fingers around its entire lower jaw, so I'm in control of its mouth, at the same time with my other hand, I'll grab its neck and pin it to the floor, then I'd get on top of it to gain complete control of that dog. Again, the goal is to achieve submission, because once that dog submits, it then knows that you're the boss. Sometimes, a little extra force is needed that causes some slight pain, which in an example like this, involves slightly twisting the lower jaw, which is a very uncomfortable thing for a dog, because their jaws are not made to twist that way. But it's important to be very careful about how you're twisting the jaw, because you could easily cause permanent damage, and obviously you don't want to do that. But the most important aspect, is once the dog submits for ten or twenty seconds, or however long it takes for you to realize that it has given up trying to fight back, then it's important to show that dog love.

This is exactly the type of behavior you would see in a pack of wolves, when they are establishing who is Alpha. Whenever one wolf wins a fight, and the other submits, you almost always see them start licking each other afterwards.

This is not so dissimilar to the approach that I took with this kid. I could've easily hurt him really badly, and by the end of it all, he clearly understood that. I didn't really hurt him, because that would have been senseless and unnecessary, and if you are thinking of the bloody lip, well, that's not really hurting him. To quote a classic line from Star Trek, when a God like entity, whisked the ship away, because of the Captain's arrogance and ignorance, believing they were ready for anything they would encounter. After they had their first encounter with the Borg, the Captain had to admit that he was wrong, so that the entity would bring them back to where they were. After, when the Captain told the entity that he understood the valuable lesson, but he felt it could have been taught without the loss of 18 members of his crew, the entity replied by saying, "If you can't take a little bloody nose, maybe you ought to go back home, and crawl under your bed. It's not safe out here! It's wondrous...with treasures to satiate desires both subtle and gross; but it's not for the timid."

The only reason why I smiled at times, and purposely did so in a calm way, was to show him that I was not at all afraid of him. But I only smiled that way, during that third encounter, unlike the first or second encounter, which was before I saw that complete fear and panic in his eyes. I don't think very many people understand how much I hate doing things like that, and how sad it makes me feel. I absolutely hate the fact, that I find myself living in a world with such people as him. But I also realized, if I had simply just kicked him out of my car, left him there, and done nothing at all, the only thing that would've done is given him more confidence, and make him feel like he got away with what he had done, which would essentially be true, if I hadn't done anything at all. I'm the first one to admit, there is no way to know what kind of lasting effect my actions towards this kid had, but one thing I do know is, doing nothing, would've changed nothing, and based on the way that kid was talking, he was definitely a potential threat to society, and I would gladly risk my own safety, just for the slight possibility, I may have helped protect someone else in the future.

I've also had knives pulled on me twice, and in those moments, I automatically knew they were afraid, if they felt they needed a weapon, and both times, as soon as I saw the knife, I immediately kicked it out of their hands.

My leg is longer than their arm, and kicking it immediately after I see it, is the best chance of knocking it out of their hands, before they tense up with the fear they clearly have. Obviously, I could have easily gotten hurt, if they had a firmer grip than they did, but again, it's worth the risk, for the sake of the greater good.

ON A DRUNK LADY'S HOOD

This one slightly rainy Wednesday night, around 12 a.m., as I was heading home, and went through an intersection, I noticed a car coming quite quickly down the street to my right, and it didn't seem like it was going to stop. Even though I had the right away, I slowed down just in case.

My dad's an excellent driver, and he's been teaching me things about driving, for as long as I can remember. One of the things he often stressed, is always look both ways when you're crossing an intersection, even if you have a green light. It's a good thing I did on that night, because if I hadn't slowed down, I most certainly would've been hit quite hard.

The car turned towards the same direction that I was already heading, so naturally, I was now driving behind it. Almost immediately, I could tell the driver was not sober. So I picked up my phone, called the police, and started following the car. As I was continuing to talk to the police, to keep them updated as to where we were at, we ended up on a road with nothing around except bushes and trees. There were two lanes going in each direction, separated by a dirt boulevard and no other cars in sight. At that point, the car was driving on the broken line, between the two lanes, and swerving back and forth slightly. Because there were no cars around, and there was a big shoulder, it seemed like a very safe opportunity to get around in front of the car, and attempt to slowly force it to stop.

Thankfully, I was able to do exactly that, and once both of our cars were stopped, I quickly got out of my car, then ran up to the other car. With a very casual and friendly gesture, I motioned with my hand to roll down the window. The lady driving the car was obviously drunk, just by the way she was looking around for the handle to roll down the window. When she rolled the window down, I quickly reached in, shut the car off, and pulled the keys out of the ignition. I then quickly ran back to my car to get my phone, called the police back, and told them exactly where we were at. While standing in front of the lady's car, facing away from it, so I wasn't blinded by the headlights; I was talking on the phone with the police, when I was suddenly surprised to hear her car start back up.

So I turned around, and saw her motioning at me to move out of the way. but I just shook my head, no. Instead, she started trying to go around me, but because of how close I was to the car, it was impossible for her to be able to get enough speed, and far enough away, to prevent me from me being able to stay in front of her car. Then suddenly, instead of trying to go around me again, she decided to just drive straight at me, and hit me with her car.

As soon as she hit me, I landed on her hood, and initially slid slightly up the windshield, before I started to slide back down again, due to the hood being wet from the rain. After I slid down a bit, I was able to grab onto one of the windshield wiper arms with my hand, but because the windshield wipers were activated and moving, it made an already difficult task, that much harder. In my other hand, I was still holding my phone, so I immediately told the police that she just hit me, was now on her hood, and she started driving down the road.

Even though there's nothing funny about a drunk driver, or a situation like this, I still found it a little amusing. I was in Québec when this happened, and the dispatch lady on the phone, didn't speak the best English, and I spoke no French at all, so when I initially told her what had just happened, it seemed like she definitely understood, but she still asked a couple times for me to say it again, since it's obviously not something that happens every day.

Eventually, the lady sped up to around 50 to 60 KM/h; then suddenly slammed on the brakes.

At this point, I started sliding off the car, but I was able to hold on to the windshield wiper arm, just long enough, so that when I finally slid completely off the car, I was able to land on my feet. I quickly ran back up to her window and managed to get the second set of keys out of the ignition, all while still holding the phone and talking to the police. Less than a minute later, I heard two cop cars redlining their engines, and racing down the highway towards us.

Again their English wasn't the greatest, but it was clear they understood right away what had happened. They still ended up making some hand gestures, trying to confirm what they thought, *really* was what happened. The one male officer, had one hand open and in front of him, perpendicular to the ground, and with his other hand lightly closed, he kept moving the closed hand towards his open hand; a clear gesture of hitting. I just kept shaking my head and saying, "Ya, she hit me.", and when he seemed to be certain, I pointed at my car, which was over a hundred meters away, to show him how far she had driven with me on her hood. Obviously the driver was arrested right away. The police then asked if I would be willing to go to the station and give a statement, which I gladly agreed to. So they told me with the little English they knew, "Follow us!"

We all got into our cars and started driving. Not far down the road from where we were, the road changed, and had businesses on each side, with a speed limit of 50km/h. I had no idea where the police station was, so when the cops started driving over 100km/h, I assumed they meant literally, and because they were respectful, so I sped up and did exactly what they asked me to do. By time I was done giving the statement, they confirmed with the breathalyzer that she was very much over the legal limit.

A moment like this, was clearly the morally right thing to do, but I've always found it interesting that most people always comment about how scary that must've been, but personally, it wasn't scary at all. If anything I'd have to describe it as kind of funny and exciting, and the only thing scary about it, from my point of view, is realizing just how easily she could've hurt or killed somebody, if she hadn't been stopped.

This wasn't the first time I pulled over a drunk driver, and sadly it probably won't be the last, and I hope one thing that never changes about me, is my willingness to act, anytime I see something like this, which puts other people in immediate danger.

ASS GRAB HEAD-BUTT

This next story, despite it being a moment where I intentionally hurt somebody, I will always feel the way I handled the situation, was the right thing to do.

While out at a bar one night, with a few friends, as we were standing on the patio, just after the bar closed, and everybody was slowly leaving, I was chatting with some random people I'd met, having a friendly conversation, when all of a sudden I felt someone grab my ass, in a way that obviously wasn't an accident. When I turned around, I was surprised to see that it was a guy. Now just for the record, I'm not homophobic at all in any way whatsoever, and the guy who grabbed my ass, I don't think was gay either, because of what he ended up saying. That night, I was wearing a nice pair of stretchy khakis, that definitely made me look a little metro, but I'm not big into style that way, I just love those pants, because they are very comfortable to dance in, and I definitely do love to dance. Back in those days, I was mountain biking a lot, and had been my whole life, so I had quite muscular legs and ass.

After the guy grabbed my ass, I turned around, and with a tone that made it obvious I was not happy, I said "What.The.Fuck.Are.You.Doing?!" This was his first warning. If he was gay, thought I was gay too, and thought I'd like the advance and find it flattering, then after the way I reacted, he obviously would've apologized, but he didn't. Instead, he replied by saying, "Well you've got a nice ass!" Then I replied with the second warning,

"I know I have a nice ass, what the Fuck are you grabbing it for?" What he said next, is the reason why I don't think he was gay, but actually made it seem like him and his buddies had a bet that I was. He then started laughing, turned towards his buddies, and said with a smug tone, "Wellll.. you're gay, aren't ya?"

In a moment like that, it's astonishing how many clear, and distinct ideas, go through my head, in a fraction of a second. It could easily seem to others, that I just reacted impulsively, and didn't really think about things very much. But in that case, it was immediately clear to me, not only that he wasn't gay, but also, he seemed exactly like the type of person to randomly grab a girl's ass in a crowd, knowing that by time the girl turns around, it would be impossible for her to know who did it. I know how often girls have to deal with crap like that, which is something I deeply despise.

So after that third warning, when he turned his head away and laughed with his buddies, like they had some kind of bet, in one motion, I took a step towards him, turned his head towards mine, with both of my hands, and head-butted him directly in the nose, knowing that I was going to break it. As expected, his nose instantly exploded, and then just like it was out of some cartoon, he began falling backwards, trying to catch himself, for about fifteen feet, only to eventually land in a half-wooden-keg-flowerpot, directly in the corner of the patio.

I will, always, find that to be a completely morally justified act, because technically, that was sexual assault. I certainly do *not* feel victimized, in anyway, *at all*, nor have I ever been a victim of any such thing. The *sole* reason for my initial reaction, is a direct reflection of how much I despise things like that being done towards women on a constant basis. No doubt, a single asshole like him is likely responsible for dozens of women having their asses grabbed in a single night at a packed club, because it's next to impossible to know who did it, when the girl turns around and sees 3 people facing the other way. Seeing that he showed absolutely no remorse after the two chances I gave him to apologize, is exactly why I decided to break his nose. I would've done the same thing, even if there was a police officer standing nearby, because there are some things you just don't do, and that's one of them. Also, from my experience dealing with police, any good police officer, even if they saw the whole thing, probably would have picked him up out of the flower pot and arrested him; then turn to me and give some sign of approval, and would likely ask, if I wanted to press charges.

Because of all these random, crazy situations, I frequently find myself in, I often feel like I'm some kind of magnet for them, almost as though the universe sends them my way, because it knows my janitorial cart is full, with all sorts of tools, for dealing with all sorts of different types of filth. Sure, I realize things like this happen to everybody, but because most people just walk away, it's hard to know how often such things actually happen to others, but it really seems like a lot more of these things cross my path. Keep in mind, for every story that I've shared in this book, I'm sure there are at least three *interesting* stories which I know of, but haven't shared, and who knows how many I've simply forgotten about altogether, and this doesn't even include the countless times, when I do as most people usually do, and walk away or not even get involved in a situation in the first place.

This next story, definitely seems like, the right thing, quite literally landed in front of, the right person, with the best shot, to target the grime, and blast the scuzz away.

READY, AIM, THE FIRE WORKS

On Canada Day one year, as my friends and I were walking back from the fireworks to their house, just as countless hundreds of other people were doing too; I was suddenly surprised by a big pile of spit that abruptly landed about three inches in front of me on the sidewalk.

When I looked up to the third floor balcony, I saw a bunch of guys in their early twenties, laughing about almost spitting on somebody intentionally. Obviously such behavior is completely contemptuous, and not at all acceptable, so of course I started shouting at them and giving them shit for being so disrespectful.

At the time, it just so happened I had some fireworks in my back pocket. They were the type which simply shot up in the air and went bang. In those days I often had fireworks like that with me, and was quite accustomed to shooting them off while holding them in my hand. They were really not very big, maybe six inches long including the little plastic spike that you're supposed to stick in the ground, and about as big around as my pinky finger.

I have no idea how many of those things I've fired off over the years, but definitely a lot, and I always shot them while holding them in my hand. Although I'd never shot them at anybody before, I still had very good aim with them, because I'd always be making sure to aim them away from anything that it could cause a problem with. I also know enough about physics, to understand that it's very unlikely to actually hurt anybody, as long as the explosive element isn't in a sealed environment, which would never happen when shooting them into the air.

Of all the times I've ever shot them out of my hand, every single one of them went straight and blew up about 3 to 5 stories up. The only exception was one time when I launched one out of my hand; it blew up immediately after exiting the little tube. Obviously, my ears were ringing a little bit for a few minutes, but it didn't hurt at all and there was no permanent damage. Everyone around, including myself, was actually laughing quite hard about it. So my decision to pull one out of my pocket and launch it at the balcony where the guys were at, was not at all an impulsive act.

I walked a little further down the street, about a house and a half away, so I had what I thought would be the perfect angle so that the firework would blow up directly over the balcony. Well, when I launched that particular firework, I swear, it must've been an act of God, because as the projectile left the tube, unlike any other time before, it suddenly launched sideways, shot across the street and blew up on the other side. Of course at this point, they all started laughing even harder.

The reason why I jokingly said, it was an act of God, was because God knew what I had in my other back pocket! This time, I pulled out a much bigger firework that did the same kind of thing, but was obviously much louder. This particular firework was about eight inches long, and was about as big around as a quarter. When I pulled this bigger firework out of my pocket, like the first time, they all ducked, as I aimed it towards the balcony at about head height, hoping it would blow up, just above their heads. Well, my aim couldn't have been any more perfect! As I launched that firework, it fired off exactly where I was aiming, and blew up, perfectly centered, directly above their heads!

Even though only one of them actually tried to spit on me, because they were all laughing about it, I felt they were all just as responsible and guilty, which is why even to this day I have absolutely no moral problem with what I did that night.

A MECHANICAL PUSH

Despite how often so many people do selfish and inconsiderate things, without any regard for other people, I still sometimes get surprised at the level of selfishness I sometimes encounter. This one day, around lunchtime, I was driving around to different pawnshops, trying to find an audio amplifier for my car. When I got to the next pawnshop, in a little strip mall, with five stores in a row, and parking spots that faced directly at the building, going from one end to the other, I drove straight in, parked my car, and went inside. Because I was looking for something specific, I was only in each pawnshop a minute or two. So when I walked out of this one particular store, no more than 2 minutes later, I was rather surprised to see, that somebody had parked directly behind me.

If there were no other parking spots available, and the person who parked behind me knew they would only be a few minutes, I could understand someone doing something like that, but the fact that there were at least three or four other parking spots empty, there's really nothing that justifies being so selfish and carelessly holding up another person. Initially, I went into each of the stores on the ground level, and asked if anybody knew whose car that was, but nobody did.

(A random thing about myself, I don't think very many people who know me even realize, is that even the thought of going in to ask a bunch of random people about the car, actually causes me a slight bit of anxiety, enough that I was little bit hesitant about wanting to do it, because I don't like to bother people with unnecessary things. The times when I do, it's because of other things that are bothering me more, which end up overriding that kind of concern.)

There was a law office upstairs, but I wasn't about to go ask, because if it was somebody that went upstairs, they would likely be in a meeting with a lawyer anyway. After waiting about five minutes or so, I started becoming exponentially more impatient, which means I was also becoming exponentially more irritated.

Eventually, I got to the point where I started honking the horn on and off for a few minutes, but still no one came out. When I stopped honking the horn for a few moments, a lady in the car next to me, had an attitude and *told* me to stop honking my horn, because her kid was in the backseat sleeping. When I looked in her backseat, I saw a kid that was easily five or six years old. I could understand if it was a baby, that might wake up and start crying, but that was hardly the situation here. I might've reacted differently, if she hadn't had such a rude and demanding attitude. But between her attitude, how old her kid was, and the fact that it was the middle the day, I suddenly found myself confronted with a second, equally ridiculous situation. After looking at her in disbelief for a moment, I reached into my open window, while continuing to stare at her, and after pushing on my horn, I didn't stop looking at her, until I finally let go of the horn, close to 5 minutes later; I'm sure I've never pressed a horn anywhere close to that long, ever before. But still, even after holding the horn for so long, nobody came out.

By that point, I'd been there for over ten minutes, and my patience had finally run out. I walked behind my car to look at the alignment of my bumper and the bumper of the car behind me. They were both about the same height, and the car behind me had a front license plate, which would protect it from being scratched. If I hadn't been driving an all-wheel-drive Subaru at the time, I don't think I would have even attempted what I ended up doing, because I highly doubt it would have worked with a 2-wheel-drive car. So I got back in my car, gently backed up, until my bumper made contact with the car behind me. Once the bumpers were touching, I proceeded to push the car behind me out of the way. I continued to pushed the car until it was about about one and a half car lengths away from where it had been, which gave me more than enough room to leave.

Although I expected the tires would screech as I pushed the car out of the way, I was genuinely astonished at how loud it actually was. Unlike the horn, it was so loud, I highly doubt there was anyone from the building who didn't stop what they were doing, to come look at what sounded like the worlds loudest car accident ever happening in slow-motion. If the owner of the car didn't hear the honking, they certainly saw me pushing their stupidity out of the way.

Morally, I don't feel bad about that at all, especially because it didn't even leave a scratch on their car, since I only touched their front license plate with my bumper. I was even surprised when I looked at my bumper later, and saw there wasn't a scratch on mine either. Moral issues aside, I've often wondered about the legality of what I did there. Because I didn't cause any damage to their car, I doubt I even broke any laws. Regardless of all that though, I'll never understand how people can be so selfish and inconsiderate like that. Interestingly, a few weeks later, as I drove by that place, I noticed that they had rearranged the parking lines, and now instead of the one row of parking spots facing the building, there were now a few rows of parking spots, all parallel to the building; it was nice to see that some positive change came from my decision to move someone's bullshit out of my way.

A DAMSEL IN DISTRESS

Of all the physical fights I've ever been in, there's only ever been one, when I felt that my life might be in danger. Even the two different times when I've had a knife pulled on me, because I was able to disarm them right away, and reacting so quickly, by kicking the knives out of their hands, there really wasn't any moment when I felt threatened, the way I did in this next story.

This happened in the summer of 2011, while I was dating this girl named Madel. This one night, my buddy Wes and I, were at my place, playing a driving simulation game, as we often would, because we are both very much into cars, and are both very good drivers. Madel was supposed to be coming over as well, and should have already been there, long before this point. Eventually, I got a call from her, and when I answered the phone, there was no response from her. All I could hear was some talking in the background, so I went into the other room, away from the noise of the video game, and started listening. It was hard to understand what was being said, but I could tell it was some kind of argument, and the other voice was a guy's. Madel had mentioned a little bit about her ex-boyfriend, and that he was stalking her for a bit, and my instincts told me that something wasn't right, so I went back to the living room and told Wes I had to leave.

The lock on the main door to Madel's apartment building was slightly broken, and I knew if I pulled it hard enough, it would open, without needing to be buzzed in. Each floor only had four units, and the elevator was almost directly across from her door. I knew when the elevator stops at that floor, you can hear the ding sound the elevator makes from inside her apartment. Because of that, I decided to take the stairs, so I could quietly get on to her floor and then stand outside her door to listen. If there didn't seem to be any kind of immediate threat, I felt it might be valuable to gather as much information as I could, in case the police got involved later.

When I got outside her unit, I could tell right away, they were just talking and arguing a bit, so I just sat there and listened for a while. There were quite a few times when she told him to leave, and I was thinking about knocking on her door the first time I heard that, but because I could tell she wasn't in immediate danger, I decided to continue listening to gather more evidence. That changed when I heard her saying, "Don't touch me", followed by, "Get off of me."

At that point, I knocked on her door in a very firm way like the police would. When she initially opened the door, it was only her and she was obviously afraid, but as soon as her ex could tell it wasn't the police, he started looking out the door as well. At that point I told him, "I believe she asked you to leave?" But then he responded by saying, "This is none of your business." To which I replied, "Actually, because Madel called me, it is my business. I've been standing out here listening for a while, and I heard her tell you to leave. So it's time to go!" He then tried saying that I didn't hear correctly, and she didn't actually say that. So I looked at her, and asked if she wanted him to leave, and she shook her head and said yes. So I looked back at him, and told him again it's time to leave, or I'm going to call the police. He then said, "Okay, just give me five minutes." I then looked at her and asked if that was okay. After shaking her head yes, I said okay five minutes, and then I continued to wait outside the door and listened. He was speaking much quieter knowing I was outside listening, but I was certain he wouldn't try anything now that he knew I was there. I actually ended up waiting ten minutes before knocking again, and when Madel opened the door that time, I went inside the apartment.

Once inside, I saw a big mess. The kitchen is pretty much the first thing that you walk into, for some reason there was flour all over the floor, and because it was a polished granite floor, it was extremely slippery. At that point, I was standing in front of the stove, which was on an island, and the wall to her bedroom was about the length of my arm away. Her ex was standing just on the other side of her doorway, inside of her bedroom, and I could clearly see him from where I was. So I looked at him, pointed at the door and said, "It's time to fucking go!" He said, "We're not done talking." Then I told him, "Yes you are. It's been over ten minutes. So either leave now or I'm going to call the police." At that point, he started slowly walking out of her bedroom and towards her apartment door.

When he got directly next to me, he suddenly grabbed me by the neck, and I instinctively grabbed him by the neck as well. I then pushed one of my feet up against the island behind me, to use as leverage, and shoved him right against the wall across from me. At that point, he began to squeeze my neck is hard as he could, and that's when I realized how serious the situation was, because he was really trying to strangle me. Thankfully, I've got very strong neck muscles, so he wasn't able to stop me from breathing. I started squeezing his neck as hard as I could too, turned to Madel, and told her to call the police. Because of how serious I felt the threat was, rather than being afraid, I found myself in a state of Zen, more calm than I'd ever been in any fight before. Because he wasn't letting go of my neck, even though I had him pinned against the wall, with my other hand, I took my thumb and shoved it straight into his eye. I was surprised that the entire length of my thumb went into his eye socket. As soon as I did that, he let go of my neck to try to get my thumb out of his head, and as he let go of my neck, there was no longer enough force to keep us pinned between the island and the wall. We started slipping on the flour coated floor and quickly fell to the ground.

Because how fast I can think about things, in moments like that, time seems to slow right down. During the single second it took to fall to the floor, to me it was a clear series of movements I intentionally made, to ensure that I would end up on top of him, once we hit the floor.

When we did hit the floor, I still had my hand around his throat, my thumb still in his eye, and was completely straddled on top of him, pinning him on the floor. He then started reaching for my face, and I could tell he was trying to get his fingers in my eyes. When I noticed what he was trying to do, I pulled my thumb out of his eye, grabbed his hand that was reaching for my face, put his thumb into my mouth, then proceeded to bite down as hard as I could, and was genuinely attempting to bite his thumb off! I then took my thumb, put it back into his eye, until he eventually started shouting, "Ok! Ok! I give up!" But I didn't let go, because he was still struggling, so I just kept telling him to submit, and stop resisting. After saying that a few times, he finally did submit and stopped resisting, but I still waited a few moments, to make sure he really had given up.

As soon as I got up off of him, I immediately backed up out of range, made sure to keep that distance, and didn't once take my eyes off his eyes until he left. Unsurprisingly, the experience of having a thumb lodged 2 inches into his skull during that quick trip to the floor, left him quite rattled, and it was clear he needed a few minutes to eye out the situation before he felt confident enough standing up again. The white part of his one eye was already completely red, and wasn't even sitting in the socket straight. He was also holding his thumb, in obvious pain, because of how hard I had been biting down on it. But still, I would not stop staring him in the eyes. I was completely calm the whole time, and every bit of my focus was on him. The whole apartment was an open concept layout, and as he went into the living room to find his jacket, he started trying to be all cool with me, even saying a few times, "Respect Man. You don't need to worry, just stop looking at me like that with those crazy eyes." At one point, he even wanted to shake my hand, but fuck that shit, I don't trust that guy. I told him, "If I ever find out that you're bothering Madel again, I'm going to come looking for you, and bring you somewhere no one will ever find you."

(In reality, that was just an empty threat, but with how shaken up and afraid he was, because of what I just did to him, I don't think he thought it was an empty threat, and as far as I know, he never bothered her again.)

When he eventually left, I locked the door behind him, and I finally knew I could relax. Even then, it wasn't until about 10-15 minutes later when I finally started relaxing enough, to even feel the adrenaline that was pulsing through my body, and that's when I started to get the adrenaline shakes, which must've lasted for another 30 minutes after that. Initially though, as soon as I turned around from locking the door, I looked at Madel and could tell she was in complete shock, and was just frozen where she was.

As soon as I walked towards her, because I wanted to give her a hug, she was so freaked out about what just happened, she was actually a little afraid of me because of how calm and unaffected I seemed, despite the violence that just took place in front of her; she even backed away a little bit as I approached her. As soon as I noticed that, I stopped approaching her, and instead, I just asked if she was okay. At first, she just kind of mumbled something I couldn't understand, and then eventually she asked, if *I* was okay. I told her, "Yeah I'm okay, he didn't hurt me." And then I added, "Why does it seem like you're afraid of me right now?" And then she just kind of started pointing towards where him and I just fought, and said, "Because… Because of that.. Because of what you just did!!" Since the adrenaline shakes hadn't hit me yet, and I was still in the calm, Zen like state that I was in, the magnitude of what just happened, hadn't yet sunk in. It took over an hour until she was finally comfortable enough to allow me to give her a hug, and almost immediately after I hugged her, she started shaking even more than I was, not long before that.

A couple months later, Madel found out through a mutual friend of theirs, that he was in jail for attempted murder, and also that his thumb and his eye were permanently damaged; I found myself surprisingly happy to hear that, knowing that he'll have a permanent reminder of what not to do, while he sits in jail for however many years.

A FLEX TO MY MORAL PERSPECTIVE

Not long after I quit my last job and began selling drugs full-time, I started picking up new customers at an almost exponential rate, at least for a period of time. Normally, when I got a referral from an existing customer, I'd always ask the existing customer two questions: first, how long have they known the person for? And second, where do they know them from? If they've known the person for a long time, and they didn't meet them in a sketchy place like jail, then my experience has shown, the new customer, will almost always be a good customer as well.

During that short period of time of exponential growth, there was this one time, I forgot to ask those two questions, because I was distracted by the excitement I had been feeling from business picking up the way it was. During a summer when most people had problems finding any weed at all, I had no difficulty, because my supplier would give me priority, since I was so consistent, reliable in my sales, and prompt when paying him. So not only did I have weed when most people didn't, I actually had really nice weed.

When I stopped by this person's house that night, he had a couple of friends over. One of them asked if he could see the weed, and after being impressed with the quality of it, he then asked if he could get my number. Between being really busy, having a lot more stops to finish that night, and the general excitement I had about getting yet another new customer, I didn't even think about asking the existing customer, those critical two questions, and I would later realize that was a mistake. After giving the guy my number, and telling him to text me right away with his name, which was "Flex", so I could save it, to know who it was when he called. I left, and continued with my other deliveries.

To my surprise, that new guy called me an hour or two later, while I was still driving around the city. He was quite impatient, and wanted to meet right away, but because of where I was in the city, and how far away he was, it didn't work out that night. A week or two later, he texted me again, and just like before, he wanted it right away, so again, it didn't work out. After this happened a few more times, and since I really hate impatient customers, I told myself, I wasn't going to deal with this guy anymore, because he was already too much of a hassle. Then a few weeks later, as I was driving around, I got a call from him again, and because I happened to be close to the area where he always wanted to meet, I decided maybe it might work out this time, and answered the call.

As usual, he wanted to meet right away, I mentioned I was only about five minutes away, and we arranged to meet in a grocery store parking lot. I told him when I get there, to hop in my car, and we would take a drive around the block. When I asked him what he was driving, he said, "A white.... umm, Malibu." I initially thought his delay was slightly weird, but then quickly dismissed it, thinking, he probably doesn't know much about cars. When I got to the parking lot, I didn't see any white Malibu, but I did see a white Cavalier, with a particular rust spot on the quarter panel, and knew I had seen it someplace before. That too was quickly dismissed, since I often saw unique cars more than once, because of how much I drove around the city.

When I saw him, I pulled up and let him get inside my car. I immediately asked what he wanted, and then handed him the ounce of weed he asked for. He then mentioned to pull over around the corner from where I picked him up. I pulled into one of the parking spots nearby, which seemed perfectly reasonable, because we were around the corner, so nobody who might've seen me pick him up, would've noticed that we just stopped around the corner.

As I pulled into the parking spot, I put the parking brake on, and told him how much he owed me. At that point, I was already starting to get a very weird vibe, which was confirmed a moment later, when he started saying, "You wanna cut grass in my neighborhood...." At the same time, as he started saying that, he also reached over and tried to get the keys out of my ignition. I got to the keys at about the same time, and during that little struggle, they got bent just enough, so that they couldn't come out of the ignition, and he quickly let go. Next, he tried to grab my phone, which was in a holder, attached to one of the air vents, in the center the dashboard. I got to the phone first, then quickly tossed it towards my driver side door and onto the floor. As I was tossing the phone, he did manage to grab my iPod, which was sitting in the cup holder just below where the phone was. At that point, I had enough of being on the defense, so I turned towards him, and with every bit of force I could apply, I lunged my whole body towards him, and head-butted him, as hard as I could, directly in his temple. It was hard enough to break the aviator glasses that he was wearing, and it was obviously hard enough for him to get out of my car really quick.

From all my experience being around super sketchy people when I was younger, I knew right away the weird vibe I got was something very dark indeed. Clearly he saw himself as some kind of gangster, and was clearly trying to muscle me into paying him some kind of tax for selling drugs, in what he thought, was *his* neighborhood. The complete confidence he had as he said that and the absolute lack of any signs of empathy for others, told me right away he was a very dangerous person that society would be better off without. What he tried to do, was one of those things which crosses many moral lines, and a person who thinks like that, is a genuine danger to society. Because of that, I had no moral issue with what I attempted to do next. After quickly starting my car, I backed up out of the parking spot, started driving towards him, and genuinely tried to run his ass over. I was only about two feet away from actually hitting him, when he managed to step up onto the sidewalk next to the building. If the curb was not unusually high at that spot, I would have driven up the curb and ran him over. I even drove around the block quickly, to make him think that I had left, but was hoping when I came back around the block, I might see him walking down the sidewalk. I knew the curbs around there were lower than usual, and would be able to easily drive up onto the sidewalk, and successfully run his ass down.

When I finally came around the block, I was quite disappointed I couldn't find him, so I continued about my night. As I was driving around, I kept thinking about all the little odd things that I noticed, but dismissed initially. Such as his, "White……ummm, Malibu", and seeing that white cavalier, with that particular rust spot, that I knew I'd seen somewhere before. At some point, I remembered exactly where I'd seen that car before; I saw it outside my buddy's house when I first met that guy. So now, I was pretty certain I knew what car was his.

A month or so later, as I was driving around doing my stops with the girlfriend I had at the time, about a block in front of where I was driving, I saw a white cavalier make a right turn onto another street, with that particular rust spot, on the passenger side quarter panel. I turned down that street as well, and as we got up to the next light, which was red, he was in the rightmost lane, waiting in a line to turn on to the entrance to the Expressway. As I drove by him slowly, in the next lane over, there he was, driving that car. After the right lane arrow turned green, which was before the light turned green to go straight, and was the lane I was in, I was watching his car in my mirrors. I noticed all of the cars in front of his, went much quicker than he was going. As he drove by my car, not only did he drive by really slow, but he was taking a really hard look through my tinted windows as well. After he passed me, I turned into his lane, and started following him down the entrance to the Expressway.

As soon as he noticed I turned to follow him, he took off as fast as he could, but because I know about cars, I knew mine was just a little bit faster than his. Once he got onto the Expressway, he drove to the next exit, took a right, and down a relatively wide industrial street, and because it was relatively late in the evening, in the middle the week, there were no other cars at the red light he had to stop at. As he was waiting in the double left-hand turning lane, and because there were no other cars going through the intersection, I knew I was putting nobody else at risk. So I came up behind him, quite quickly, and rear-ended his car hard enough to spin him around in the intersection. He then tried to take off in the direction we just came from, and because my car was a little bit faster, I was quickly able to catch up to him, and I tried to sideswipe his car. Unfortunately, he moved over just in time, only to see me looking out the window and yelling, "**You want to try being a Fucking gangster, you piece of shit?**" After I passed him, he started trying to chase after me, but I was quickly able to lose him. I then called him up on the phone, and warned him, if I saw him walking down the street, I'd run his ass over, and if ever saw his car again, I'd hit him even harder. I never did see that car on the road again, despite me actively looking for it. When I got home and looked at what damage there was to my car, there was only a small crack in my front bumper, and I was quite happy to see, a piece of his bumper stuck inside that crack; I still have that souvenir to this day.

If I had gotten that shoe from Rico Sauve, the shoe would be sitting right next to that piece of Flex's car, on my bookshelf, as a talking piece and reminder, just as any other souvenir; in this case, of why it's important to stand up to assholes like that!

Considering what I wrote in this chapter, if there was ever a time to have a conversation about morals, that time would definitely be now. I'm pretty sure most people will agree that trying to hit him with my car was more than excessive, but certainly almost everyone would agree that trying to run him over and actually killing him would have definitely been morally wrong. When I was younger, I would have completely agreed with that as well, but that night was another definitive moment that would lead a lasting impression on my moral perspective. This was the first time I knew for sure that I would be able to kill someone if I thought the reason was just.

As I'm reflecting upon this, I find myself thinking about the passive kid I used to be, the stark contrast between then, and the specific list of things that turned me in to such a vigilante at times.

Despite the almost daily bullying I experienced up until grade 8, and the countless fights others would start, up until jail, I knew I had never hit anyone nearly as hard as I felt I could. Even though I'd be defending myself against someone who attacked me, any time I'd throw a punch, I could always feel myself backing off just before hitting them. I distinctly recall doing that during the very first proper fist fight I had ever been in, despite how many years I spent preparing myself for that moment. It always seemed rather strange, that even in self-defense, I knew I was backing off because I didn't want to hurt the other person. The positive aspects of empathy are so numerous, obviously it's a good thing over all, but it's interesting the way it can also cause us to do things that does nothing to add to the greater good, and sometimes, it can even cause harm to the greater good.

Not hitting a bully as hard as I could is a great example of such a harm. If I had always been able to use my full strength to defend myself, not only I'm sure I would have been picked on less over all, which obviously would have contributed to my greater good, but if I had been able to hurt any of them badly enough, I'm sure they would at least think twice about picking on random people in the future.

I first started examining empathy more closely during the 10 months while I was in jail. Before then, everything I had learned about empathy could easily make anyone think there is nothing negative or concerning at all about it, and from an empathetic point of view, that totally makes sense. The problem with that utopian point of view, is something I realized quite clearly while I was in jail: some rare people completely lack empathy, and have no concern about anyone other than themselves. Such people are commonly referred to as narcissists, sociopaths and psychopaths. As much as I believe in the possibility of rehabilitation, modern research has shown from MRI scans of such people who are in prison, is that the area of their brains that deals with empathy are all very small compared to normal people; clearly no amount of rehabilitation is going to change that.

This is why I had no moral issue about trying to run Flex over. Legally, when it comes to protecting your property, the law states you can use "a reasonable use of force." If I had managed to hit him, and someone saw it happen, then called the police, it would ultimately be up to the courts to decide, if I used a reasonable amount of force to get my property back. But considering his gangster talk, it's not unreasonable for me to have thought he might have a gun on him. I also have no record (because my past record had been pardoned by that point), and I look like the poster boy of someone who wouldn't harm a soul. Combined with what I found out from a friend of mine later, I found out just how accurate my intuition was. When I told him this guy's name, what he looked like, and the area of the city we were in, it turns out, this guy is actually a gang member in one of the most notorious gangs in the city, and his brother is currently in jail for murder, so I wouldn't be surprised, if a court would have ruled in my favor.

Last of all, if you truly believe we all live other lives, then suddenly hitting the reset button for someone like this who will always lack such basic empathy for others, is not such a morally questionable thing to do.

THE 40 FOOT JUMP

We're finally at the point, where things start to get really interesting. There was no way for me to know, when this next event happened, that it would set off a chain of events, that have continued up until the present day, and I'm sure my life would be drastically different, if this single event didn't happen. It's quite possible, I wouldn't even be writing this book right now, even though I had been planning it way before this event took place. If I ever did write a book, most of the rest that follows from here would not have been in that book.

Before I get into this next story, I want to include a few seemingly random details, but they actually relate to the circumstances of what happened next. At the time this event took place, I had a fairly new Subaru Impreza, that I financed and bought brand-new. This was my first brand-new car, and compared to the two used cars that I had owned before this one, I was quite disappointed with the way this one handled in its stock form. These next details will likely only be interesting to other car enthusiasts, but it won't take long, so I'll include them anyway, but hopefully, I can still explain things well enough to make it interesting, even if you don't know much about cars.

My first car was a 1999 Dodge Stratus, that I never modified in any way, other than the sound system. The suspension that comes on those cars, is a double wishbone suspension in the front and back. These are the same kind of suspensions that are used on Formula-1 cars. An F1 driver actually helped design that car. Needless to say, it handled impressively well from the factory. My second car, which is the one I had when I rear-ended Flex, was a 2002 Mazda Protégé-5 hatchback, which had 192 000 kilometers on it when I got it. All of those cars rusted quite easily, which is why I didn't care if I Flexed the front end, slamming into some assholes car. The protégé didn't handle nearly as well as the Stratus, but it still had a very sporty suspension on it, and still handled better than the Subaru. The stock suspension on the Subaru was something that grandma and grandpa would be happy with.

As a result, not only was it the first of my cars that I ever modified, but I modified almost every aspect of the suspension. Most of the soft squishy bushings were replaced with much stiffer ones. The shocks I put on, were over twice as stiff as the stock shocks. I even put a mild lift kit on the car, which raised it about an inch. This may not seem very practical, but considering how much fallen snow can be compacted into an inch, the car can drive in significantly deeper snow before getting stuck. I also added a whole bunch of chassis braces, and basically, I set the car up knowing that I'd be doing some minor jumps with it off-road.

As I mentioned in one of the previous stories, my buddy Wes and I are really into cars. The game we use to play a lot, is called Gran Turismo™, and is considered by driving enthusiasts and racecar drivers alike to be one of, if not, the most accurate race simulator on the market. Combined with one of the high-end racing wheels and pedals, which I had, driving a particular car in the game, is very accurate to how it is to drive in real life. So after I put all the adjustable aftermarket parts on my Subaru, Wes and I loaded up my car in the game, and spent countless hours tweaking the suspension settings, before taking the car in for an alignment. Well just as I'd hoped, once I got that alignment, my car handled just like it did in the game.

The reason I felt particularly compelled to include such extensive details about cars, is because of how inherently dangerous driving can be. Most of the specific details I decided to use, could be replaced with other car related details and still achieve the same purpose. This is because the purpose is to illustrate the level of understanding I have of the mechanics of vehicles and driving in general, but despite how good of a driver someone is, mistakes can and do still happen. I mentioned, my dad has been teaching me to drive for as long as I can remember, and not only is he an excellent driver, but he's an excellent teacher as well; if I had the money, I'd get into racing, and I'm sure I wouldn't come in last on my first race. However, my dad also stressed the importance of safety, to be mindful of other drivers on the road, and never to play around on public roads, when there are other cars or people around that you could put at risk. Since it's one thing to put yourself at risk, but it's a whole other thing to put others at risk. The latter of which, is clearly a morally wrong thing to do, but if you are only putting yourself at risk (which includes not doing something that could damage private or public property either), then I don't see any moral issues. I felt it was really important to stress that, not just because of the moral aspects of it, but also, for any of the fellow car enthusiasts, who may be reading this and also play around on public roads at times. I cannot stress this enough to any of you, *Don't Put Others at Risk!* Just don't do it! Because if you ever killed somebody by playing around, that's something you would have to live with the rest your life!

As a final note, before I begin, relating to that psychological assessment, that was done of me when I was in jail, back when I was 17, my second highest score, which wasn't that much lower than my highest score, describes the exact type of abilities that would be needed to be a good driver. But like I said, it doesn't matter how good of a driver you are, even the best make mistakes, and the mistake I made the day this story occurred, was a mistake of a few thousandths of a second.

The story begins one Friday morning, in the spring of 2012, as I was driving a friend home from downtown. Because we were going in the opposite direction of the morning rush-hour traffic, there were very few cars on the highway in the direction that we were going. The exit we would need to get off at, to go towards his place, was one of my favorite 270° exit loops in the city. I knew from previous experience while playing around many times late at night, when there were no other cars around, that I was able to go around that corner from the entrance, all the way through to the exit, at just under 120km/h, with only all-season tires, which had an average grip rating. Towards the end of the loop, I still had enough grip, to be able to turn in a little bit more than I needed to.

Well on this particular morning, the tires that I had on the car, were high-performance tires, and had much more grip than the other tires I just mentioned. Again, I want to stress this, it doesn't matter how good of a driver you are, because of the highly dynamic nature of driving itself, even the best drivers can, and do make mistakes; this is why there's so many crashes in motor racing. As my dad would say, "You've got to pay, to play." Part of what makes a good driver, is the ability to analyze your mistakes afterwards, identify what you did wrong, learn from them, and hopefully not make those mistakes again. (This is also the same philosophy I take towards life itself, which I hope is evident from the stories that I've shared and the things that I've learned, from the countless mistakes that I've made.)

The first mistake I made that day, actually started the previous fall, before I put my winter tires on. After having driven my car with my winter tires for the past 4 months, on this spring day, I'd forgotten that I'd only driven with these new tires, for less than two weeks before the snow came. As a result, the tires were still a little squishy, and hadn't been fully broken in yet. This is something everyone should keep in mind when they buy a new set of tires; they need to be driven a certain amount of kilometers, before all of the manufacturing oils wear off, and the tires start to stiffen up. So as I came up to the exit that spring morning, I was only doing 100km/h, which I knew for certain, because I looked at my speedometer as I was entering the final straight before the turn, and I knew the car could easily go around the corner at that speed. Just before the turn, I said to my buddy, "Are you holding on?" Since at a hundred kilometers an hour, we were going to experience enough side G-Force, that he would want to be holding on. I should've said that a little bit sooner, because I was slightly distracted by saying it.

When you downshift into a lower gear and let the clutch out, unless the engine RPM is matched perfectly for the lower gear, there is a good chance the car is going to dip forward just a little bit, which causes weight to transfer from the back of the car to the front. As I let the clutch out and let the car stabilize, the mistake that I made, was starting the downshift a couple thousandths of a second too late. Just as the car dipped forward to its maximum, was the moment I needed to start turning. Because of that mistake, as I started to turn, the rear end of the car was momentarily lighter, which meant as we started to turn, the back end of the car had slightly less grip due to the reduced weight pushing down on the tires. So the moment I started turning, the rear end of the car immediately broke loose just a bit, but that little bit, was way too much. In that fraction of a second when I first noticed it, I knew we were about to take a big jump.

Off to the side of this exit ramp, there's no guard rail thankfully, or else I wouldn't play around on that ramp, but instead of a guardrail, there was a big grass field without any trees. Between the shoulder of the road and the field, there's a very gradual ditch that is about as deep as my car is high, and if I was going slow and straight I would've been able to drive down into it and up into the field. But we were going neither slow, nor straight, and because of how quickly I can analyze these kinds of things, within a fraction of a second, I knew we would be hitting the other side of the ditch, where it starts going back up into the field, completely sideways. I also knew that hitting the brakes, would've been the worst thing to do, because if I had hit the brakes, and locked up the wheels, when we hit the grass sideways, the tires would've dug into the grass, much deeper than they were already going to, and that would likely have would've sent the car tumbling sideways, and rolling over a number times, considering we were going 100km/h.

I knew the best thing that I could do at that point, was to steer directly towards the ditch as far as the wheel would turn, and rather than breaking, because it's an all-wheel-drive car, I actually pressed the gas pedal to the floor, hoping that the front wheels would help straighten out the car and minimize how sideways we were going to be, once we hit the hill on the other side of the ditch. I was trying to gain as much forward momentum as well, which would help spread the sideways momentum over a slightly longer diagonal distance. All of this would help reduce the chance of rolling the car on its side when we finally hit the hill

As we slid down the ditch and hit the hill going up into the field, the moment we hit that hill, the driver side quarter panel in the back, smacked into the side of the hill, and so our initial clockwise rotation, was *instantly* reversed, and we suddenly started spinning counterclockwise, while simultaneously, the moment the car was shot up into the air, because I was hard on the gas, thankfully that gave us forward momentum as well. As we left the ground, the car did a 180° turn in the air, and when we landed about forty feet away, with the front of the car pointing up in the air at around a 45° angle, we ended up landing on the back bumper. It actually crumpled the rear end of the car about an inch forward, and because the car was a hatchback, it also bent the hatch about an inch forward too.

When we landed, my first instinct was to try to start the car back up, having no idea that we wouldn't have been able to drive it away anyway, because of all the suspension parts that were completely bent. Because the side airbags went off, the car wouldn't start. Thankfully, neither of us was seriously injured, the only mild injuries we had were stiff necks, because of the way the car suddenly went from clockwise to counterclockwise, as we hit the side of the hill. My poor Chihuahua, actually suffered the worst injury, because the bitch got slapped by my buddy's guitar case, and left her with a black eye. Of course, I couldn't see the black eye because of all her black fur, but the white part of her eye was red, so it was safe to assume, she had a black eye under her fur. My friend's guitar case was also damaged when it smacked into some of the plastic panels in the back of the car, and he was surprised when I gave him enough money to replace it. It actually surprised me, that he was surprised, but because it was my fault, I wouldn't feel morally right not replacing it.

I knew I wasn't speeding. When you look at the speed limit signs on exit and entrance ramps, you'll notice that they are a yellow/orange color, instead of the traditional white. The reason for this, is because it's a suggestion, and not part of the Ontario Highway traffic act as a law, which was confirmed in the reckless driving ticket that I got, which had the posted speed limit written as being 100km/h, even though the yellow sign stated a recommended speed of 40km/h. Thankfully, when I went to traffic court, I was able to beat that reckless driving charge, because that obviously would have had a huge effect on my insurance.

Despite all the damage to that car, I was actually able to fix it myself, and have a lot of funny pictures of the process. At times, I had to park the car at different angles, between two support columns, in my parking garage. I had a chain hooked up to my trailer hitch, and wrapped around one support column, to stop the car from sliding, and I used a winch, which was chained to the other support column, and the other end to the driver side quarter panel, behind where the plastic bumper cover goes, because that quarter panel was pushed in about three inches, and I was able to use the winch, to pull that whole quarter panel back to where it was supposed to be. There's obviously a lot more details, but this isn't a story about how I fixed my car; I still have that car to this day, simply because it's not worth anything to sell at this point, but I was able to straighten everything and drove it for a few more years after that jump.

Getting back to the accident, after we got out of the car, I looked around and I didn't see anybody around looking at us. Even though I wasn't panicking, and I knew they would have no legal right to search the car, simply because of an accident, but still, for some reason that I still can't understand to this day, I asked my buddy, to take my bag of drugs, and go hide it behind the sound wall a couple hundred meters away, and just make it look like he's going to pee. Well, as it would turn out, somebody was looking at us, and he happened to be an off-duty firefighter.

When the police showed up, he mentioned that my buddy had gone and hid a bag over behind the wall. Once they got the bag, and saw the drugs inside, I had to admit the bag was mine, so that my buddy did not get charged. Once I did that, they now had a legal right to search the car. In the car, I had a little notepad, with half a month of day-to-day transactions written in it. We were both still arrested, and because it was on the highway, it was the Ontario Provincial Police's jurisdiction, which was much better than having to deal with the city police. To my surprise, they basically arrested my dog too, and let her come with us to the OPP station, instead of calling animal control, and bringing her to the pound. Ironically, that wouldn't be the last time my dog was arrested, but we'll get to that later.

Once at the police station, I eventually met with a detective who was in charge of drug offenses. He was actually a really cool and respectable guy. I knew they had arrested my buddy too, despite me telling the arresting officers that the bag was mine, so I stressed again to him, that it was my bag and he had nothing to do with it, and that he shouldn't be charged. He respected that, and ultimately my buddy was allowed to go.

During the interview with this detective, of course he was doing his job and mentioned that if I helped him, he could probably help me, because he saw that I had no record. But even though I had no record, and any lawyer would tell you not to mention anything that you been pardoned for, I mentioned it anyway. I knew it wasn't going to make a difference in court, and I wanted him to understand, this is nothing new to me, because he was really trying to scare me into giving up my sources, and out of respect, I wanted him to realize he was just wasting his time. I told him about my past a bit, and that the people I deal with are cool people, so there's no point in asking me to betray them, regardless of how he might be able to help me, but I was very respectful with the way I declined his offer.

I asked him at one point, if he likes Star Trek. When he shook his head yes, and asked him if he liked The Next Generation, and again he said yes. So I asked him, if he remembers a particular moment in the very first episode, and he did, so I pulled out a classic Picard line from the show, as an example of how I felt about the potential consequences I was going to face. To partly paraphrase the line, I said, "If I'm going to be damned, I'm going to be damned for who I really am." He kind of laughed and smiled a bit, and said, "I completely respect that!"

I then made a random comment about how I felt, and said, "You seem like a really interesting guy, I bet in different circumstances, you and I could sit down, have a few drinks and have some really interesting conversations." To my surprise, he said he totally agrees, and that we should do that sometime. After, he gave me his personal cell phone number on the back of his business card, and a few days later, we met up for coffee.

We chatted about a bunch of random stuff. I told him about what I knew of the Charter, and the new way I discovered to challenge drug laws, and I was going to fight the charges that way. At one point, he even agreed that drug laws should be changed, but added, as long as they are as they are, he's required to do his job, obviously. That admission was very respectable, and told me my intuition about him was right. I also found out that before he was a detective, he worked as a counselor dealing with ex-cons and drug problems.

Ironically, after we had coffee at Starbucks, I went directly into the Future Shop next door, to buy another identical bag, as the bag they kept, because I wasn't about to stop selling drugs, since I'm certain the drug laws violate the Charter and therefore the Constitution.

A DECISIVE MOMENT

During this period of my life, I was single, as were many of my close friends, and we had our weekly routine. One of our friends was a karaoke host, and also a musician/lead singer and my buddy Wes was his drummer. So between karaoke and their live shows, there were four days of the week, where we would be at one of four bars. Over the next two weeks since the date of the accident, every night we would go out to a different bar, I was basically having the same conversations with lots of different people that we were friends with. Of course everyone knew what had happened, and were asking me what I was going to do and how I was going to fight it. Because I didn't have a record, I knew the amount of drugs that I had on me was not a large amount, and from the notepad, it was clear I was only selling to end-users and wasn't some kind of big drug dealer. I also knew from all of my years of experience dealing with courts, if I pleaded guilty and made a deal with them, I could have easily just gotten probation or worst case probation with a little bit of house arrest and likely some community service. But I definitely knew if I made a deal with them I wouldn't go to jail. So there was that choice on the one hand, but then on the other hand there was this choice with potentially historical consequences.

My whole family knew that I sold drugs. Even one of my uncles, when he was mad at my dad for some reason, tried to get my dad in trouble with their mom, by telling my grandmother, some comment about how I'm a drug dealer. Now if there was ever a comment that can illustrate how my family is, it would be one such as this, spoken by my grandmother, this sweet little French lady from New Brunswick, that's been living in the Detroit area with the rest of my extended family, since shortly before the Detroit riots in 1967. When my uncle told my grandmother that, she replied by saying, "Oh, he is not! ... And even if he is, it's none of your god damn business!" Oh how I love my family.

Anyway, not only did they know that I sold drugs, but ever since I got out of jail, before I even started selling drugs, and was only using them, I had been telling them about what I learned while I was in jail, about this new way to challenge drug laws under the Charter, that has never been attempted before. So now, there I was, faced with that moment of choice. I hadn't yet decided which way I was going to address the charges, because I knew if I tried to fight it under the Charter and lost, it would almost certainly make the sentence a lot harsher than if I'd made a deal with them at the beginning. After two weeks of thoroughly discussing this with lots of people, I still hadn't made a decision. But I will never forget the moment, when that decisive choice was made.

The reason why I was driving my buddy home, that fateful Friday morning, was because we had just left a friend's house downtown, that we went to after the bar Thursday night. We had been up all night, continuing the party, and of course, waited long enough, so that I was legally safe to drive, and when the accident occurred, I did pass the breathalyzer, since they obviously smelled alcohol. So two weeks later, it seemed quite fatefully appropriate, that I would come to the decision while at this same friend's house, once again for another after party. There were four of us there that night, all who I would consider to be intellectuals. The owner of the house, was the lead designer/marketer behind one of the most well-known female clothing brands in the country, I'm sure anybody reading this would recognize the logo, but of course I'm not going to mention what company it is. The other guy that was there, was a robotics engineer, who worked for a local company, and does work for NASA. The fourth person was his girlfriend, I forget what she does, but she was also a very intelligent person.

So that night, the four of us continued having drinks, as well as some very high quality cocaine. The only conversation we basically had, from shortly after 2 a.m. when we got there, until about 10am, was just about how I was going to deal with these charges. In a very intentional way, they all played devil's advocate, and on the other side of the debate, there was only me.

Something to keep in mind, is that I've been thinking about this issue at that point, for a bit over thirteen years. Not only did I have similar debates with others, countless times over those previous thirteen years, but I had also spent countless hours debating the issue with myself, and when I get into a debate with myself, of course I'm completely unbiased, objective, and do my best to win! Since it's with myself, you might think that I would win either way, but you have to keep in mind, that in order to win, someone must also lose. So what it really means to win with yourself, in an unbiased and objective way, is that for every point that you think about, on one side of the argument, you must also genuinely try to defeat that point as well. This is, in essence, the foundation and fundamental principle that underlies the scientific method.

After the debate started, and continued that night, there wasn't a single counterpoint, that any of them brought up, that I had not only thought of already myself, but had already successfully refuted as well. As the hours passed by, and more empty baggies of cocaine littered the table, because after all, it keeps us awake and alert, provided you don't do too much, and get all spacey in your head. Being the group of people that we were, none of us like to get to that point, so we regulated our use accordingly, as most people that I know who do cocaine, also do. Finally, late into the morning, after the sun had come up, one by one, the three of them slowly, all had nothing else to say. Then suddenly, we found ourselves all sitting in silence, and me realizing, I had successfully countered every single thing they'd said. But still, I hadn't yet made a decision.

After a few minutes of silence, when I think we all realized there was nothing more to be said, somebody suggested that we put on some music. The space engineer went over to the sound system, and suddenly said to me, "In ten seconds or less, give me the name of a song to put on!"

Typically, I don't do well with the sudden pressure of needing to decide something like that, and to this day, I have no idea what made me think of the song. Not only had I not listen to it in probably over a decade, but even when I did listen to this band a lot when I was younger, this was never a song that I ever thought of putting on, and was really only a song I listened to, when I put on the whole directory from this band. Additionally, listening to, and remembering lyrics of any song, has never come naturally to me, and even when I consciously attempt to listen to, and understand what's being said in the lyrics of the song, the autistic side of me, is always so mesmerized by the actual beat, timing and the mathematical structure of the music itself, that even when I try to listen to the lyrics, it's always extraordinarily difficult for me to maintain that focus, and listen to the lyrics and meaning of the words.

Within seconds of being asked to name a song, suddenly the words that came out of my mouth were, "Pink Floyd's, On the Turning Away".

For legal reasons, I obviously can't quote the lyrics without needing to jump through a bunch of hoops, and finding out who I need to get permission from, and likely pay some kind of royalty. I was considering reaching out and asking, and if it was one of the original band members that was in charge of making that decision, considering this was an issue about drugs, I think they would probably say yes, and might not even ask for a royalty, but unfortunately, it's managed by some kind of company, and so it's unlikely they would be sympathetic at all, and just think about making some more money. But there's nothing preventing me from paraphrasing and summarizing.

For all the grammar police out there, (I say that jokingly of course). I want to comment about how the following chapter is written. I realize that there are some broken grammar rules, and some odd structure to how I've written it. When I initially wrote it, I had the lyrics to that Pink Floyd track on the monitor next to me, and because I remember that night so vividly, I started writing the following paraphrased version of those lyrics, reflecting the context and feeling of what was going through my mind at the time. After I finished writing what follows, I went through it quite a number of times, adding a comma here, using a slightly different word there, because I felt such changes better reflected how it was in my mind at the time. There are times when I could've used less commas even, that some would consider to be more grammatically correct. But any time I started trying to "fix" any kind of incorrect grammar, I always found that it started losing some of the essence of what, and how I was feeling at the time. So in that respect, it should be read in a slightly poetic way.

Also, if possible, I suggest pulling up the lyrics to the song while you read the next part.

WHICH WAY SHOULD I TURN AWAY?

So there I was, at the end of this multi-hour debate, all of us sitting in a silent discord, and me, thinking, about this fateful decision... then the song starts to play.

As I'm listening, I find myself unusually focused and consumed by the lyrics, as if the universe is suddenly speaking to me. I'm hearing this song talking about the way, people often turn away from us downtrodden, who are abused and oppressed by the power of laws, which I know to be unjust, and how not to accept these bad things that are happening, or I'll notice. that I'll also be turning away from them. And somehow, it's kind of sinful to just stand there and do nothing, knowing that, light is being overpowered by the shadow and the shroud that it casts over all that I know. And how blinding it can be, when we let our hearts be cold and hard like a stone, and essentially how, allowing ourselves to turn away, because we feel the words we have to say won't be understood, and ultimately, how alone we could suddenly find ourselves feeling, about everything that we know.

Effectively, that summarizes the first half of the song, at least in the context of the decision I was being faced with, and that's how I essentially interpreted it, as I was sitting there, listening, to this song I hadn't heard in over a decade. And as I'm listening to this during that fateful morning, I suddenly feel myself being filled with this emotion, so intense, that it brought tears to my eyes. That emotion fills me even now, thinking about it once again, as I'm writing this to each of you. Most, if not all of the people that I had been talking to, about this choice I had to make, either directly or indirectly, suggested I make a deal with them if I knew I wouldn't be serving any jail time. While listening to the first half of this song, I'm sitting there thinking, about how pretty much everyone has been, suggesting that I turn away, from this thing that I've known, by making a deal, instead of standing up to that which I know our Charter of Rights says is unjust.

My eyes already filled with tears, and experiencing this intense feeling of sadness, knowing that I've just spent two weeks, essentially listening to people tell me that, I should turn away, simply because, that's what they would do. But if there's one thing that should be clear, to any of you who've read that which I've written thus far, is that turning away from something unjust, is not really in my character to do. Even about things that are way less important, than an issue such as drugs, which I can confidently consider myself to be an expert on, from the end user, to the other end of the spectrum, and the global consequences and harms that are being caused to Third World Countries, because of our laws here, in our comfortable First World Countries.

And then as the song continues, I sit there silently, filled with this sadness, and listen to what the universe wants to say to me next… I hear what it says, as the tone and perspective of the song changes. It then begins to transition…

It speaks of a dream and pride. I think of the dream I have, that one day these unjust laws will change… and I hear the universe tell me, that I should stand with pride and not turn away from this dream, which I have had for so long. And as though with wings, I should fly through the shroud and shadow of the night that is always casted, over the light and goodness that we know, whenever we turn away. I hear it speak to me of hope, because the daytime will soon be stirring. It talks about the speechless, and I think about how many people agree that drug laws should be approached differently, but out of fear, they all continue to turn away, united in their silent accord. And how because of this silence, everyone is unaware of how big the ranks truly are, how much they've grown, and how many people would be united, in this fight, if I were to decide, to turn away, no more.

It continues, and speaks of using, words that I'd find to be strange, and even though I understand the words of law, I also know, that such words, are quite strange indeed, as they are words those united speechless do not understand. But if I use these strange words, that I do understand, it seems to say to me, that I'll be mesmerized by a flame that it lights. And then, if I make this decision to fly with wings through the night, suddenly, I'll feel the wind, of a new change in sight.…

Then, the message I hear, it becomes quite clear, when it tells me, turn away no more, from those who are weak and weary. Turn away no more, from the coldness, hopelessness and feeling, of the silent weak and weary. It speaks of the universal truth that, this world must be shared by all, and that standing and staring, is simply not just, and it's definitely not enough.

Then it finally ends, by asking me one question, as though it's not even sure what my decision will be. So when I hear, what it finally asks: Is it only a dream, to believe, that I will do, no more of the turning away?

In that moment I knew, what my decision must be.

THE DIE HAS BEEN CAST

Now that I had made the decision, that I would fight it the way I've always said I would, if I ever got caught, I was immediately faced with another choice. Do I attempt to find a lawyer to represent me in a way that has never been done before, or do I represent myself, in this unprecedented fight?

After thinking about it for a while, I realized I wouldn't even be able to make a decision until I at least spoke with a lawyer. I knew, even if I did hire a lawyer, I would insist on being more actively involved in the whole process, than they would normally be accustomed to, because after all, nobody else has ever done this before, so I would almost certainly understand it better than any lawyer would. I did know one lawyer from a past issue I had to deal with. I picked that lawyer by sitting in court, and watching the different lawyers that were there and how they presented themselves in front of the Judge. I was definitely happy with how he represented me in the previous case, because I ultimately won. So I called him up, made an appointment, and then finally went and spoke with him.

The conversation was awkward, to say the least, because I started off by insisting, that if I did hire him, I wanted to be more involved with the process. After explaining how I wanted to fight it, under Section 1 of the Charter, I was surprised by his reaction. He told me that Section 1 is not used that way. When I asked him why not, he really didn't seem to have a very good answer, or even know why. So instead I asked him, "Is there anything preventing Section 1 from being used defensively?" But again, he seemed confused, and instead of giving a yes or no answer, he was a bit insulting, and in a slightly arrogant kind of way, he responded by saying, "It's just not done like that. If you had gone to law school, you would understand that. Section 1 is just not used defensively." I ignored the insulting way he said that, and persisted. Eventually, he admitted that there's nothing technically preventing Section 1 from being used defensively, but then again stated, "…but it's just not done like that!" After seeing how persistent I was about the issue, he ended up saying, flat-out, that even if I paid him, he wouldn't be willing to represent me that way. So that ended the conversation right then and there, and because of the way he reacted, it was clear I would be representing myself. So over the next eight months, I was enrolled in the Google law school.

Thankfully, I am more than an expert with finding things with Google, and if there is something out there, I can usually find it. But initially, before the first court date, I had no idea what I was even looking for.

When I went to the first court date, I got into quite an interesting argument with the Justice of the Peace. During any kind of first appearance like that, the courtroom is always packed with other people, but because I have a lot of experience going to court, I knew that the lawyers always go first, and then once the lawyers are done, it's essentially a free-for-all, first come first serve kind of thing, and whoever's the most assertive, usually gets seen first. The most important thing, if you're there without a lawyer, and you don't want to be there all day, is to sit as close to the front as possible. When you see that the lawyers are almost done, already start to make eye contact with the Crown and the Judge, lean forward, and sit upright in the seat, like you know what you're doing, and you're ready to talk to them. So after the lawyers were done, I think I was the first person without a lawyer to go up and speak to the Justice of the Peace. I began to have this very unusual, and at times, slightly funny conversation with her, in front of this packed courtroom, but of course there was never any kind of hint on my face, that I found it to be at all humorous.

It started off with the Justice of the Peace asking me how I was going to plea, to which I obviously said, not guilty. She then asked, if I was planning to have a lawyer represent me, to which I obviously said no. I then explained that I would be fighting the charges under the Charter of Rights, and at that point, she inquired about what section, or sections, of the Charter I was planning to use.

Before I continue, I'm going to quote Section 1 first, and explain a few things, since I'm sure it'll make it easier to understand why this was a bit unusual.

> 1. *The Canadian Charter of Rights and Freedoms guarantees the rights and freedoms set out in it subject only to such reasonable limits prescribed by law as can be demonstrably justified in a free and democratic society.*

The first important thing to understand about Section 1, is that Section 1 of the Charter is *supreme* law in Canada, and all other law must conform to it. Some of you may have heard about the notwithstanding clause (Section 33 of the Charter), which gives the government powers to override Section 2 and Sections 7 through 15, but it doesn't apply to Section 1, which means Section 33 also has to comply with Section 1.

The next thing that you might notice about Section 1, is that it's a bit different than any of the other rights. It's not a directly obvious right, as all of the other rights are. For example, Section 8 of the Charter, which is a lot of lawyers' favorite section to use to defend against a drug charge:

> 8. *Everyone has the right to be secure against unreasonable search or seizure.*

Obviously that's pretty simple and straightforward, and you don't need to be any kind of expert in law, to understand what it means. Most of the other rights in the Charter, are also relatively straightforward like that, and speak of something specific, that pretty much everybody can understand without having a law degree.

However, Section 1 basically states that we are guaranteed all of the other rights in the Charter, and that any limit which is placed on any of those other rights, has to be deemed reasonable, and that it must be demonstrated why it is reasonable.

Because it's not directly stating an obvious and straightforward right, is the reason why it's never been used defensively. Normally, for example, if a defense lawyer files a Charter Application under Section 8, because they believe the evidence against their client was obtained from a search that was unreasonable, if the Crown disagrees and believes that it was a reasonable search, then the Crown will counter with a Section 1 Charter Application. Then a Charter hearing would take place, before any trial or sentencing, and a Judge would have to decide whether or not, it was in fact a reasonable search, which involves a test, commonly referred to as the Oakes test. The Oakes test, is from a case in 1986, and was the first time there was a debate in court about how to determine what is "reasonable" as Section 1 mentions, and since then, that is the gold standard, and only standard, that is used to test if a limit to any of our rights is in fact "reasonable".

So there I was, before this Justice of the Peace, being asked what sections of the Charter I would be arguing were violated. I began by first paraphrasing Section 1, and rhetorically asked, what is the government's demonstrably justified reason for limiting our other rights by putting people in jail for something like marijuana, when a thing such as alcohol is legal, which clearly causes more problems to people and society, than something like marijuana, which was still illegal at the time.

But I was also charged with *possession for the purpose of trafficking* of cocaine, speed, MDMA, and OxyContin (because I happened to have some Oxy pills on me, which I never actually sold, because I know how easy it can be to get addicted to any kind of opiate, and can be an extremely hard addiction to break, due to the physical dependence that it creates, and even though I don't believe the laws against things like heroin are just, from a personal, moral point of view, I would never want to be responsible in any way for somebody developing an addiction like that. I only had them on me, because I like doing small amounts myself anytime I'd be doing cocaine, but it was still something I was charged with.

After explaining that first argument with respect to marijuana, I basically repeated, that the same argument applies to the other charges as well. She then seemed very confused for a moment, which wasn't surprising, considering nobody's used Section 1 like that before, and then after a moment she replied, in a stumbling kind of way, by asking, "So what you're saying sir, and if I'm understanding you correctly, you're planning to argue, …and if I have this right, that essentially *all* drug laws in Canada are unconstitutional?" And of course, I answered, "Yes, that's correct." At that point there was obviously a bit more confusion, and then the Justice of the Peace, and the Crown attorney started chatting back and forth for a few minutes, and then the Justice finally said to me, "Well sir, if that's what you want to argue, that's your right. I also want to make sure you realize, if you plan to represent yourself, that it's your responsibility to submit the Charter Application ahead of time, and you can't just wait until the day of your trial?" Again I replied by saying, "Yes, that's fine."

I then asked, "Where do I go to get the Charter Application I need to fill out?" Suddenly she got quite annoyed, then gave me a little speech about how she's not there to give me legal advice or do things for me, and if I plan to represent myself, it's my responsibility to know what to do.' And then, understandably, I got a little defensive and said, "I'm not expecting you to do things for me. All I asked was where I get this form I need to submit. By law I'm entitled to a fair trial, and I don't think it's fair to expect somebody, that's representing them self, to know where to get this form." At that point, she then explained, it wasn't some form, and that it is a document that I must create. I then replied by saying, "Ah! Excellent! Thank you."

She then continued by saying, "I also have to inform you, because of the nature of the charges against you, you have the right to have your trial in provincial court, or you can have a trial before a Judge in the Superior Court, or you could have your trial before a Judge and Jury in the Superior Court.

How would you like to proceed?" Now considering that this is my first time being a lawyer, I was delighted to learn I had so many choices, so of course, I said, "Superior Court, with a Judge and Jury!" At that point, there was some more talking between the Crown and the Justice, and then she finally said to me, "Okay sir, but of course you realize that the Charter arguments are only heard in front of a Judge, and not a Jury?" (Which I definitely didn't understand at the time, but I did now that she told me,) so I wasn't lying when I said, "Yes, I understand." She then confirmed by asking, "So then you still want to proceed with the Judge and Jury trial?" To which I obviously replied, "Yes, that's right." So then, they talked to each other some more, and it seemed pretty clear, I was causing a headache for them, by selecting the Jury trial, and eventually the Justice told me that my case is going to go upstairs to a different courtroom, and instructed me were to go.

As I started to leave, she told me to hold on a moment, because the Crown was saying something to her, and then a few moments later, she said to me that 1 of my 5 charges (the weed charge), had some kind of absolute jurisdiction, which meant that it had to be seen in this lower court, and to simplify everything, considering that was the least serious charge, they were going to drop the one charge that couldn't go up to the superior court, and then she sent me on my way.

So my first day as a lawyer, I scored a point already. Now, I also knew how to begin my research on Google, by searching for "Charter Application", and then selecting image search. After starting with that one little piece of information on what to search for, eventually, after countless hours of researching and learning everything I could, about the whole process and everything I needed to do, and after few additional court dates along the way, once I finally felt I was ready to proceed, a date was finally set for the first pretrial.

Before I go further, I should explain a few more things. First of all, the point of the pretrial, is for the Crown and the defense, to be able to get together, and discuss trial matters, in order to make sure that both sides are ready for trial, before a trial date is set, witnesses are booked to come in, and all that complicated stuff, since the last thing the court wants, is for there to be a mistrial, because someone was not completely ready. This would mean all the witnesses and everybody involved would have to be scheduled to come back another day, and obviously that's a big hassle and inconvenience to a lot of people. The pretrial is basically just the Crown, the defense, and a Judge, plus a court clerk and a security guard. The judge that's going to be residing over the trial, will never be at a pretrial, so that the Crown and the defense can talk openly with each other, without the risk of creating any kind of biased in the mind of the Judge.

The pretrial is also an off record, and informal hearing. Nobody stands up when they talk, kind of like a casual conversation between friends. Even though it's off record, there's still a record of what's said, which is the reason for having the court clerk there, but nothing said in the pretrial can be used at the trial, unless both sides agree to it. The only point of recording everything, is that there is often more than one pretrial and it's often not the same judge, so the record of the pretrial, is just there so each judge knows what happened at the last pretrial. I also knew ahead of time, that the pretrial is not the place where you submit a Charter Application, or any other motions for that matter. It's only about trial matters.

In the case of my trial, the bag of drugs and the notepad, with the record of half a month of day-to-day transactions, were all admissible in court. I also knew if the Charter application failed, it would be an open and shut trafficking case at trial. But I still didn't want to go to the pretrial empty-handed and make it seem like I hadn't been doing anything, so I wanted to bring the Charter Application anyway. So of course, in my usual style, whenever I have an assignment due for school the next day, I would always wait until the night before to even start writing it, and this court case was no different. So quite literally, the night before the pretrial, is when I decided to start writing the Charter application. And in a 12 hour, Ritalin fueled writing binge, I eventually completed the Charter Application, with a few hours to spare.

A LICENSE TO SELL;
THE SECRET THEY DON'T WANT YOU TO KNOW

The morning I got to the courthouse, even before the pretrial started, I already learned something new. At the time, a very close late friend of mine was living with me, and was in law school at Ottawa University, so I invited him to come along with me, because I knew it would interest him. Well when we got to court, we both learned that nobody else was allowed in, even though it's off record and informal, so he had to wait outside. The pretrial started out with the Crown saying a few things, laying out the details of the case, and eventually it was my turn to do the same. But remember, I expected to be found guilty at trial, so I really had nothing to say, but it seemed kind of awkward if I would've said nothing at all, or told them that I had nothing to say. So I was being kind of coy and indirect in response to what the crown was saying and asking me.

Eventually, I noticed he was starting to get a little annoyed and irritated, and that was the last thing I wanted to do, so eventually I told him exactly this, "Ok, put it this way. If the Charter Application fails, I expect to be found guilty at trial. I won't be contesting any of the evidence; basically, your job will be really easy." As soon as I said that, simultaneously, both the Crown and the Judge flinched their heads, obviously both shocked that I just admitted to drug dealing. They will quite likely never hear the defense say something like that again, at any pretrial, because if you were expecting to be found guilty at a trial, typically you wouldn't be having a pretrial at all, you would just be pleading guilty. This is exactly why the Crown then replied by asking, "So then why are you pleading not guilty?" To which I replied, "Because even if the Charter Application fails, it doesn't mean I think it's just." At that point the Crown and the Judge looked at each other and shook their heads, in a way that obviously expressed, "Ok, Fair point."

After that, it basically ended the pretrial. But the Crown and the Judge knew that I was going to be doing something under Section 1 of the Charter, and because nobody has used Section 1 defensively before, no doubt they were very curious. They also knew that I had the Charter Application ready, and with me. Even though that wasn't the official place to submit a Charter Application, we still had about 45 minutes of court time booked, and if we all left at that point, nothing else would be going on in the courtroom anyway. So just as I had hoped for, their curiosity led to them asking if they could see a copy of it, which I happily agreed to. If you are interested in knowing more about the full legal details, please visit the website I've set up for that purpose: www.daffa.org. For now, I'll just explain that it's a three-page document, with most of the first page, being a header and necessary formal requirements a document such as that must begin with, and most of the last page contains references to supporting evidence that I was planning to submit. So basically, there is only about a page and a half of actual content.

I also want to remind everyone about what I explained, when I was telling the story about when I was in jail, regarding my highest score on the psychological assessment. I'm not going to quote it again, but I do want to stress again, I'm not saying this out of pride, but rather because it helps put into perspective the response from the judge, when he first glanced over the Charter Application, after I gave it to him. My highest score was earned on a very specific verbal subtest, which basically relates to exactly what would make a good lawyer. I scored 183 on that specific type of thing, which means, based on the population of the earth, there would only be about 12 000 people, who could score that high, or higher on that specific type of subtest. This helps explain why I was able to discover how to use the Charter in this new way, that nobody else has before. I also want to point out, if I hadn't written that Charter Application, and it had just been given to me, and I needed to understand it, I would need *at least* an hour, but perhaps longer, by myself, to make sure I was able to wrap my head around the nuances and how everything is written. Additionally, if I had to argue against that Charter Application, I wouldn't be able to successfully defeat it, and I know, because I was trying to do that the whole time while writing it, which is why it took me 12 hours, to write only a page and a half.

So after I gave a copy to the Crown and the Judge, the Judge started looking at it, then quickly began flipping the pages, then pauses and kind of tilts his head back a little bit, and then starts saying, "Would you mind explaining this in ummm…", And I could tell immediately, that he was trying to say in layman's terms, but none of us were layman, when it comes to the law, and as far as I know, there's no professional equivalent of the word. So I interjected by saying, "….you mean like I'd explain it to my friends?" At which point, he smiled, and said "Yeah." So after I explained it, like I'd explain it to my friends, he just nodded in a way that indicated he understood, and then he asked if he could keep the copy I gave him. Which I obviously agreed to, because that's exactly what I had hoped for, since I knew this wasn't the formal place to submit it. I then turned to the Crown and told him he could keep the copy I gave him as well; they both seem quite satisfied and intrigued. We ended up setting a date for another pretrial two months later, and that was it for that day. Not only did I admit to drug dealing, but I also showed them all my cards.

It's also noteworthy to point out, this was a Federal Prosecutor, which is the highest in the land, in Ottawa, which is also the highest in the land, from a legal point of view, since Ottawa is where Canadian laws are made.

Two months later, I went back to court for the next pretrial, and because I had been extremely sick for the past month, and was still sick enough that you could obviously tell from my voice, and the way I was kind of sweaty, that I was obviously still sick; if I didn't have to go to court, I would've been in bed all day. I intentionally got there a little bit early, because I wanted to have a minute to talk with the Crown before court, to explain why I hadn't done anything new, but even before I finished saying that, he interrupted me by saying, "If you're about to explain why you haven't done anything, don't bother. I can't really say much right now, but let's just say, something's going to happen in there, and well, basically, you're not going to be a lawyer for much longer."

I was pretty sure what that meant, because unless I showed some kind of extreme incompetence or mental deficiency, I knew they couldn't take me off my own case. But between not wanting to get my hopes up, and also not wanting to seem cocky, I put on my best Forest Gump face and pretended like I wasn't quite sure what he just meant.

This was the third or fourth time I'd dealt with this Crown Attorney in a courtroom. Every time I met him, he always looked the Judge in the eyes, held his head up high, and spoke with the kind of confidence you would expect from a lawyer. Usually there was even a slightly cocky vibe towards me, kind of like "What's this kid think he's doing?" sort of thing. But this time he's got a very different vibe about him. He's not really looking the Judge in the eyes, slouching a bit, and mostly looking down at his papers, kind of like a dog with its tail tucked between its legs. When the Crown starts talking to the judge, he says, "Ummm…. Your Honor, ah.. this isn't going to take very long, so ummm…   I'll just get right down to it. Ummm. Essentially, after multiple conversations, with umm.. many people in my office, we've decided to stay the charges against the defendant." At that point, I noticed the Judge flinch his head in surprise, because no doubt he read the details of what was said during the last pretrial and saw that I had admitted to drug dealing. I suspect that the Crown anticipated the Judge was going to react that way when he told him they were staying the charges, because of what he said next. "The reason being… [for them staying the charges] …..and if I could just explain to the defendant what this means." At which point the Crown explained to me what a stay of the proceedings meant, which I already knew, but I didn't interrupt, and the Judge either didn't notice, or didn't care, that the Crown never went back and finished his incomplete thought about the, "the reason being". At that point, I was told I was allowed to leave, and quite surprisingly, I suddenly found myself to be a free man!

Current score: Unlisted: 1. Her Majesty the Queen: 0.

Not bad for my very first court case!

As I left the courtroom, you could easily think that I would have been very excited. I was obviously happy the charges were just dropped, but I think the best description of how I felt initially, would be closer to confused and slightly dumbfounded, because I was not at all expecting that, especially after admitting to drug dealing during the previous pretrial. As I was driving home, a particular part of what the Crown said, kept running through my mind, more specifically the part about, "multiple conversations with many people in his office." This told me one thing for certain; at least three Federal Prosecutors have seen the Charter Application, in addition to at least one Judge. Now keep in mind what I said about how I would not be able to successfully fight against that document, not even if my life depended on it.

After thinking about his words a little bit more, I was trying to picture what took place in his office, involving those multiple conversations with many people. Not only does that mean *at least two* other Federal Prosecutors have seen the Charter Application, but it kind of sounds like more than two other people. Another interesting thing about the way my mind works, is how often I will get very detailed impressions about people and situations. The impression I eventually had about how this likely unfolded in his office, which may or may not be accurate, essentially goes like this: at some point the Crown sat down by himself, perhaps even took it home, poured himself a liquid drug, called alcohol, then sat back in a nice comfortable chair, and spent a bit of time, really thinking about, exactly what I had written, what it says and what it really means, paying attention to all these subtle nuances.

I have no doubt he eventually understood, and after understanding it, if he felt he could beat it at a charter hearing, then it doesn't make sense why they would drop the charges. It doesn't make sense at all. The only logical conclusion is, that eventually he not only understood what I'd written, but realized the historical significance if it were to go to an official hearing and win. If it did go to an official hearing and win, not only would it overthrow essentially all illegal drug laws in the country, but they would actually have to go rewrite pharmaceutical laws as well. Since if the laws against something like cocaine, were suddenly deemed to be unjust, then how would it be just to require somebody to have a prescription, for something like Ritalin? Because of how long it took me to come to that detailed of a realization, I doubt he thought about it enough to see the pharmaceutical complication, but no doubt he understood the basic significance that it would overthrow all illegal drug laws. Upon realizing such a thing, he would have this moment of "Oh Shit!"

So what does he do next?

Remember pride is a powerful motivator, and lawyers are usually very proud people, generally speaking. Because of pride, it's quite unlikely he's going to go to into the office and say something like this to anyone, "Hey man, this kid, who is representing himself, has got me stumped with this Charter Application he's written, would you mind taking a look at it and tell me what you think?" Instead, it probably went more like, "Hey man, can you take a look at this and tell me what you think?" Then eventually, the person comes back, and now they're both feeling the same way. Next it was probably something like, "Oh Shit! Let's go talk to the boss!"

Regardless of how things actually played out in their office, with the multiple conversations and many people, what all that made me realize, was that essentially, it gave me a license to sell drugs; I even took his business card to staples, had them laminate it with the thickest stuff they had, and from then on, I kept that in my bag of drugs, as my license to sell, and if I ever got caught again, I'd tell the police to call him, and he'll explain why they are wasting their time.

After I got home from that second pretrial, my buddy that was in law school was still living with me, and as I walked in, he looked at me, then asked how it went. At that point, I was still so shocked by what happened, I didn't seem excited or happy at all externally, and I responded by saying, in a very mellow and mundane mono-tone, "they dropped the charges." He then just kind of looked at me, clearly unsure if I was being serious, and then asked, "They what?" And then I confirmed what I had just said by saying, "I won." We actually went back and forth for a few minutes like that, because he was in disbelief just as I was, and like me, he was also trying to understand the significance of what had just happened, which wasn't hard to figure out, it was really just more about truly accepting, that yes, that's what just happened.

He started talking about what happened in all of his law classes, and in every class that he brought the subject up in, it caused quite a debate. Most of the students were polarized and either believed that there's more to the story, and the other half of the students realizing the significance of somebody using Section 1 defensively. Eventually, I found out that two of his law professors wanted to meet me. Law professors have what's called a 'Doctor of Law', which is the highest level of legal education you can achieve. One of the professors that wanted to meet me, was his ethics professor, and the other professor, was one of the seven Supreme Court judges. Tragically, my buddy was killed in a car accident, so unfortunately, I was never able meet either of them, but I was definitely more than willing to.

UNEXPECTED FREEDOM

After the unexpected victory, I suddenly found myself slightly unsure of what to do next with my life. After the initial accident, when I got charged with drug dealing, for the following ten months, I was spending most of my free time researching and learning about law. I expected this fight to last for many years and was assuming it would likely end up in front of the Supreme Court. I knew if I had lost at an official Charter hearing, I would've appealed the decision, and if I had won, I'm positive the Crown would've appealed the decision as well. Then the appeal would take place at the next higher level of court, which would've been the Ontario Court of Appeals. And just like before, regardless of who would have won, I'm sure there would have been another appeal, and at that point, the final appeal would take place in the Supreme Court of Canada. Because I was expecting to be fighting this legal battle for the next few years at least, I was also expecting I would be spending more time learning about the whole process each step of the way, so any kind of long-term personal plans, were not at all on my mind. After they unexpectedly dropped the charges so early on, I suddenly found myself wondering what I wanted to do with my life next. But because I just spent most of my free time over the last 10 months educating myself in law, I figured I deserved a break to relax, and simply enjoy myself for a bit.

Even though I'd won, a big part of me was actually disappointed that they dropped the charges, since I truly believe that drug laws are unconstitutional, and because I can consider myself to be an expert on the topic, all the way from the end user, to the global issues surrounding the drug issue. As with any subject matter that I find interesting, I've spent countless hundreds of hours over the years researching all aspects surrounding the drug issue. Not only does it concern me knowing how many lives are ruined within our own country, when people are sent to jail simply because of drugs, even though they haven't harmed anybody else, but even more concerning, is knowing that drug laws in our comfortable first world countries, are causing wars around the world in numerous Third World countries; our drug laws are even contributing to the loss of the rainforest as drug cartels continue to burn large swaths of forest to grow coca plants each time the local government finds one of their existing plantations. Because of the aspect of my personality that so often stands up to even minor issues that I feel are unjust, I couldn't help feeling selfish if I were to do nothing, especially knowing that I've got a get out of jail free card, if I were to ever be arrested again for drug dealing, while also knowing how many people in the world are suffering because of our senseless and unconstitutional drug laws. So over the next 5 months, I kept thinking about wanting to still fight this issue, especially now that I felt even more confident that it would win, if it were to go to an official Charter hearing.

Before they unexpectedly dropped the charges, I realized that I would have a better chance of winning, if there was public awareness of my specific case. This is why I came up with the idea for www.daffa.org.

During those 5 months after they dropped the charges, I kept feeling like it would be very selfish of me not to continue the fight, and I was still thinking about forming the apparel company I had in mind. I decided that I would take some time for myself, and then after the fun of the summer was over, I would start building the site in the fall. But then in the middle the summer, near the beginning of August, an unexpected opportunity fell into my lap.

A CLUB TO THE SIDE OF THE HEAD

All that changed, when one day in the middle the summer, a good buddy of mine presented an opportunity to me, that I couldn't say no to. He mentioned that the owner of the only after-hours club in the area, was planning to close the club, because he wanted to go to Australia. The reason why he was going to close it, was because he didn't feel he could find a buyer, due to the legality surrounding the club. In case you're not familiar with the Ottawa area, Ottawa is located in the province of Ontario across the Ottawa River from the city of Gatineau, which is located in the province of Québec.

The main legal issue relates to certain bylaws, that both cities have similar versions of, which essentially prohibits dancing between certain hours, which are the exact hours that after-hours clubs operate at. Because Ottawa is the capital of Canada, it's a very political area, and I'm sure the bylaws were put in place because of the stigma surrounding after hours-clubs, due to everybody knowing that people do a lot of illegal drugs in such places. I've read each of the bylaws from each city, and I'm sure they're both unconstitutional, but as I mentioned I really don't like conflict or needing to deal with it, so I only looked into the bylaws just in case I would need to fight it in court.

The way the old owner got away with having the club for five and a half years, was by making it a private club, which meant he wasn't able to advertise, and it was by membership only. Essentially, the membership terms were no more complicated than paying the nightly "membership fee", which was just the cover charge to get into the club each night. Obviously it was a legal loophole, and not very many people would want to risk buying a business that operated in such a gray area. My friend knew that I wouldn't have any problem at all with that, and so when he heard the old owner talking about closing the club, he mentioned that he knows just the right person.

There was also another issue involving the local biker gang, that would often cause issues at the club, and as well as a few other little odd quirks, which all made him further doubt he could find anybody to buy it. But after all the bullying and bullshit that I've went through as a kid, and the way it's toughened me up, I wasn't at all concerned about the bikers. Essentially, he didn't know anybody that was crazy enough, and bold enough, that would be willing to deal with all those issues, so when my buddy said to him, "I know the perfect person!" he couldn't have been more right.

When my buddy came and talked to me about it, I was immediately intrigued, and after I heard how much he was asking for the club, which was 30 000$, and included all of the equipment, I wanted to meet with him right away. A lot of people have this idea that drug dealers make all sorts of money, but in reality most people that sell drugs, don't make very much money at all. Like with most businesses, It's really only the people at the top, that make most of the money, and I never had any kind of desire to put myself in that kind of position. As I mentioned before, I initially started selling drugs as a way to make a little extra money to make ends meet, and then eventually started doing it full-time, simply because I kept losing jobs, due to my sleep-related issues, which I didn't even realize at the time were related to being slightly autistic. I never made that much money while selling drugs, sure, I made enough to live on, but I didn't have 30,000 dollars sitting around, that's for sure. But I did know, my credit with the people I bought drugs from was very good, and I felt that I might be able to borrow the money from one of them.

After meeting with the owner, and finding out all the financial details, based on what the old owner said, I should be able to pay off the 30,000 dollars and a bit of interest within a year, provided that what he said was true and the club was actually making between 20 000$ – 40 000$ a year as he claimed. But that was a big if, because he didn't have any financial records. Thankfully, my buddy would often manage for him during nights when he'd be out of town, or just didn't want to work at the club some night. My buddy never added up the profits from each night, and compared it to the expenses and all that stuff, but what he did know from managing the club enough times, is looking around at how many people are there, and know if that was a busy night, a slow night, or an average night. So after I met with the owner and found out all the financial details, my buddy and I started going there each night it was open, and each night I would ask him if it was an average amount of people, below average, or above average. Then at the end of each night, I would look at the actual number of people that paid and the amount that they paid. After I felt like I had enough data points, I did some calculations and because I also knew what the expenses were, I was able to come to the conclusion that the owner seemed to be honest about what the club was making. After talking with one of my suppliers, I was able to borrow the money, and then made a gentlemen's agreement over a hand shake with the owner while we waited for the contract to be drawn up.

I immediately started taking detailed measurements of the entire layout of the rented space, brought those measurements home, and because I'm really good with AutoCAD, I first started by creating a 3D model of the entire space. After, I started designing some renovation plans that I had in mind, because I saw an opportunity to make a lot more money than 20 000 to 40,000 a year. What I immediately realized, was that the space was only being used during the most inhospitable business hours imaginable, which was Friday night (or technically Saturday morning), from 2 a.m. – 7a.m, and then Saturday night (or technically Sunday morning), during those same hours. The space itself was located directly downtown and completely surrounded by government buildings. I also knew that because the club was already paying the rent and the expenses, anything else I did with the space during the week, would be pure profit.

The entire rented space was 3500 square feet, but the club part of the space was only using about a third of that, and that's including the bathrooms. The rest of the space was pretty much unused and it was just random rooms in the back. The main room of the club with the high ceiling, was a perfect rectangle basically, but the DJ booth area took up about a third of one end. I realized if I were to move the bathrooms into the back area, and then put the DJ booth where the bathrooms currently were, that would open up the main room and create a perfect size room to create a fitness/dance studio during the week.

I spent countless hours over the span of about six months, from when I initially made the deal with the owner in August, to January 1st, which was the official transition day. The designs that I had made in AutoCAD, I would later learn, while showing a bunch of people after I first took over the club, what the value of the drawings were, when one of the people I ended up showing it to, seemed unusually impressed, compared to everyone else that I had shown it to. After asking why he seemed so impressed, I found out that he does AutoCAD stuff as a job, and he told me that the amount of detail and work that I had put into these designs, would cost somebody about 30,000$ if they came in and asked for that kind of work to be done. It was the first, and only time any sort of value had been given to anything I've done in AutoCAD, which definitely felt better than coming in first place in some competition I wasn't even able to attend. I also made sure when I met with the owner of the building, that I would be allowed to do the renovations I had in mind, and he had no problem with it. But as I'll eventually explain, all that went sideways, because of things outside my control.

But before I get too far ahead, there are a few other things that are significant, which happened pretty much from the beginning as soon as I made the deal with the old owner.

I have hinted at this before, in other contexts, but it seems important to stress that I really have never been very comfortable with being at the center of attention. Sometimes it can easily seem that way, especially when I get really excited and into a story that I'm telling people, if they seem interested in hearing the story. People often tell me that I'm a good storyteller, at least in person, and I know at least sometimes with writing, so hopefully this book is one of those times and you enjoy reading it.

The important thing that happened the day I met with the owner and made the initial agreement to buy the club, there was only him, my buddy, and myself in the room. The very first thing I asked them after we made the agreement was, "How many people know about me buying the club?" They both told me that nobody knew it was me, and the only people that knew he was even selling it at all, was his sister and his parents. My other buddy hadn't told anybody at all. So I asked them both to promise me that they wouldn't tell anybody that it's me, and even not tell anyone that he's even selling it, if it doesn't need to be said, but definitely don't tell anyone it was me. After they promised me they wouldn't, I then made them promise me two more times, because I really didn't want anybody to know. They even got curious and asked why, but I simply told them I wasn't quite sure, it just seemed better that way. Even though I told them that, I knew I had a few reasons. I mainly just didn't want to be harassed, and all of a sudden have a bunch of people acting like they are my best friend and didn't want to deal with being in the center of that kind of attention, especially knowing that I was going to have to deal with that eventually. The important point is, both of them kept their promises and as far as I can tell neither of them told even a single person.

Before I made the agreement to buy the club, I actually very rarely went there. Partly because I found it to be a little sketchy, which says a lot from somebody who grew up in the Windsor/Detroit area, but more importantly, there was no hardwood dance floor; it was just vinyl tile, on top of cement. And because of how much I love to dance, if I was going to be up all night partying like that and dancing, I'd rather drive to Montréal two hours away, and dance on a proper hardwood dance floor, with a much better sound system. Anyone who has danced a lot on both hardwood and cement floors, knows how much better your knees and body will feel, after dancing twice as long on a hardwood floor, versus half as long on a cement floor.

Of the times when I would go to the club I was buying, I'd say I was just as likely to pay cover and go in than not pay cover and just hang around outside, just because I'm more of a night person than a daytime person, and I'd be up anyway, but one thing I wasn't, was any kind of a "regular". In fact, if it wasn't for a couple things that stood out as unique, I think most people would've barely remembered me.

The things that stood out would be either, my black Subaru Impreza with gold colored rims (that would be noticed by anybody that's into cars), or else I'd be driving a bright red 1990 Miata. But even for those who aren't into cars at all, I pretty much always had my 15 pound Chihuahua with me, who is not only exceptionally cute (and I'm not just saying this because she's my dog), but she's incredibly intelligent too. She's also very well trained, because I've had her since she was three and a half months old, and I'd been drug dealing full-time before that, so she literally goes just about everywhere with me, the only times I leave her at home is if I know it's too hot out during the day, and I will be going to a store or someplace where the car will get too hot, however even though Chihuahuas hate the cold, I'm still able to bring her and leave her in the car in the winter, because she has a big bed and then a smaller bed that goes inside the big bed, that I'll cover with a really thick warm blanket, and so no matter how cold it gets, she's still super warm inside of her little den.

Now before anyone starts thinking, oh poor dog for leaving her in the car like that, you shouldn't make such judgments until you know the dog. If I leave her at home in the apartment, and I go downstairs to work on my car for thirty minutes, by the time I get back upstairs, she will almost always be crying at the door, and then burst into excitement the moment she sees me, as though she hasn't seen me in forever. The separation anxiety only gets worse the longer she's left home alone in the apartment. However, because she's been accustomed to going in the car with me pretty much her whole life, and being left in the car for extended periods of time, she never gets separation anxiety. I know this is true, because of the countless times I tested it, especially at first, because I wanted to know. But no matter how many times she's been in the car for an extended period of time, and I've quietly snuck up on the car on the way back, even making sure to hold my keys so they didn't make any noise, every single time I've done that, and I look in the car, she was always curled up sleeping, either in her bed or more often in my seat, probably because it smells like my farts, and we all know dogs are funny that way. ;)

So basically between either one of my distinct cars, or my dog, there were a fair amount of people at the club that recognized me, even if they didn't know my name.

Once I made the agreement to buy the club, and I didn't have to pay cover anymore, I started going almost every night it was open, even if only for a few hours. The very first night I went to the club after the deal was made with the owner, I intentionally went there to start a rumor. The first person that I saw when I got there that I knew, as soon as he was alone, I quietly took him aside, and in a secretive kind away, I asked him, "I heard Phil is selling the club, and someone bought it, but nobody knows who it is. Have you heard anything about this?" Because this particular guy happened to be the gossip King of that club, he was understandably shocked that me, this person that barely goes there, knows about this thing before him. He was so shocked and in disbelief, he just kind of looked at me like I was crazy and I'm just hearing rumors. When he asked me where I heard it from, I said, "I can't remember the person's name. It was towards the end of the party last week, but if I see them here today, I'll point them out to you."

After I went upstairs, I patiently looked around for another person I kind of knew, and when nobody was around, I spread the rumor a bit more. By that point, I was still thinking about the first person I told, Mr. Gossip King, and realized I definitely told enough people that first night; the last thing I wanted, was for anybody to figure out that I was the first one to be asking people about it. I continued telling one or two people each night the club was open until eventually, the first time I asked somebody new, who responded by saying, yes they have heard about it. At that point, I knew I didn't need to keep telling people anymore, because the rumor was obviously spreading on its own.

When I first started spreading the rumor, there wasn't any kind of master plan behind it, I just figured it be a good way to create some hype and excitement, because I knew I was planning a lot of changes to make the club better. In fact, if I had spent any amount of time really thinking about some grand plan, I'm not sure if I would've done it in the first place, because of how unexpectedly far and wide the rumor eventually spread, as I would quickly learn the first day I took over the club, once the New Year's Eve party ended.

By the time the New Year's Eve party arrived, there were a few people at that point who knew I was the new owner, but even then I triple swore everyone that knew it was me, to complete secrecy and to not tell anybody else, and for good measure, even reminded them, with a smile, that they don't want to betray the new owner and get on his bad side; as far as I could tell, that worked. Even though not that many people knew it was me, essentially everybody knew that somebody bought the club, because that New Year's Eve party was also advertised, as the old owners going away party, and everybody knew the club was staying open.

It was really interesting to see how distorted the rumor became, by the time New Year's came around. There were so many different ideas about who bought the club. Some people thought it was the bikers, some people thought it was some DJs from Montréal, and a whole bunch of other ones I forget, but almost nobody suspected it was me. Even when the New Year's Eve party finally arrived, there was no big announcement. Even by the time the party did end, there were still very few people that actually knew it was me, but as I would soon find out, the rumor that I started, spread much further than I ever considered.

A NEW KIND OF CLUB

After all the random customers left, the only people who remained were my buddy Wes, my buddy Issa, and myself. Then there was also the old owner, and a few of his friends, who were all in the office doing the final cash out. As me and my two buddies were waiting in the main room for the old owner to be done in the office, I went to the back area quickly to grab a 40oz bottle of rum, because me and my friends were planning to start our own party, as soon as the owner was done.

After grabbing the rum from the back, I started walking towards the main room, just as I walked out from the hallway and into the main room, I started saying in a slightly loud voice so that my friends could hear me on the other side of the main room, "Are you guys ready to party?" As the arm that was holding the bottle of rum swung out into the main room first, followed a split second later by the rest of my body, just as my eyes were fully past the wall of the main room, and my other arm and leg still swung backwards and hidden behind the wall, I instantly froze, standing on one foot, mid-walk, as I suddenly saw the most unexpected site of two police officers casually walking in the door.

That was one of those moments when, within a second, a massive amount of ideas suddenly went through my head, in an attempt to make sense of why they were there right now, after the party was over. During that brief moment while I stood there like a statue, beautifully representing a party in motion, one of the things that went through my head, was realizing that they seemed just as surprised by my sudden appearance, as I did theirs, and they too paused in their tracks the moment I did, as two statues representing an official scene of uncertainty over what to do next.

Then about a second after my initial pause, feeling as though I had figured out why they were there, I started to say, as I continued moving to into the main room and slowly came to a normal standing position, "Heeeyy Guuys! ... I'm assuming you've heard there's a new owner?" At that point, the look on their faces and body language told me a silent, but affirmative yes. So I continued by saying, "Well, that would be me." As I slowly begin walking towards the closest officer, I said "Let me introduce myself..." And then now that I was close enough, I extended my hand, and as he extended his hand to shake mine, I told him my name is Adam and it was nice to meet them. He then just looked around for a moment, seemingly thinking about what to say next, because I'd already answered the initial question he wanted to ask. He then asked a few generic questions, which kind of felt like he only asked because I'd already answered what he really wanted to know, since it might've been a little bit awkward and rude if he just went directly to taking out his notepad, which is what he did after asking those few generic questions. He then asked if he could get my number, which I was happy to give, he also asked for my last name, which I would've preferred them not to have, but with my phone number I knew they were going to find out anyway, so I gave him my last name as well. I then made a joke that I would ask for their number, but I've already got it, which he didn't seem to get or didn't find funny, but still overall he seemed like a nice guy and was very polite.

We chatted a little bit more and I mentioned that I was going to be fixing the place up and doing some renovations, and hopefully make the place much less sketchy. He smiled a bit, as though he was happy to hear that. He apologized for interrupting our New Year's Eve celebration, then they walked out the door and left.

I turned and looked at my friends, to see a slightly confused look on each of their faces, which helped confirm what I was feeling and thinking, that it was indeed a bit odd that they would come at the end of the party, after everybody had left, to find out if the rumor they heard about a new owner was true. Then a few minutes later, when the old owner finally came out of the office, I mentioned the guests that we just had, and when I saw that he seemed a bit surprised as well, I asked him if they had ever come at the end of the party, after everybody had already left. After thinking for a second, he said "never". When the old owner left, me and my two friends went into my new office, and started our New Year's Day party.

At this point, the incident with the cops coming in unexpectedly, set the initial conversation in motion, and influenced the conversation, for most of the remaining time we were there that day. The first obvious thing that we could conclude, was that the cops had heard about the rumor that

I started. I immediately realized that the drug charges which had been stayed, happened less than a year before that day, ten months and a couple days to be exact. I also knew that when charges are stayed, they don't go on your record, since you were not found guilty, and technically the charges could be reactivated within 12 months. However, even though nothing would be on my record, there would still be a record of the charges being stayed on the internal police database, until a short period after they are no longer able to reactivate the charges. Because of all that, I knew within a few days at the very most, the Gatineau police were going to realize that the owner of the new local "drug-club", recently had five counts of trafficking dropped. After sharing this revelation with my friends, they actually seemed much more concerned than I was. It's not that I wasn't concerned, it's just that I believe most problems have a solution to them, or at the very least, most problems have multiple ways to deal with them, and often the most obvious one that come to mind, is usually not the most effective.

Their initial suggestions mostly included ideas, such as lying low with selling drugs, or that maybe I should not bring my bag with me to the club each night, and a few other similar suggestions. They even asked how certain I am, that the police are going to find out that I recently had the 5 counts of trafficking dropped, which I told them I felt was 100% certain. During their initial questions and suggestions, I was also processing this issue, and had already started thinking about, a very radical and unorthodox approach, for how to deal with the situation. After hearing all of their suggestions, and not being able to think of anything better, I eventually shared what I had in mind. I clearly realized that it was a risky choice, and that the only way it would be the best choice, was if two assumptions I had were actually true. If either one of the assumptions were wrong, I realized what I was planning to do, would probably not have been the best decision.

The first assumption, involves the reason why the Crown decided to stay the charges. Over the previous ten months, since they initially dropped the charges, I'm not sure how many countless people I've talked to about it, and most people, by far, seemed to feel that they dropped the charges just because they didn't want to deal with the hassle, rather than actually feeling that they would've lost if they proceeded. Personally, I can't see that being the case, because in all my years of going through the court system, and also being around a lot of people who have also gone through the courts a lot, I've never once heard anything, from anybody, or seen anything myself, that comes even close to seeming like some charge was dropped for a reason such as that. Additionally, I realized nobody else that I've talked to about them dropping the charges, understands the Charter Application in any sort of way, that even came close for them to be able to understand the significance of that document. In fact, most people haven't even read it, and the few that have, I'm sure don't fully understand it. Even my late friend who was in law school, kept inaccurately referring to it as a loophole, when a loophole is a very different thing. A loophole is when someone finds a way to do something a law was specifically intended to prevent, such as the bylaws preventing an afterhours club from operating in the city. In the case of Section 1 of the Charter, it was intended to prevent any law placing unjust limits to our rights, which my Charter Application proves drug laws are doing, and therefore, it isn't a loophole.

The second assumption is a much simpler one, which is that they will indeed go back to the police station and quickly realize that I had five counts of trafficking recently dropped. I really had zero doubt about this second assumption.

There was also the one thing that happened shortly after the charges were initially dropped, which made me feel confident that the Crown dropped the charges because they didn't feel they could win; the fact that two of my buddy's law professors wanted to meet me.

So based on those assumptions, I concluded that the Gatineau police, would in fact quickly realize that I recently had five counts of trafficking dropped. It really couldn't seem any more obvious to me, unless they came out and directly told me. I also knew that the Gatineau cops are mostly bullies, especially with only English-speaking people, even more so if you are a guy. So if I were to just try to lay low and keep my head down as my friends suggested, my experience with bullies told me, that it would almost certainly encourage them to try and catch me, especially if they felt that I was a little worried about that; keeping my head down would be the best way to make it seem like I was worried. Even if I were to just act normal and not change anything, it probably wouldn't seem any different to them. However, there was the much bolder option, which was, to let them know, that I know, that they know. But if I'm going to be that bold, might as well take it a step further, by letting them know, that I know, that they know, and also, that I want them to know, that I don't care that they know, and even want to make sure that they know this.

Since I knew that they've got their ear within the gossip circle very well, I knew exactly how to accomplish this goal. So I decided to bring a copy of the Charter application to the club and kept it in my office. Then similarly to how I spread the rumor about the new owner, I started to spread a new rumor, by explaining to everybody that came into my office, about what I had done with the Charter, and how I have a license to sell drugs. I would even go so far as almost making it a requirement for anybody that wants to hang out in my office, that hasn't been there before, that they first have to listen to this explanation about my license to sell.

Remember though, most of the people in that community didn't really know me at all. Over the next few months, the misconceptions and false ideas that people had of me, were almost universal. Some people thought I was being cocky and foolish, and would try to caution me, as though I didn't realize what I was doing. Other people would think I was being arrogant to think that my bold approach would actually discourage them, or make it less likely for them to bother me. But I didn't think it would make them less likely to bother me over all, I just felt that it would make them less likely to come after me for drug reasons. I felt that by spreading the rumor about my license to sell, it would make them evaluate the whole situation more thoroughly, by looking into the reason the charges were dropped, than if I had said nothing at all. If the Crown and the Judge needed to put some effort into really understanding that document, then unless there was somebody in the Gatineau police station, that was really good with understanding the nuances of law, I felt they would almost certainly be more likely they would dismiss the importance of it, if they didn't take enough time to really try to understand the significance of it.

So despite all of the attempts by other people to convince me to stop telling everybody, I continued with the choice I felt was best. Eventually it started getting to the point where a lot of the people who were regularly in my office, were starting to get so annoyed by hearing it again and again, that they would often try to insist that I just stop, simply because they were in the room, in *my* office. But I quickly explained that it doesn't work like that, and if they don't want to hear me say something, in *my* office, no one is forcing them to be there. Ironically, what they didn't realize, is that it had long gotten past that point, and I was even finding it tedious and annoying to continue telling every new person that hadn't heard about it yet.

When the day I was waiting for finally came, I was so relieved that I could finally stop telling everybody. The day I was waiting for happened one night when one of the regulars stopped by my office and asked if she could talk to me alone, when I have a moment. I gladly agreed not knowing what she had to say. Eventually, when everybody was gone, she came into the office and shut the door behind her, which really got my attention because the door to my office was rarely ever closed. She told me that just before coming to the club, she was at a bar, and as the bar was closing, she was talking to two girls that she knows, and while they were chatting she mentioned that she was going to BPM, which was the name of my club, and neither of those two girls had been there before. Then one of the girls told her, that she should be careful about going there, which shocked her, because she knew how much less sketchy the club had become since I'd taken over. When she asked why, the other girl replied by saying, "Oh haven't you heard? Apparently the new club owner is an open drug dealer!" As soon as she finished telling me this, she was completely surprised when she saw how excited and relieved I was to hear that.

That obviously warranted an explanation, because of how confused she looked. So I explained to her, that I've been waiting for somebody to come in and tell me just such a thing. I then asked her if she remembered how I started that rumor about the new club owner, and when she acknowledged that she did, I further explained that I wanted the rumor about my license to sell to get out there, because I wanted the police to know I'm not afraid that they know about that. So now that I knew somebody that hadn't even been to the club had heard that rumor, I was certain it was just a matter of time until the Gatineau police heard that rumor as well. Then suddenly I was no longer telling anybody about that, and no one seemed to even notice. Mission accomplished!

By the time I knew that this new rumor was definitely solidified in the gossip circle, it had already been a few months since I took over the club, and during that time, the cops started coming every weekend, on both days, and definitely going out of their way to make their presence noticed.

For the first couple of months or so, when the police would come in during a party, I would make it a point, every single time, to come out and greet them and ask if there is anything I can do for them. They always declined, but also seemed to have an unusual vibe towards me. The weird vibe that I got from them most closely felt like annoyance and contempt. If that really was the vibe I was feeling from them, the only thing that would really make sense for them feeling that way would be if they knew that I'm a drug dealer, but knew that they couldn't do anything about it.

As a final note, I want to share a quick story regarding a time when a cop stood in the middle of the dance floor with his flash light on. I was in the office at the time, when someone came in and told me the cops where there, "doing their thing." This time, one of them was standing in the middle of the dance floor with the light on. I immediately knew that was not at all acceptable! I went out to the main room, saw that the cop was still being an idiot, and unsurprisingly, everyone else on the dance floor, gave him a nice 2-3-foot space all the way around him. So I went over to the lighting controls, and showed him, quite literally, that mine is bigger than his. I put the movable spot lights into manual mode, put them initially on a dim red, aimed them both directly at him, widened the beams just enough to cover the whole area around him, where no one else was. Then in one moment, I made the whole room dark, and put the spot lights on full white!

Needless to say, he stopped being an idiot a moment later, turned his little bright idea off and quickly left.

House: 1, Visitors: 0

BY-(WHAT?)-LAW

Eventually, perhaps maybe a month or two after that girl told me what the other two girls at the bar said, a friend of mine called me up one Friday evening before the club opened, and told me that he heard from someone that the police were going to come by and try to shut us down. So Friday as we were preparing to open the club, I held a short little staff meeting that included a few of the regulars that we would let in early, and quickly said: "I heard from a friend that we should expect this to be an interesting night."

About halfway through the night, somebody came into my office to tell me that the police were there and they wanted to speak with me, which was a first. Before I continue a quick important point about one of the changes that I made to the club since I took over. As I mentioned, only about a third of the 3500 square feet, was actually used for the club. The old owner never really allowed anyone in the back area, but I started handing out keys to people that I felt were trustworthy, which would allow them to get into the first part of the back area which I made into a VIP lounge, and each key holder was allowed to bring one non-key holder with them, but the non-key holder had to leave if the key holder left too. Because the cops had been coming regularly since I took over the club, they obviously noticed that suddenly, there were lots of people coming in and out of that back area, that they couldn't get into.

After I was told that the cops wanted to speak with me, I walked out of my office, down the hallway, and exited through that door that they were seeing lots of people come in and out of all the time. As I exited the door there were six cops all standing not too far from that door, but I knew this ahead of time because of the cameras that are all over the place. When I walked through the door, I intentionally closed it quite quickly behind me and I then walked up to the officer that seemed to be in charge. He was very polite and fairly young, and definitely seemed like the least alpha of the group, but I got the impression he was in charge, because he probably did well at the Academy, and got a promotion early on.

So I start off by saying, "I heard you wanted to talk to me?" He replied by saying, "Yes, but is there a place we can talk, somewhere quiet?" Even though I immediately realized he was hoping I'd bring them through that door they were so curious about, and despite the fact that it was extremely close to where we were, I smiled and happily said, "Of course!" I then motioned with my hand for him to follow me, then proceeded to march them all back through the dance floor and right back down the stairs that they'd just come up. Even though they were all behind me, because there were so many mirrors in the club, I knew exactly which angle to look at, without needing to turn my head around, to be able to watch them, and quickly notice by their reactions that things were already not going according to their plan. We started walking down the three flights of stairs of a single file stairway, and as we got about halfway down, the non-Alpha Alpha, stopped me by saying "this is good."

At that point, I turn around, with a big enthusiastic smile on my face, like I'm very interested in what they have to say, which was true. He began by saying to me in his uncertain, not very practice English, with a heavy French accent, "Yes, we are here on behalf of the city of Gatineau, regarding bylaw issue" which I totally understood, but because of his very broken English, and how uncertain he was that he was even speaking it properly, I just looked at him with this very confused expression, as though I had no idea what he just said, and just waited.

He then starts saying. "oh.. well. ahh, umm…" and then turns around and says a few things to his partners in French. Even though I don't understand very much French, it's very clear to me that none of them know how to say it better. He then turns back towards me and says something simpler, by saying. "Oh, well, are you the, ah, owner?" I then responded with a big smile showing I understood this time, and very enthusiastically I said, "Oh! No, I don't own the building."

Considering that was obviously not what he meant, but was still technically true, he did his um, ah thing again, and then turns around, says a few more things to his partners in French, and when he finally turns back around he says, "Well, do you, ah, Run this place?" And then I reply, with a very confused look on my face, by repeating, "Run. This. Place?"

I just look at him, waiting for him to clarify what he means by that. Then I stand there, patiently looking at him all confused, but very intently like I really want to understand what he meant. He again turns around to his partners once again, but this time they all kind of shrug their shoulders without even saying anything, and so he quickly turns back to me and starts repeating the same umm and ahs, and then just as it seems like he is going to say something new, I say, with a very uncertain expression and tone, as though I wasn't quite sure if I am answering the question correctly, "Well, I rent the upstairs.. I do engineering stuff, and build electronics and lights that I want to sell eventually as a product, and so I invite a lot of friends over to have these parties, and then I can test out these new lights that I build, to see if everybody likes them, before I try to sell them to the stores."

He then pauses, while he's obviously processing what I had said, and then his face lights up as though he got it, and then he says that in a slightly excited kind of way, "Oh. Well, ok.. ummm, well thank you very much, you have a very good night." I then wished them a very good night too, and I politely smiled at each of them as they walked by and headed on out the door!

House: 2, Visitors: 0

THE RIGHTS PREPARATION

Because my experience owning the club started with the police from day one, and the decision I made to address the issue head-on, by spreading the rumor about my *license to sell*, I assumed from the beginning, the club would most likely get raided at some point or another. After I'd made the decision to spread that rumor, I also decided it would be a good idea to start preparing as many people as possible, by teaching them about their rights guaranteed under the Charter. However, I felt it would be better to wait until I felt people were comfortable enough, and had more time to get to know me better, to build enough trust, before telling them, that I expected the police would raid the club at some point, because the last thing I wanted was to scare people away.

After I heard from that girl that the *'license to sell'* rumor was self-sustaining, and seeing that more new people were still coming to the club, despite likely knowing about the rumor, I felt it would be okay to start telling people that I expected to be raided at some point. From that point on, I started teaching countless people who came in my office about the Charter of Rights, the specific rights that are most useful in everyday life, and what they should say to anyone that does violate their rights, which would include the police if they ever did end up raiding the club. I even made sure to explain the differences in how they should respond, depending on whether or not the police would have a search warrant. I assumed if they ever did raid the club, they would obviously have a search warrant, but because of how often they were coming in while the club was open, I realized the importance of explaining the difference.

A SHORT RECESS

After the 6 police officers came in that one night, wanting to speak with me, and failed in their attempt to shut the club down for bylaw reasons, the police suddenly stopped coming to the club, almost entirely, and for the next 8 months, things were relatively calm, in that regard. But even though the police were not around for a while, during the 2 ½ years that I owned the club, I don't think there was ever a period of time, when it would be accurate to say things were *calm*. Owning a regular dance club that serves alcohol, would no doubt be pretty chaotic, but owning an after-hours club makes a regular dance club seem like a daycare. Even though an after-hours club doesn't serve alcohol, people often show up completely hammered, because they often come from a bar, and then most people start taking other drugs as well. Interestingly, things usually became less chaotic as the alcohol wore off and only the influence of *other* drugs remained.

A TABLE, A TABLET, AND TOO MUCH TALK

Early on when I owned the club, I felt it was really important during those early days, that people understood certain things about my character. I knew that not only were the police watching, and testing me, I also knew that the local biker gang was trying to figure out what kind of person I was, since there was quite a mystery surrounding me due to the fact that nobody knew me. I also knew that the whole after-hours community was paying close attention to me as well, and trying to understand what kind a person I am, especially considering it started off, with me spreading this rumor about my *license to sell*.

As I've mentioned multiple times in this book, not only do people often misunderstand me, but because of my physical appearance, and how innocent and harmless I look, combined with how polite and friendly I am (provided that nobody provokes me and crosses any kind of moral line), and finally because of my experience being bullied so much when I was young, I was very aware of the fact that I needed to present myself in a certain way, in order to try to minimize the chance, that anybody might get any sort of idea that might make them think I'm some kind of pushover, or type of person that wouldn't stand up to any kind of injustice. Because of these concerns, I definitely took any opportunity that I saw during those early days, to really make a strong point about my willingness to stand up to whatever bullshit I might encounter. I also felt it was extremely important, that people knew that I was a man of my word, and if I said something, that I meant it.

Well on one particular day, during and after-after party, there were only 6 of us there at the club and we were all sitting in my office. Because everybody was high at that point, and had been up all night, the conversation that was taking place, I eventually became disinterested in, because it required just too much effort to try to say anything, since everybody was trying to say everything they had to say too, and not really listening to each other. So I took out my tablet computer that I had, and started searching online classified ads for any kind of cool club stuff that I could buy, that would make the place better.

One of the 6 people that were there, was sitting on one of the couches quietly, just kind of watching everybody else have their conversation, while I was sitting quietly using my tablet. Because of my natural tendency to hear what's going on, even if I don't want to listen to it, I was still aware of the conversations that were taking place, even though I was distracted with what I was doing on my tablet. At one point, I was suddenly distracted from what I was doing on the tablet, when I thought to myself, "Are there 4 different conversations going on?" This immediately got my attention, because there was only 4 people talking! After thinking that, I quietly peaked up from my tablet and started actively paying attention to what the 4 people were talking about. It didn't take long for me to realize that, yes there were indeed, 4 separate conversations taking place, and each of the 4 people, were essentially talking to themselves, and nobody was listening to each other.

I sat there for a moment, thinking about how to approach the situation, but I knew I didn't want to just tell everybody to stop, and simply point out that nobody was listening to each other. I was hoping I'd be able to think about something, that would leave some kind of lasting impression. When I first thought about this unorthodox idea, I honestly didn't expect it to turn out the way it did, if I had, I'm not sure if I would've taken that approach in the first place.

After deciding how I was going to proceed, I started off by very quietly saying, "Can everyone stop talking for a second?" But because I intentionally said it quietly, I didn't expect anybody to pay attention to it, especially considering they already weren't listening to each other and were talking much louder than I initially said that. So then I quietly said a slightly different thing, "If you guys don't stop talking for a second, I'm going to break my tablet." Again because I said it quietly, I still didn't expect anyone to stop talking, but I still wanted to see if they were just ignoring me, and felt adding that tablet detail would help confirm that." So then I said it a little bit louder, "Guys I really don't want to break my tablet, can everybody just please stop talking for a moment?" That time as I said it, I motioned with the tablet in my hand as though I was going to break it against the corner of the desk. That still that had no effect, so I said it a little louder than the previous time, and continued motioning with my hands. I continued repeating this quite a number of times, each time saying it just a little bit louder.

Eventually after repeating it more times than I counted, while saying it louder each time, by the time one of them reacted, it was clear that they'd heard it quite a few times already, due the obvious frustration that came out when one of them finally said, "Oh! Enough with the tablet already!" When I first thought about doing this, I knew that I would only break the tablet if 2 things were confirmed. First, somebody needed to acknowledge that they understood what I had said, and second, they needed to essentially dismiss what I'd said. In this case because of the way he responded, both of those things had been confirmed within the single statement that he made. I did hesitate ever so slightly, because as I mentioned I wasn't expecting to have to actually follow through with that, but I realized if I didn't, then it would set a really bad precedent about how meaningless my word was. So after that slight hesitation, I slammed the tablet into the edge of the desk and bent it in half.

At that point everybody suddenly stopped talking and had a look of shock on their faces. When one of them asked, "Why would you do that?" I immediately place the blame on the guy who said the comment, "…enough with the tablet…", because based on what I was saying I was essentially making it their choice. I also quickly pointed out that the reason why I started saying that in the first place, was because I noticed that the 4 of them, were having 4 different conversations, and that none of them were actually listening to each other.

Of course they all kind of realize that, and had some very uncomfortable and awkward looks on their faces, and although I had just basically thrown away 200 dollars, I still feel today that it was worth every penny of it to make a point to them. Of course the guy never felt it was really his fault, but it was definitely something that they talked about with other people, and that helped plant the seed that I'm a little bit crazy, because they obviously saw that as a crazy thing to do. It of course also sent a strong message that if I say something, I mean it.

After that incident, I intentionally left that tablet on display in my office, expecting many people to ask about what happened to it, which would give me an opportunity to share that story of principle with other people as well.

Additionally, because of that and other similar things I had done, I would eventually learn that part of my concern was no longer an issue, when I found out that the bikers wanted nothing to do with the "crazy" new club owner; I never once had any sort of issues with them.

STUDIO UNLISTED

Another thing that I started realizing early on, was the amount of people that started getting a key for the VIP area, was growing quite large. This was not at all a bad thing in my eyes, but I also felt it would be convenient to have a way to be able to contact any of those (relatively) trustworthy people, in case I was ever throwing a private party during the week, or just simply wanted to send a message to all of those people at once. When I took over the club, it was initially called BPM nightclub, but shortly after I took over, I dropped the nightclub from the name, and changed it to BPM Studios, since I felt it fit with the *private club* philosophy, much better than calling it a nightclub. I've also been using Unlisted as my last name on Facebook for countless years. I've even toyed with the idea of officially changing my last name to Unlisted, simply because of how amusing it would be any time I'd be filling out any sort of official paper work. The other person: "Oh, I need to know what your last name is." Me: "It's Unlisted." Them: "I understand that, but I need to know what it is to submit the paper work."....

Eventually, I decided to make a private group on Facebook, to be able to get in contact with all of these key holders to the VIP lounge, and I decided to call that private group, Studio Unlisted. I suddenly had this idea, while I was doing some work at the club one night during the week. As soon as I'd thought about this, I took a break from the manual labor I was doing, and decided to go create the Facebook group quickly, before I'd forgotten about it. After I made the group, which only took a few minutes, I wanted to write something about it, just so everybody that I added to the group, knew what it was about. But me, being the way I am, I didn't want to just write some simple generic statement, but wanted to write something interesting, and have a little fun with it. Well instead of a few minutes, it was closer to about 6 or 7 hours because of the intricacies of what I ended up writing, I wanted to make sure that the logic was perfectly sound, and the emphasis that I added by capitalizing certain words mid-sentence were on point.

The following is what I ended up writing:

STUDIO UNLISTED

"If you have been added to this group of Us Unlisted, it is because I have personally added you. It also means that I have personally met you and would now feel comfortable enough to trust you in my home even if I were not there with you.

To those of us whom have been added thus far, it is likely you already have an idea of the purpose for this group's being. But just in case, and in the spirit of clarity, it's being included here anyway.

In short, if I trust each of you enough to be in my home without me, then you are definitely trust worthy enough for The Party Unlisted, future Deals Unlisted, and any what-ever-other Unlisted perks not listed in this list of Unlisted.

As a privilege of being listed here, a member of Studio Unlisted, any guest of yours, to any Party Unlisted, is actually a guest of ours, and as such, upon arrival, they are invited to enjoy the same Deals Unlisted we ourselves enjoy, but ONLY if the nature of my trust in you, is mirrored, by you, onto them, and can be reflected back to each of us by saying; Yes, you would trust them in Our House of House, even if you are not there.

However, as it has been said before, if Trust was a certain thing, it wouldn't be called Trust; it would actually be, just, a simple, Fact.

Therefore, the most certain way of dealing with that which is uncertain, is by The Unlisted being the only one of the listed members of Studio Unlisted who is allowed to add guests of the Unlisted to this list of us friendly Unlisted.

...Oh, and if for some clear reason you are unclear about anything listed in this clear list of the unlisted list of Unlisted, come talk to me next time you are here and I'll attempt to make clear that which would then be clearly unclear.

Cheers!"

ACTUATEDLY MISUNDERSTOOD

This next story doesn't really have any kind of moral principle behind it at all, and even the type of misunderstanding that occurred, isn't like any of the other misunderstandings that I repeatedly referred to, but this was still quite an interesting misunderstanding, and was one of those times where the obviousness of why I was misunderstood wasn't at all initially apparent to me. More importantly, it's quite a funny story, which is the main reason why I am including it.

It all started this one day, when I came back from a surplus store, with an actuator that I had purchased, for a project idea that I had in mind. A quick explanation of what an actuator is, for anyone who doesn't know; it's basically just like a hydraulic piston that's used on heavy machines that allow the different parts of the machine to move. You'll notice them by a shiny silver tube that goes in and out of a thicker cylinder. An actuator is basically the same thing, but instead of using hydraulic fluid to move the piston in and out, it uses gears and an electric motor to do the same thing, and the one I had was only about 16 inches long.

Because I purchased the actuator from a surplus store, I wanted to test it to make sure it worked before building something with it. So on this random Tuesday afternoon; I was sitting at my desk at the club listening to a folder of some old electronic music that I had, because I wanted to find some tracks that were still good to mix with at the club. I was holding this actuator between my legs, and using a random power supply that I had plugged into an extension cord on the floor. I used one hand to hold the cord of the power supply, and the other hand to connect the 2 wires to the 2 different metal pieces on the power supply connector.

As I started testing this actuator, sure enough it worked, and as I was holding it between my legs, the piston started going in and out. I wouldn't have thought anything perverted about that, if it wasn't for the song that was currently playing while I was testing it, which was called "Bedroom Sessions". I don't think I need to start quoting the lyrics of the song, for anybody to get the relationship between this thing going in and out between my legs, and the lyrics of such a song. Even though I was sitting there by myself, I ended up laughing so hard, my stomach was hurting because of this completely random coincidence.

At the time I also wanted to learn more about video editing, because I now had almost 40 cameras in the club, and I knew already there were funny things happening that I wanted to create stitched together videos of. So I figured I'd make a funny short video, using part of the audio from that song, and a short video I recorded of this piston going up and down between my legs; it seemed like a fun way to get a little bit of practice using the video editing software. I also knew that a lot of the regulars would often make very perverted jokes, so I figured posting a video like this on my Facebook page, would get lots of laughs.

Finally, after a few hours, I completed a short little video and had the movement of the piston from the actuator lined up with a certain section of the song. Personally I thought it was hilarious, even though I'm not usually one to make perverted jokes like that. By this point of owning the club, I was definitely having a lot of people adding me as friends on Facebook, and it got to the point that it didn't seem to matter what I posted on Facebook, regardless of what it was, it would still get a bunch of likes.

To illustrate that point when I mentioned this to someone one day, I immediately made a post on my Facebook page of something as stupid as, "Orange". Just as I predicted, a number of people liked it. So when I posted this video on that Tuesday afternoon, by the evening I was quite surprised that not a single person had liked it yet. Then as the days went by and Friday approached, the only person that liked it happened to be my mom, which didn't really surprise me at all because I know how my family's sense of humor is. Before my mom had liked it, I was starting to wonder if something was broken with my Facebook page, but at that point I knew there wasn't; I still knew there was something strange that I obviously didn't understand.

At the beginning of the night that Friday, when people started coming in, I intentionally had the video up on one of my monitors in the office, to ask people if they'd seen this funny video that I made. After noticing that every person that I tried to show the video to, appeared to be slightly uncomfortable, finally the one person I felt certain would find it hilarious, Mr. Gossip, who was also the king of perverted jokes, finally walked into the office, but surprisingly, he seemed to be more uncomfortable about it than anyone else. So I persisted, and then persisted some more, until finally he said in a very awkward way, "I don't want to see that shit." Suddenly, in that moment, it all made sense.

What I realized, was that nobody knew about the coincidental thing that happened, which inspired me to make the video in the first place, and it wasn't some weird perverted thought that I randomly had. But more importantly, the awkwardness had to do with how I had been towards all of the girls that were hitting on me since I took over the club. I knew from the beginning that I should expect a whole bunch of women basically throwing themselves at me, considering that I'm a decent looking guy and, more importantly, the club owner. I'm sure even if I was really ugly, I'd still have a whole lot of girls throwing themselves at me, simply because I was the owner. But I'm not a slut, and I wasn't about to be known as the slut club owner, more importantly, I'm just not that kind of guy; I've always known how much I wanted a relationship and family, and obviously I would want somebody to love me for who I am and not only be interested in me because I'm the owner of the club. Because of the awkwardness of acknowledging somebody's advancements, but then dismissing them, I decided that the better way to approach that issue, was to just pretend like I didn't even notice they were hitting on me, and put on my best Forest Gump face.

I did this so well, over the 4 or 5 months that had passed by this point, that even the guy that was now sitting across from me who was super uncomfortable about the video I'd made, at one point after a very attractive girl was massively hitting on me in my office, and I still gave the same blank look, like I'd just didn't notice, after she had left and it was just him and I in the office that night, he leaned over to me, and asked, "Do you realize that she was hitting on you?" But in that same nonchalant, oblivious kind of way I'd been, I simply said, "Ya, I know". Confused, he then said, "I mean she was like *really* hitting on you." I replied in the same kind of way, "Ya… I get that." And then just continued doing what I was doing as though I didn't understand the significance of why he was pointing it out.

After realizing all these details in that moment when we had this video in front of us, it suddenly clicked that a lot of people were probably starting to think that I was gay, which I have no issue with, but I could see how all the sudden people could be weirded out by that video, especially considering I didn't show any interest in guys either. Once I told them about the coincidental way the video got inspired, and mentioning the fact that I'm actually very attracted to girls, but that I've just been acting towards them that way because I don't want to be involved with a girl that's just interested in me because I'm the owner of a club, in that moment there was this sign of relief on his face, and suddenly he found the video funny!

EMPTY THREATS AND A TIP

The next legal issue that occurred because of the club, started near the beginning of the first summer while owning it. But this time, instead of it being from the police, the city decided to take a new approach in their attempt to shut us down. This time they sent the landlord a cease-and-desist letter, threatening to fine him 675$ for each night that the club was open.

This obviously caused issues between me and the landlord, and suddenly the landlord told me that the renovations that I had in mind were not going to happen. This was obviously a big deal for me, because that's the main reason why I wanted to buy the club in the first place, since I knew my plans could allow me to make enough money, in a completely legal way, which would allow me to start having a relatively normal life and stop selling drugs. Needless to say, it made me quite sad and a bit depressed when this happened, and from that point on, I kind of said "Fuck it".

That's when we really started to party hard, since I no longer cared about being exhausted during the week, and not having the energy to keep working on the renovations that I'd slowly started doing. The landlord also started asking me to start paying him more rent, with the extra amount of money being held in a trust, and that it would still be my money, but it was there just in case the city decided to start fining him.

This went on for a few months, and during that time I started researching all of the laws surrounding this issue. Eventually I discovered that the city threatening to fine him was a very shaky legal argument, since I was the one renting the space and responsible for what was taking place. So once again, I took advantage of this indirect communication channel I had to the city and the police through the gossip circle, and started telling everybody, I knew I could easily fight the city using the Charter of Rights. Ultimately the city never did fine him, and eventually I convinced him to stop requiring me to give him that extra money, because I wouldn't be able to keep the club open if I had to keep giving him that extra money.

Also right around the time when the city initially gave the landlord those notices, I also got a tip from a friend, who was talking to a lawyer friend of his, who heard that the Gatineau police were making plans to raid the club. My friend also found out from the lawyer friend of his, that apparently I'm quite notorious within the legal community, because of what I had done with the Charter and the drug charges. Of course this further boosted my confidence about that issue, and made me more certain than ever that the police and the city were definitely hesitant to come after me directly, which was also confirmed by the fact that the city gave the landlord the notices rather than me.

Over the following 6 months until the new year, the police only came in to the club maybe one or two times, and each time it seemed obvious they were looking for somebody specific, rather than trying to give us a hard time.

PROGRESSIVE RESTRICTIONS

As I've previously mentioned, based on what I've learned from owning the club, if I were to open one again, there would be a number of things I would do differently. I still would create a VIP area, in that same Studio Unlisted philosophy, because I saw the positive impact it had on the whole community's interpersonal relationships. But one of the key mistakes that I made from the beginning, was not creating a separation between the VIP area, and the very back area where my office was. Initially this allowed people to come and go into my office as they pleased. Eventually, a lot of people started becoming rather disrespectful while in my office and developed a sense of entitlement like they had a right to be there.

   It got to a point where I'd ask someone to leave my office because they kept doing something I repeatedly asked them not to do, often just talking too loudly, that they wouldn't initially leave. Of course that is not at all acceptable and caused me to have to become progressively harsh, and aggressive towards them, and usually end up yelling at them; a few times I even had to physically throw people out of my office. Even more astonishing, is how many people felt I was in the wrong for doing so, even though I started out asking nicely. It's absolutely astonishing how people can be like that, and I'm sure I will never understand what types of things go through a person's head, that leads them to think, they have some kind of right, to stay in somebody else's office, when they are a guest that has been invited to be there.

Because of how much I hate having to deal with confrontations like that, and also because of how many people would view me as the bad guy, I eventually addressed the situation by installing a door in the middle of the back hallway, that separated the VIP area, from my office area, which also included a room I made into a kitchen, since I knew of how often I was going to be there. By that point people were so accustomed to coming in my office, initially everyone just started knocking on that door, so that quickly led to me putting up a sign that said "DO NOT KNOCK ON THIS DOOR!" in big bold letters, filling up a whole sheet of paper. I even had to put a light on the door, shining down at the sign, so people could see it, since the hallway was fairly dark while the club was open. For the most part that fixed the issue, but even then some people still had such a feeling of entitlement, and would still knock on the door.

The people that knew they were allowed to come back, understood not to knock on the door, and instead just announce themselves by saying their names. Eventually, most people got the point, but if I had put that door up at the beginning when I first took over the club, the majority of the social issues that caused a lot of people to dislike me, almost certainly never would've occurred. Some people from the club had this impression of me, that I was some kind of master manipulator, and had these grand elaborate plans, but in reality, the only big plan that I had ahead of time, were my plans to renovate the building, and turn it into a fitness studio during the week.

For the most part, I just went with the flow and dealt with issues as they arose. If I was really such a master planner that way, I clearly wouldn't have missed something as obvious as putting that fucking door up from the beginning. Admittedly, because of my tendency not to show any kind of weakness or vulnerability, I did intentionally give off the impression that I had a lot of these things planned way ahead of time. But even the example of the first rumor I started about somebody buying the club and nobody knows who it was, if I'd really thought about it even a little bit deeper than I did, I probably would've realized that the cops might end up hearing about that too. That almost certainly would have changed my decision, knowing that these trafficking charges could've still been reactivated and were still on their internal database.

If the cops hadn't heard about that rumor, and only found out that there was a new club owner after 2 months of me owning the club, when the charges would've been off their internal database, then they probably never would've found out, I recently had 5 counts of trafficking dropped. If they had never found out those details, then I definitely wouldn't have spread the rumor about my license to sell, and there's a good chance that the police never would've started harassing me the way they did, and it's possible that the club would still be open today, and the renovations and plans to turn it into a fitness studio during the week, probably would've been successful, and no doubt my life would've been quite a bit different right now. It's hard to say if it would've been better or worse, but things would certainly be different, that's for sure.

DON'T DEE DISHONEST

Once again, going back to when I first made the deal with the old owner, and I started spreading the rumor about a new owner, but nobody knows who it is. As I mentioned the main reason why I didn't want anybody to know, was just because I didn't want to be harassed and bothered, not have all sorts of new fake friends, and was trying to delay being at the center of any attention that I knew I would feel uncomfortable with. Beyond that, there wasn't any grand plan for me choosing to start spreading that rumor. I did however, learn a lot of things from doing that. One of the things I noticed almost immediately, after people started finding out that it was me, was how certain people's attitudes suddenly changed towards me. I remember a lot of people that I would tell the rumor to, had an attitude towards me like I was bothering them, and were not at all very friendly towards me, because I was just some nobody to them.

But every single one of those types of people, once they realized I was the owner, were suddenly acting like they were my best friend. Immediately, I knew I couldn't trust them, and they were really just selfish, and likely had psychopathic/sociopathic personality types. The main bouncer, Dee, was one such person, and if it wasn't for the political consequences that I would've had to deal with, if I simply fired him from the beginning, that's exactly what I would've done. Everybody that went there, all liked Dee, and not just that, but he would often talk about his chronically sick kid, so people were very sympathetic towards him. Clearly, if I would've fired him from the start, without any real reason other than I don't trust him, no doubt that would've caused a whole lot of people to not like me. If it was just a simple issue of them personally not liking me, I could have easily dealt with that, because I've been use to that my whole life, but knowing how it would affect business, I realized a compromise was needed, and I'd have to figure out another way to deal with that issue.

Usually, I'm the type of person that will give others the benefit of the doubt, when I have doubt at least. Initially, I did consider different reasons for why my impression of him might not be accurate. The only reason I could really think of, that could have caused him to be kind of dismissive towards me, up until the point he found out that I was the new owner, and then suddenly being one of those people, that started acting like my best friend, was the fact that he is a bouncer, and has to deal with a bunch of idiots on a regular basis; countless people that try to be all friendly with him, hoping that they'll get something out of it. That definitely could've been the reason, he was the way he was towards me, before he found out I was the owner. But because of all of my experience around thieves and other criminals, and even living with them for extended periods of time while I was in jail, my gut instinct not to trust him, was too strong to ignore.

So right from the beginning, I was keeping my eye on him, but without making it seem like that at all. I was still open to the possibility that my instinct about him was wrong, but every time I've ever ignored that kind of gut feeling, without exception, I've always regretted it later. After getting to know him better, once I took over the club, and spending a lot of time thinking about how to address the issue, I eventually figured out a way to test him to see if my instinct was correct.

When I first took over the club, the old owner had separate sheets for both the bar and the coat check/door. The purpose of the sheets, were simply to track inventory and sales at the bar, the amount of coats that people paid to have checked, or the amount of bracelets that were sold and at what price. Within a few weeks of seeing how those sheets worked, I noticed that there were some flaws, that could allow somebody to manipulate them in such a way, that would make it impossible to notice if somebody was taking money out of the cash, and simply lying on the sheets in a certain way.

As soon as I noticed that issue, I immediately made new sheets. I also noticed that the bar and coat check staff, would want to switch halfway through the night, but with the old sheets, it made it very difficult to do, so the old owner usually wouldn't allow it. Because I wanted the employees to be happy with their jobs, I designed the new sheets to allow them to be able to switch halfway through the night, and so instead of 2 different sheets, there was just a single sheet that they would use for both the bar and the coat check area. Given my ability with things such as law, it wasn't very difficult for me to design the sheets, that would make it impossible for anybody to fill out in such a way, and allow them to steal money, without me noticing. Even after I created the sheets, I spent quite a bit of time trying to see if I could find any loopholes, and after not being able to, I was pretty confident that no one else would be able to either.

Once I was comfortable that the new sheets I created were working smoothly, I decided to give Dee some extra responsibility, which would speed up getting things ready at the beginning of the night, by giving him a key to the bracelet box, and allowing him to take out how many bracelets we needed for that night. After a few months of allowing him to do this, I suddenly decided to do an audit on the bracelets, knowing that I had records of every single sheet, from every night that we were open. I also had records of when, and how many bracelets I bought, and based on all of those pieces of information, it was simply a matter of using basic arithmetic, to figure out if any bracelets were unaccounted for. So one night by myself during the week, I spent many hours going through all the records and eventually came to the conclusion that there were a lot less bracelets in the bracelet box then there should have been.

I had already heard rumors that Dee was selling bracelets outside the door, but he wasn't an idiot, and would often tell me he would do that to speed things up when it was busy, but then it would get recorded on the coat check sheet after. The problem I noticed with that logic from the beginning, was if it was that busy down there, and he was outside helping out with getting people in faster, then who was actually at the entrance to go upstairs patting people down for drugs and weapons and doing what the bouncer was supposed to be doing? So yes he was "clever" but not really very clever. That immediately made me suspicious that not all of the bracelets he was selling outside were actually getting recorded on the sheet. So when I initially did the audit of the bracelets I expected some to be missing, but when I finally added everything up, there were so many missing bracelets I not only triple checked all of my calculations, but I asked somebody else to as well, and they came to the same number that I came to. In total there was close to 15,000$ in bracelets missing, and suddenly he's got his hand caught in the cookie jar.

That Friday, when he got to the club, I casually told him that I didn't need him to be doing the bracelets anymore, since I was not as busy as I was when I first asked him help with the bracelets, and I'd be taking care of that from then on. I didn't even bother asking for his key back to the bracelet box, I just simply changed the lock with another identical looking lock. There were other people in the room when I said this to him, and afterwards I found out, they were equally as surprised by his initial reaction as I was. Immediately, he became very defensive in a way that seemed suspicious, not just to me, but everybody else who saw that. During the course of that night, while he was downstairs doing his job when I wasn't around, he kept going on about that issue in a way that a lot of people felt was a little weird and suspicious.

Eventually one of the regulars came in and asked me what that was all about, and I explained to him exactly what I discovered, and even showed him all the numbers. Well long story short, after talking with enough people that night after the club closed and Dee was gone, I explained to everybody how I didn't trust him from the beginning, but knew if I fired him from the start a whole lot of people would been very upset with me. Everyone agreed that they would've been without having some kind of overwhelming proof like I now had. The next day when Dee came in, I wasted no time firing him right on the spot. Afterwards, over the next few weeks, I still needed to explain to countless people all the details about why I was certain he had been stealing, and eventually everyone I showed the evidence to was shocked.

THE HOUSE DOES NOT ALWAYS WIN

Before I continue the rest of the stories about the club, I want to jump back a few years to an incident that happened at the casino one night during my birthday. The incident happened after I was first charged with drug dealing, and a few months before the charges were ultimately dropped. I didn't include this story in the chronological order in which it occurred, because I felt it would interrupt the flow of the entire story, from when I took the 40-foot jump, to when the charges were ultimately dropped. But it's an important story to include, not just because of the very big moral issue and the gross violation of the Charter of Rights, which occurred that night, but 2 of the arresting officers that were at the casino that night, would be two officers I would soon have reoccurring problems with, a year after I took over the club.

Not long before the drug charges were dropped, this very significant event took place on December 11th, 2012, while my girlfriend at the time and I, were out at the casino one night. We really didn't do very much gambling, but mostly just sat in the bar area, having a few drinks and chatting with another couple at the table next to us. I was driving that night, so I didn't have too much to drink, and even after last call, we were still there for a couple hours. We weren't exactly being quiet, but we never got told we were being too loud. At one point a security guard came over, and randomly started chatting with us. He never asked us to be a little quieter or anything like that, he just seemed like he was being friendly.

Well, remember how I mentioned that sometimes I get random impressions of people and things, this happened to be one of those times, and I got a very specific impression of the security guard. As I often do, out of curiosity, to see if the impression is accurate, I just kind of blurted it out, and asked, "Excuse me, but are you Jewish by any chance?"

Admittedly, this was definitely one of those times where I put my foot in my mouth, but what I asked was not at all, in any kind of way, racist, prejudice or discriminatory. In fact, my really close friend I mentioned, that was in law school, was actually one of my very closest friends, and he was Jewish. He was the first friend I had that I knew was Jewish. Since I've always enjoyed learning about different religions, I'd often ask questions about Judaism, and one of the unique aspects I learned, was the importance Orthodox Jewish people place on the mother. Essentially if your mother was born of a Jewish mother, and her mother was too, then you'll be considered properly Orthodox as well. This is the only religion that I know of that has any kind of genetic link like that. After I first met my buddy, and getting to know a lot of his Jewish friends, I started feeling like I can sometimes notice with some of them, certain physical traits a lot of them had in common with each other. This is what led me to have that impression of the security guard that one night.

I could see how someone could take that the wrong way, especially from someone who looks like me. My buddy even started making a joke after we found out that there's a good chance I'm Jewish, because of Polish ancestry that went at least as far back as my mother's grandmother. When we realized this, he started jokingly calling me the Aryan Jew. Even the girlfriend I was with at the casino that night, immediately looked at me with one of those looks like, I can't believe you just said that. It was hard to tell if he was offended or not, but I kind of got the impression he might've been. I thought about saying something, but I didn't want to make it worse by apologizing for something I wasn't even sure if he was offended about, and felt it was better just to let it go. Eventually he walked away, and we went about our night.

A few hours later, as we were outside walking towards my car, that security guard suddenly showed up and asked me, if I was planning to drive. I told him I was, and then despite him having no idea how much I had to drink that night, and not showing any signs of intoxication, for some reason he felt that he was going to make an issue out of it, and I'm pretty sure I know what his motivation was. I also know that even when I'm completely "hammered", I still walk straight and never stumble, or show any kind of sign of being as drunk as I am. Even though I knew I didn't have that much to drink, I also know that it doesn't take much to blow over the legal limit. Since he was threatening to call the cops if I drove my car, I asked him if they had a breathalyzer inside. When he said yes, I offered to go blow into it. But I was also very irritated by the fact that he seemed to be coming out and harassing me for no particular reason, other than possibly because of what I asked him, but that was obviously pointless to bring up at this point. If that was his motivation, it definitely doesn't justify his actions.

Right from the beginning, I started insisting he give me his security number, which by law he has to do. But he refused, and then as we were walking back towards the door, I continued to insist about his security number, and went further by saying if he didn't give it to me, I was going to talk to a manager to make a complaint. At that point, despite neither my tone or behavior changing, he suddenly decided that I was too drunk to go back in, and told me I had to leave immediately. When I continued to insist that he call a manager to come out, he started telling me, if I didn't leave immediately, the police were going to be called. I said "great, I'd love to talk to the police if you're not willing to get your manager."

When I saw a police car pulling up, I calmly started walking towards the police car. The driver of the police car and I were making clear eye contact with each other, but despite him obviously seeing me, he still sped up to me, and slammed on his brakes at the last moment; he drove close enough for me to jump back suddenly. The moment the officer got out of his car, he started walking towards me in an aggressive way.

This caused me to immediately start backing up, put my hands up in the air, and say, "No confrontation. No confrontation. Why are you coming at me like that?" And then his response was, "Because let me see your hands." despite the fact that my hands were already up in the air, in a non-confrontational kind of way. Then without saying anything else, he suddenly grabbed me. But because of my understanding of the law and the Charter of Rights, I immediately knew that this was completely illegal for him to do.

As I've mentioned, because I seem to be a magnet for things like this, that is exactly why I had a tiny, 300$, high-tech, digital recorder in my pocket. This thing is so accurate, if I were to leave it in one room of my apartment, with nobody in that room, it will clearly pick up a conversation on the other side of my apartment, around thick soundproofed walls, provided the doors are open. But then, in extremely noisy environments, it'll lower the sensitivity of the microphones, and still clearly pick up conversations, rather than sounding very distorted. There are two microphones, because in addition to all the other fancy features, it uses the two microphones to compare any kind of little noises that might be picked up from being in a pocket, and then it can subtract that from the actual audio you want to hear, resulting in a very clear recording.

When the first officer grabbed me, I immediately tensed up, out of instinct, because of the problem I have with my shoulder. The traditional way police will grab you, is exactly the type of movement that is likely to cause it to dislocate. More importantly, I knew he had no right to be touching me at that point, because I hadn't done anything wrong. Since I was resisting, eventually when his partner realized he needed help, she started trying to restrain me as well. The two of them weren't able to fully restrain me, even though by their own words in their statements, I was only trying to passively resist them, and not actually try to hurt them or anything. Then another cop car showed up, with two other officers, and then a third officer started trying to restrain me with the other two, but that wasn't quite enough either. Finally, a fourth officer got involved, and eventually they were able to get the handcuffs on me. At that point one officer was holding one of my shoulders and arms, another officer had the other shoulder and arm, then the other two officers each had one of my legs. Then they carried me over to one of the police cars.

Obviously, I'm not stupid, I knew I was being arrested and brought to the police station, but I wasn't going to make it easy for them, because they were in the wrong, and I knew this was being recorded. Not just by my audio recorder, which by that point, I had tossed to the girlfriend, just so that there wasn't some kind of "accident" with my recorder when I got to the police station. I also knew the casino had a lot of security cameras, even outside.

I proceeded to make a very *big* scene. I started shouting that I'm being assaulted and my rights were being violated (all of which was 100% true), and even told the girlfriend to call the news. Because I'm good with physics, one of the things I understand, is that trying to lift a stiff person, is very different than how you pick up a limp person. So as soon as they got me to the back door of the cop car, which took them about three minutes, I suddenly started randomly switching between stiff and limp, but in a controlled way. Eventually, I threw them off balance so much, that I was able to get the 5 of us about ten or fifteen feet away from the cop car.

I know all these details so clearly, because during the trial, my lawyer took the audio from my recorder, and lined it up with the video footage from the casino, which matched up perfectly because I didn't remove anything from the audio.

After I was able to get the 5 of us about ten or fifteen feet away from the cop car, you could see how exhausted the 4 cops were, and they had to set me down for a couple of minutes to catch their breath. They were all breathing heavily, but with my body's ability to produce adrenaline the way it can, you could clearly see I was still ready to go. After their break, they picked me back up again, and it took them another few minutes to get me back to the cop car.

Even once they got me to the car door again, I was able to stick my thumbs out just enough, that they got caught on the side of the car, preventing them from being able to put me into the back. The security guard from the casino even reached in from the other side of the car, and tried pulling me as well. But still, just my thumb sticking out, was enough to prevent them from getting me in. Once they realized it was my thumb, it still took one officer about a minute, using both hands to force my thumb out of the way, until I obviously wasn't able to hold my thumb in that position anymore.

Anyone who has heard the audio recording from that night, never wants the keep hearing it after a certain point, when you could hear how much they were strangling me. They stepped on my lower back so hard, that the entire lower half of my back was one big bruise. You could even see a distinct boot print over one of my lower facet joints, that was so distinct, it would be easy to determine the size and type of boot. I could tell right away that there was some kind of damage to the joint. I paid for a private MRI within a week or two after that, because I knew I was going to be filing a lawsuit, and there was a 6-12 month wait in the public health system. The MRI did show damage to it, and that facet joint still hurts to this day.

Eventually, I was charged with resisting arrest, and assaulting a police officer, because I supposedly spat at the female officer, which I definitely didn't do. That is even a bit inconsistent with their statements that I was only "passively resisting" and not trying to hurt them. Technically, from a legal point of view, if a police officer is attempting to arrest a person, but the arrest is not a just arrest and violates the Charter of Rights, then a person can actually use as much force as is "reasonably" necessary to prevent the unjust arrest. Obviously spitting wouldn't qualify, since it does nothing reasonable towards helping prevent the unjust arrest, but because of how much they were hurting me, legally, I could have used as much force as necessary to defend against that unjust attack. During the trial, the Judge even made that exact point, but if I did everything I could to defend myself, they only would have called for more backup, and I still would have been arrested.

Because of the ongoing issues I would eventually have with those cops, I'd truly love to be able to go one-on-one with any of those assholes and put them in their place; people like that should not be cops! Morally, I would have no issue with that, just like I had no issue with trying to run Flex over; thugs are thugs, regardless of what kind of clothes they wear, and people like that need to be stood up to.

With the audio from my recorder, and the video footage from the casino, together it showed, that the four police officers and the security guard from the casino, all conspired to fabricate evidence, due to the obvious inconsistencies between the recordings, and their statements. Because of the severity of the situation, I went and found one of the best lawyers that I could, who obviously wasn't cheap, and that was a bill that took a while to pay, but when dealing with corrupt cops who all clearly lied on their statements, it was obviously a serious issue that justified the cost.

The case itself, actually took quite a few years before it was resolved. Part of the reason it took so long, was because it had happened in Québec, and the trial was mostly in French. Due to the necessity of a translator, essentially everything was said twice. Despite the severity of this case, there was still a particular moment in court that was both hilarious, and quite absurd at the same time. It happened while the first officer who grabbed me was testifying. Since everything needed to be translated, only a few sentences were said at a time. The first cop's description from when he initially decided to arrest me, until they finally got me into the back of the cop car, essentially went like this:

> After he grabbed me, he almost had control of me, but then he didn't.
> (Translator would translate.)
> Then the next officer got involved, and they almost had me, but then they didn't.
> (Translator would translate.)
> The third officer got involved, and they almost had me, but then they didn't.
> (Translator would translate.)
> The fourth officer got involved, and they finally managed to get handcuffs on me.
> (Translator would translate.)
> They struggled to get me over to the police car, almost got me in the back seat, but then they didn't.
> (Translator would translate.)
> And suddenly, for some reason he couldn't understand, we were far away from the car again.
> (Translator would translate.)
> They set me down on the ground, rested for a moment, then brought me back to the car.
> (Translator would translate.)
> They got me back to the car, but were still struggling to get me in the back seat.
> (Translator would translate.)

At this point, the Judge was looking at him a bit funny, with an obvious look, wondering why it took them so long to get *me* in the cop car. The expression was so apparent, even the testifying officer noticed, and obviously felt he needed to justify why it took them so long. He clearly became a bit nervous, because he paused, looked down for a moment to think, and for some reason, thought this next thing would be a good way to explain:

"Il semblait avoir des superpowers."

(Even though I was the only one in the courtroom that didn't understand the French, everyone still had the same expression on their faces as I did, including the translator: "Did we really just hear that?")

And then the translator says:

"It was as though he had superpowers."

In that moment, the question that was on everyone's face, had just been answered: "Yes we really did just hear that!" Then suddenly, the entire courtroom erupted with laughter! But since we were in court, just as quickly, like a well-rehearsed orchestra, everyone instantly stopped. This was followed by a really awkward pause, as everyone looked around at each other for a moment.

I can only speak for myself, and my lawyer (I asked him afterwards), but that was by far, both the funniest and most absurd thing, I have ever heard in court! This was made even more funny when you could see how awkward and uncomfortable the testifying officer was, realizing what he just said. He even tried to "fix" what he just said by saying a half formulated idea, which the translator said as, "Maybe he was on drugs, or something like that. Obviously I don't know of course."

Unsurprisingly, I told all my friends about this, that it's official, I have superpowers!

To have a bit of philosophical fun with this, I realized something not long after this happened. Of anybody in the world, police officers, might just be the foremost experts in overall human strength. Despite how much I've tried to think of other professions, such as professional fighters, or military personnel, or people that work in this psychiatric departments of hospitals, or prison guards. Prison guards would be the most comparable to a police officer, but a professional fighter is really only going to be knowledgeable about other fighters for the most part. Similarly, military personnel would generally only have experience with other trained military personnel. A police officer though, over the course of their career, essentially deals with the whole range of human strength because they deal with all sorts of different people. This definitely qualifies them as being an expert witness in the area of human strength, and such an expert, just declared, on record, that I seem to have superpowers. This actually presents a very funny question; does that make me some kind of lethal weapon? ;)

Despite how funny that was for everyone in the courtroom that day, I'm not sure how well the humor of that moment translates into a book. Besides the humor of it, there is a practical point of why brought that up, which has to do with the character of that officer. After he realized what he said, he even started blushing, but then to try fixing the stupidity of what he said by suggesting I may have been on drugs, just further makes him look like an idiot, and shows he has no issue saying whatever he thinks is "best", rather than simply speaking the truth. Of course, there is the absurdity of his comment, since I *obviously* don't have superpowers. One of the first things I thought after he said that in court, was how it is kind of an insult to him and his partners, suggesting they are weak, which is likely what motivated his following comment about drugs.

When we got to the female officer's testimony, which is who I was accused of spitting at, and she pointed that moment out in the video, I realized that yes some spit did come out of my mouth. Initially, because of the other things they said in their statements, which the audio and video prove were lies, I just assumed that the spitting thing was a lie too. But after seeing the moment in the video when she wiped her face, I do believe some spit came out of my mouth. But you can also see that I was shouting when she wiped her face off, which should have made it apparent that the spit was not intentional. That kind of accidental spitting is so common, everyone has accidentally spat on someone during a conversation, and has also accidentally been spat on. It happens all the time, but we generally just dismiss it, because of how common such a thing is.

This case went on for a number of years before I was eventually found not guilty. The Judge actually had so much to say during his final statements, that we were all in the courtroom until close to 7 at night. After he said I was not guilty, he continued talking a bit longer. I was surprised that he essentially gave the cops shit, by expressing his concern regarding the inconsistencies between all four of their statements and the evidence from the audio and video. After everything that the Judge said to the cops, I have no doubt that all four of those cops lost credibility in that Judge's eyes for any future case they may be in front of him for.

ILLEGAL ENTRY OF THE LAW

The following occurred just over a year after I took over the club, on Saturday, January 11, 2015, around 2 PM, during a private party, when the doors were locked. I was DJ'ing at the time and quite high on Ketamine. As I was DJ'ing, not long after I snorted a rather large line of Ketamine, in my peripheral vision, I suddenly thought I noticed an unusual flicker of white light near the back door. As I looked over, it was a bit hard to focus clearly on the door, which was only about 40 feet away, because of how high I was on Ketamine. After squinting my eyes and looking at the door for a few moments, I was pretty certain I saw what looked like police officers on the other side of the door. I was so certain, I immediately put down my headphones, went to the back and into my office.

There were a bunch of people hanging out in my office, and without stopping on the way to my computer, to look at the camera feeds, I casually said, "Cops are here." After not being able to see any kind of sign of the police on the cameras, as I turned around and looked at everyone in my office, I saw everyone staring at me in silence. I then said, "I think I may have just had my first hallucination." Everyone knew I had been doing a bunch of Ketamine for the last 11 hours, and even though I'd never had anything that would come even close to being a hallucination, on any drug ever, none of them knew that, so it didn't seem like an unreasonable possibility. At that point, there were no cameras looking at the other side of that door, so I asked someone if they could go make sure.

Less than a minute later, the person came back into the office, and confirmed that the cops were indeed there.

Pretty much everyone who was still at the club, was high on some drug or another, so without looking through the window on the door to see who was knocking, someone accidentally let them in.

The middle door in the hallway was shut and locked, and after the cops were let in, one officer walked to the middle hallway door, knocked, and then patiently waited. I did have cameras in that area, so I could clearly see he was there. But in that Ketamine induced state that I was in, not only was my perception of time altered, but logic is a bit different as well. I knew I had been preparing everybody for this moment, and as I started going through the details in my head, I started organizing everything that I needed to deal with the situation. The main thing that I needed, was the Charter application, but try as I may, I couldn't find the copy that I had been showing people, since it had been so long since I showed it to anyone.

So I loaded up the Charter Application on the computer and printed out a fresh copy. The printer was a rather noisy laser printer, and was in a utility room that had vents on the door, just next to the middle hallway door, directly on the other side of where the cop was patiently waiting; no doubt, he could clearly hear the sound of the printer. I went over to get the fresh copy of the Charter Application out of the printer, came back to my desk to staple it together, then suddenly realized it wasn't on legal paper. In a sober state of mind, this wouldn't have been an important detail at all, especially considering I was not submitting it to a court of law, but in that state, I just wanted to make sure that everything was proper.

Despite knowing the officer was waiting on the other side of the door very patiently, it made perfect sense to me that I should go change the paper tray in the printer, which he could obviously hear as well. So I put the legal paper in the tray, slid it back into the printer, went back into my office to switch the settings on the computer, and printed another copy on legal sized paper. I then went and got the freshly printed legal size copy, went back in my office to staple it together, neatly folded it into thirds, picked up my vaporizer, set my keys on the desk so they couldn't use them to get back in through that door, put my little 300$ audio recorder into my pocket, and then headed out the door.

As soon as I went through that middle hallway door, I quickly closed it behind me, and then politely began by stating, "We have a problem here." He replied by saying, "We *do* have a problem!" I then suggested that he go first with the problem that they had, and then just before he started speaking, I interrupted by saying, "First of all, I want to ask you, do you have a personal problem with what's going on here, or are you just following orders?" He then said, 'he has a directive, and that he was there to investigate reports of an illegal nightclub.' I then quickly pointed out that it was 2 o'clock in the afternoon, and so anything that was taking place right now, clearly had nothing to do with reports of an illegal nightclub." He then explained, that he was still required to investigate due to his directive, and they are just going to take a quick look around and it won't take too long. I then asked him his name, which he told me was Dan, at which point I gave him my name as well. I mentioned that he seemed like a nice guy and I can respect the fact that he's following orders, and I hope he doesn't take anything that I was about to say personally. I asked him if he had a search warrant, but he told me that they didn't need one. I told them that actually he did, according to section 8 of the Charter of Rights, but that I understood he was just following orders, so I'm not going to give him a hard time about it, and I'll bring it up with the appropriate person in his department. He thanked me, and said he appreciated that. He then looked down at the paper I was holding, and asked me if I had something to give him. But because he hadn't mentioned anything about drugs, I just dismissed the paper, and said it was unrelated. From that point, they took a quick look around in all the rooms that were unlocked, and didn't go past the locked hallway door into the back office area.

They also got the names of everyone who was in the main club area, which was actually in violation of section 9 of the Charter of Rights, and they got my full name as well. Then they ran all of our names through their computer, to see if anybody had any warrants or conditions. Personally, I knew I had a condition not to be drinking, because the charges from the illegal arrest at the casino were still pending.

As I was waiting in the main room with everybody else, for them to get the results of all the record checks, there were 8 police officers in total, and I noticed 2 of them, were 2 of the police officers who arrested me at the casino. One was the initial officer that got out of his car and grabbed me illegally, and the other was his female partner, that I was accused of spitting at. After the female officer recognized me, she immediately walked out the door, and when she came back in a few minutes later, she had a box in her hand, which I assumed contained a breathalyzer. After they finished getting the results back from all the record checks, the female officer looked at Dan, and asked, "Now can I?" Then in a reluctant looking way, Dan said "Yeah, sure."

At that point, she approached me and said that she was going to breathalyze me, because I have a condition not to be drinking. I objected to that, on the grounds that nobody had seen me drinking, and I show no signs of intoxication. She then replied by saying that I smell like alcohol. I explained that's because the whole room smells like alcohol, since people had been drinking all day since the club closed, and somebody spilled a beer, but that didn't dissuade her at all. I was told if I didn't blow into the breathalyzer, I would be arrested. Because I knew the arrest at the casino was illegal to begin with, I didn't feel the restriction that I couldn't drink, was a just restriction, so of course, I had no moral problem about not obeying that condition. And because they were also violating the Charter of Rights by coming in the club illegally that day, just like I did at the casino, I gave her a hard time about the breathalyzer as well.

    I started to gently blow into the machine, with my cheeks puffed completely out, as though I was blowing extremely hard, but after a few moments, the machine beeped in a way, that told the girl I didn't blow enough, and she told me I have to "Blow harder." *Of course*, I had my best Forest Gump look on my face the whole time, because the last thing you want to do in a situation like that, is give off any kind of smirk, since that would only piss them off more than they already would be from such an attempt to blow into a breathalyzer. As this went on for a couple of minutes, she became increasingly frustrated, but this was not at all a bad thing, because of the excellent audio recording I ended up getting, of this female officer, with a very cute French accent, saying things that, if you didn't know was about a breathalyzer, sounds like a very odd sexual thing was going on. During one of my attempts to blow into the machine, you can hear her saying "Blow. Blow. Harder, Harder", and many other funny things like that. Absolutely nothing in that audio recording sounds like official police business.

    Keep in mind that this was all taking place in front of about a dozen of my friends, as well as the other 7 male officers. Because she had her back to those 7 male officers, she couldn't see what I could see, which were clear smirks on their faces as they were trying not to laugh from what she was saying. At one point. she turned and asked the other officers if I was messing with her, and one of the officers nodded that I was, but they only kept watching.

    Still, with this perfect Forest Gump persona, I continued to "cooperate". I knew I was going to have to make the thing blow properly, and finally, after a little over 2 minutes of this, I eventually did. Of course it registered some sort of alcohol, because I had been drinking that night. At that point, she informed me that I was being arrested for violating my conditions of bail. I was handcuffed, brought down to the police car, had to sign a paper to go to court about that new charge, and then was released right away. (Because they were in the club illegally, the charge was ultimately dropped.)

    After I went back into the building, I headed straight into my office, and immediately transferred the recording of what just happened to my computer. I cut out just the 2 minutes of the hilarious dialog from the breathalyzer moment, analyzed it with some music software, to see which musical key it was in, which happened to be F minor, and then looked at which tracks I had that were also in the same key, and found the perfect track to mix it with. I put the recording on a USB drive, then immediately went back out to DJ, snorted some more Ketamine, turned the music up a little bit louder than it had been before they showed up, and proceeded to mix what she said into this perfectly suitable track.

The song is, quite appropriately, called, "Everyday". After a short musical intro, a guy starts saying, in a casual, non-musical tone: "You'll probably never believe, how much I did and do still love you baby….. But it's not important anymore…… I just wanna survive… I'm thinking about you, Everyday." Then he stops talking, and when the next musical verse starts, I mix in, "Blow. Do it! No, you don't blow….You need to blow harder.. Blow, Blow.. Do it.. Harder…. " And from then on, anytime I was DJ'ing, I always had the recording of her and that one specific track ready to play, *Everyday*, the cops would come back in, which of course, ended up happening. From that point on, any time I ever referenced that particular time when they came in illegally, everyone in the club knew what I was talking about when I mentioned, "Blow Blow, the remix."

In case anyone is wondering about the legality of recording someone without the person knowing, in Canada, the law states that as long as one person who is part of the recording knows it is being recorded, then it is perfectly legal, and because I always know when the recorder is in my pocket, I don't need to say anything about it.

Some of you might feel I went a bit far with that, but I'm sure most of you will find it as funny as we did, and still do, Everyday. But from a moral point of view, I can't imagine how anyone could feel that was morally wrong at all. Not only were *they* in the wrong, both at the casino and that after-noon at the club, but also lied on their statements from the casino, and then the fact that she felt she needed to go even further and try to pin another stupid charge on me, leaves me having absolutely no sympathy for her at all. If she's not going to be considerate of other people's rights, she has no grounds to complain about me using her funny comments, to bring joy to all of the people that would come to the club to dance, and forget about their problems in life; only to need to deal with police harassing us and violating our rights, when we were not bothering or hurting anyone, simply because we enjoy different things than they do.

Now that I think about that story, this is a good example of how I will redirect one emotion into another; in this case I'm redirecting anger and frustration into humor, and at least in this case, that doesn't seem like an unhealthy thing to do; at least as long as one is aware they are doing it.

House: 3, Visitors: 0

ACCIDENTAL BREAK AND ENTERING

By the end of the party that following morning, most of the people that were there that night ended up hearing about what happened. But not only did that not discourage any of them from wanting to stay for the after-after party, Sunday morning, but there were about twice as many people than the day before.

Around 8 or 9 in the morning, I got a call from a friend of mine, saying that he just got a call from a Quebec Provincial Police Officer he knows, was told that the police were planning to come back again, and that we should probably all go home. I politely thanked him for his courtesy call, but explained, I saw no concern that would cause me to want to leave. This time, as soon as the private party started, we made a point to explain to everybody, that under no circumstances, do they open the door for anyone, regardless of how hard they're knocking. We also put up a black garbage bag covering the window, and made sure to have the music quite a bit louder that morning.

At precisely 11 o'clock a.m., as I was sitting in my office with a number of others, suddenly everyone from the main room started pouring into my office. We were quickly informed that the police were there, and just broke the window on the door. I immediately started looking at the cameras, but didn't see any police officers in the main room yet.

I would later learn, when I examined all the footage in detail once they left, they had been pounding on the door, so hard, for so long, it left well over a dozen deep dents in the brand-new steel door. They were pounding on the door with enough force, to cause a camera, mounted on the wall 30 feet away, to shake each time they hit the door! The camera was shaking for quite a while, but everybody was still dancing, because they clearly didn't hear it over the music. After the shaking stopped, there was a brief pause, and then suddenly after that pause, everybody on the dance floor, all at once, quickly headed towards my office, as in some kind of great Exodus.

After the excessive and repeated pounding failed to achieve their goal, the officer that was pounding on the door, most likely turned to the commanding officer, Dan, to ask what to do next. After that pause, everybody started rushing out of the main room when they heard the glass break. I suspect that breaking the glass was an accident, because once the glass was broken, there was another longer pause, before they started clearing away the rest of the glass, so they could reach inside and open the door. This suggests the officer who broke the window, likely didn't mean to, had an "Oh Shit!" moment (or in French, "Tabernac!"), and then turned to Dan again, to ask what to do next.

The officer was likely pumped full of adrenaline and was frustrated after pounding on the door for so long, he probably unintentionally used too much force when he started tapping on the glass. If they were really planning to break the window, not only am I sure they would have had a search warrant, which they didn't have, but no doubt they would have broken the window almost from the start. As any good commanding officer would do after such a mistake was made, he probably quickly considered his options, which in this case, would be to either leave, or proceed to go in, even though it would be technically breaking and entering, unlike the day before, when it was just an unlawful entry. It doesn't require very much imagination to realize how much worse it would have looked on them, if they had run away after accidentally breaking into a place.

Once inside, unlike the day before, they were moving in a stereotypical, secure the room kind of fashion. It's hard to tell from the videos, because of the low resolution of those cameras, if they actually had their guns out, or if it was just them holding the flashlights in a similar way, but they moved in away as though there were in full tactical mode, clearly because of the obvious threat from a bunch of people dancing and minding their own business, on that lovely Sunday morning. For the record though, I never saw any guns drawn. This time, they didn't stop at the locked hallway door, and ultimately searched the entire place; they even forcefully broke into the rooms that were locked. I still have pictures and the videos of all of the damage they caused.

This time, we were all made to sit on the floor in the main room. But because I had been preparing most of these people for almost a year, for just such an occurrence, everyone was completely on point. As we were sitting on the floor, *everyone,* except me, was talking to someone they were sitting next to, about how wrong the cop's actions were. As each officer tried telling people to stop talking, everyone responded by saying they didn't have to be quiet, because the cops are violating their rights! Upon witnessing this beautiful moment, I decided to lean back against the wall, to relax and enjoy the show, wishing for nothing more than a bit of popcorn.

After about 10 minutes, when the cops seemed to have given up telling people to be quiet, and were all having a humble conference in the middle of the room, I could see how frustrated Dan was, and because Dan was a respectable guy, I decided to end my brief sabbatical. I sat back up, got Dan's attention, and asked him if I could say something to everyone quickly. After he agreed, I said to the group, "Can everyone be quiet for a moment?" but nobody seemed to hear me. So I did what I learned to do in my office, any time I wanted to quickly get everyone to quiet down, and said, "EVERYONE SHOOOOOOOOSH!" And like a well-trained army, immediately everyone was absolutely silent; you could've a heard cricket sleeping in the other room. Even the officers were shocked. and they looked around at each other for a moment, clearly surprised I was so easily able to do, what they could not.

I then said to the group, "I know you're all aware that a number of our rights are being violated, and I'm sure none of these officers want to be here…" then I paused for a moment, looked directly at the 2 officers from the casino, and I continued by saying, "…well at least most of them, but we can deal with the legal issues later. To get this over with as quickly as possible, I kindly ask everyone to cooperate with the officers, so they can be on their way, and we can continue our party." At that point everyone respectfully did what I asked, and started cooperating with the police.

Shortly after that, I noticed the female officer coming back into the club, once again with the breathalyzer. As the other officers were getting everyone's names, she was sitting in front of the door, staring directly at me with a smug look on her face, and slightly swinging the case she was holding in front of her. She knew, if I had 2 breaches in a row, unlike the day before, when I was released as soon as I signed the paper, this time, I would have to be brought down to the jail and wait to see a Judge Monday morning. I knew this as well, but because I just did Dan a favor, and I knew there was mutual respect from the day before, I politely asked him, if I could get a drink from the bar. He turned and said, "Ya, no problem."

As I walked towards the bar, which was right next to the door the female officer was standing in front of, she immediately started trying to get Dan's attention, because she wanted me to blow into her little toy again. As soon as I noticed Dan wasn't responding, as I was walking towards her, I looked her directly in the eyes, and smiled with the same intensity as the stupid, smug look she no longer had on her face; I'm sure she realized what I wanted to do. I knew exactly what was in the fridge, but I'm sure she was still shocked at what I did next. I knew the best chance I had of messing up the results of the test, would be to do something I wouldn't normally ever want to do!

When I got to the fridge, I made up for the lack of chemistry between her and I, by creating quite the chemical reaction inside of my stomach. First, I grabbed a protein drink, and guzzled that down in about 5 seconds. Next, I took a V-8, and chugged that down just as quick. Finally, I picked up a can of coke, turned and looked at her again, so she could see what *my* smugness looks like, then I casually walked by her and went to sit back down to enjoy my refreshing beverage.

By the time I got to the other side of the room, as I turned and sat back down, there was just enough time for me to see how pissed off she was, as she turned and shoved the door open, to go outside and put her perverted toy away. Despite how defiled my mouth felt, after the flagrant culinary transgression I just subjected myself to, I decided to courteously wait until she returned. As she walked back in, I looked at her once again, gracefully opened the can of coke, took a sip, and washed away what remained of the vile hope she had.

House: 4, Visitors 0

MY FRIEND, DAN THE COP AND I

(This particular moment was actually a direct continuation of the same event from the last chapter, and happened just minutes later, but it seemed special and unique enough to separate it under its own heading.)

After I finished savoring the blow and pop of the female cop's ego, and were now just waiting for all the record checks to come back over their radios, I asked Dan if I could go to my office to get my vaporizer, and again, he politely affirmed. So I got up off the floor, headed towards my office, and Dan followed behind me.

At the time, I was selling E-smoke vaporizers at the club, because a buddy of mine owns one of the big chains of E-smoke stores in the city, and I got them slightly above his cost. My motivation wasn't actually profit, since I'd only be making 10 $ on each of them, and would never be something I'd be able to sell enough of to make any sort of noticeable amount of money. My only motivation was the desire to potentially help people quit smoking. Sure the vaporizers are still harmful, but they're not carcinogenic at all, and are way less harmful than cigarettes.

When we walked into my office, I picked up my vaporizer off my desk, turned around to walk back out, and in the audio-video recording from inside my office, you can hear me start saying, "Do you know anybody that smokes?" because I was going to try to sell him a vaporizer, simply because it seemed like a funny thing to do.

He either didn't notice, or merely dismissed the trivial question I asked, because as I finished asking, he started saying, "Adam, you know, off the record… That's not good…" as he pointed to 3 small piles, of 3 different drugs, on my side of the desk. He then points at a sign I had just put up on my desk that weekend, which read, "By the Gram, Marijuana for Sale!" (Which was truly meant as a joke, because everyone there knew, weed isn't a club drug. And further, as an inside joke, because there were definitely more than a few people, who would often be way too wired, from doing too much speed, and that sign was offering a thing that would calm those space cadets down.)

So when he pointed to the sign, and said, "What's up with that? Come on." I let out this huge smile, and truthfully said, "That's a Joke! It's satire!" He then says, "Ok, ok, whatever." He then started to say something about how I run my establishment…" that he never actually finished, because at the same time, I asked, "Is any of your stuff recording?" He then replied by saying, "No, this is all off the record." Then I continued, "Ok, just between you and me…(and countless others, since I knew my stuff *was* recording.)", then there was a slight pause, as I gathered my thoughts, and then I continued, "I've always loved experimenting with drugs." Then he tried to interrupt, but I insisted, and when he allowed me to continue, I said "I don't know, but you probably did some stuff when you're younger." But I saw the look on his face as I said that, and then I said, "Ok, maybe not, but you know friends…" And his reaction that time, made me think that yes, he definitely does. I further added, "Some people can drink all their lives, and never have a problem. And other people, they have a problem with it."

As he agreed, I carried on, "Any other drug, from my experience, being around, because I like dancing, and stuff like that. Being around it, I'll do a little bit here and there, but I'm a healthy individual, I'm 34, but I don't look like it… and what I've found, is that most people, just like with alcohol, will regulate themselves." During this whole time, he said yes and agreed multiple times with what I was saying. Then I finished what I wanted to say, "… and the whole drug issue is really what this is all about. You know how it is with politics?" He then said, "Yes, I know how it is!" And then the conversation changes, because he could tell I made the point I wanted to make. He then said, "So what I want to do, is to take a few pictures in here, because I'm allowed… " (Which isn't true, because they broke in illegally, without a search warrant.) then tried to justify his actions, by saying, "because of what is called the Plainview theory." But that would only be valid, if they were not violating Section 8 of the Charter.

Before we left the office, I actually told him something that was partly true, and partly a lie. It was true, on a personal level towards him because he was a very respectful person, but wasn't true from a legal point of view, because of the unjust orders he had been given. I mentioned that I felt his conduct was very admirable, which he thanked me for saying. I then made a comment about how I'm sure he appreciated what I did out there (by helping them get everybody to stop talking.) And then quite passionately, he said, "Yes, I do appreciate it. A lot actually. It was Very admirable."

As we started walking out of the office, I asked him who I should be getting in contact with, about this incident. He replied by telling me that I'm not being charged. But if I was being charged, he gave me the name and number, of the person who's in charge of penal accusations.

Not long after we got back in the main room, the 8 of them left, once again, accomplishing nothing, other than putting smiles on our faces. At least they got some nice souvenirs from the pictures they took, which I decided not to charge them for, that they could hang on their wall back at the station, because of the pictures they got, as evidence of a great party.

A few days later, I had my "secretary" (girlfriend) contact the officer he referred me to, because I wanted to address the issue head on. I thought the secretary calling, would be a ridiculously professional touch, on par with how ridiculous their professionalism had been. And after a week or so, without my call being returned, I had her call again to leave another message, but they maintained their same level of professionalism, and never did return my calls. Considering the magnitude of their fuck-up, no doubt they were worried I could file charges against them at any point within 2 ½ years from when they broke in.

No charges were ever filed against me, and they didn't even take my drugs that were on my desk. Gee, I wonder why?

House 5: Visitors 0

A FEW OTHER RANDOM EVENTS

In reality, there were so many crazy things that happened during those two and a half years I owned the club, that it could easily make an interesting book all on its own, and who knows, if this book is successful, maybe I'll write one just about the club another day. But for the purpose of this book, and not wanting it to be too long, I've only picked the stories that I felt fit in with the theme of this particular book.

One incident that I forgot about, involving a knife, actually happened at the club. So technically, I've had two and a half knives pulled on me. I say "half", because it wasn't really pulled *on me*. During one of the private after parties, this one guy, was having a serious mental health problem, and although, he did pull out a knife, it wasn't at anyone specific. It was obvious that he was in a complete state of panic and full of fear. The afternoon when this happened, there was less than 10 people at the club, and while I was DJ'ing, someone came and told me about what was happening. Of course I immediately stopped and attended to the issue. As soon as I saw the state that he was in, I realized a very non-aggressive approach would be best, rather than trying to disarm him with force, like I had done the previous two times knives were pulled on *me*.

Initially, I just tried talking with him, very calmly, trying to reassure him, that we were all friends, and nobody wants to hurt him. To further help reassure him, I made a decision that certainly put myself at greater risk, but in that moment, it seemed like the right decision. What I did, was basically sit down in front of him very slowly, but I sat in such a way, that I could easily jump up in a moment's notice, hoping that moment would not come. It seemed to help, because it definitely caused him to become a bit confused, and less afraid; he even took a step back, as though questioning what he was doing. At that point, he lowered the knife a bit, and told me he just wanted to leave. So we unlocked the door, and off he went.

As soon as he left, I had a quick conversation with everyone who was there, because I didn't want to call the police, to report such a troubled soul, and I was hoping there was a small chance someone might know something about him, that would make me feel less concerned and change my mind about calling the police, but the conversation only made me more certain that I needed to report him. To ensure the police understood clearly, I asked someone who was fluent in French to call, and made sure they really stressed the fact that he wasn't being violent or aggressive, but only pulled the knife out, because he was panicking, and very afraid someone was going to hurt him, even though there was absolutely no threat towards him. We never found out what ended up happening with him that day, but eventually we did hear that he got some help, in some kind of mental institution. Needless to say he was never allowed back.

One more quick thing I'd like to briefly touch on, but don't feel is necessary, to go into any kind of lengthy detail.

After the police broke in to the club illegally, those two afternoons at the beginning of the year, the police essentially stopped coming all together, for the remainder of the year and a half that I own the club. They didn't even do the regular patrols anymore and it seemed like they had finally just given up. There was one specific time though, when the cops came in, and once again violated section 8 of the Charter of Rights. This time, it was a new group of young cops, and it kind a seemed like they wanted to try to make a name for themselves, and do what none of the other seasoned cops had been able to do. Essentially, as a buddy of mine exited the VIP door, even though my buddy tried to close the door quickly behind him, you can see in the video footage, that the female cop that was right next to the door, quickly put her foot in front of the door, preventing it from being closed. After that, they went and searched around the back, again without a search warrant, and even went all the way into my office, but once again left empty handed.

House: 6, Visitors 0

OFFICER SIMON'S UNEXPECTED TRIP

The last 2 stories I will be sharing about the club, both involved police officers, and was ultimately what made me decide to finally close the club.

This particular event happened on May 29, 2016, and was a night where I once again say "as luck would have it". The reason why I say this is because it was the first night in the almost 2 and a half years that I own the club, when I had taken LSD. It's typically a very hard drug to come across, and there wasn't even any going around at the time, it just happened that while cleaning one of my drawers of goodies out at home, I discovered 20 or so hits of really good acid that I forgot I'd been saving for a special occasion, and this night, would turn out to be a very special occasion indeed.

Shortly after the party started, my amazing girlfriend, Karo, and I, decided to do about 5 hits of acid each. At approximately 5:30 in the morning, when the acid was in full effect, and the black-and-white video feeds from the cameras in the club, were actually very colorful to watch, but just like with most drugs that I take, I have a surprising ability to be able to still function quite well, and often even after doing a lot of a drug, it's still hard for a lot of people to notice that I'd taken anything at all, at least if I don't want them to notice.

As I was sitting in my office with Karo, and 2 other friends, suddenly my bouncer/manager, came into the office and informed me that the police were there and wanted to speak with me. Now every time the cops had ever came to the club, and wanted to speak with me personally, every single time I have asked, "Did they ask for me by name, or did they ask to speak to the owner." Just like they did every other time, this time they also asked to speak with the owner. The reason why I always asked that question, without exception, is because if they came in and asked for me by name, it could be seen as harassment, especially considering the incident at the casino.

After hearing that one of the officers wanted to speak with me, I got up and followed my bouncer down the hallway, through the door that separated the club from the VIP area, and to my surprise, I couldn't see any officers around. I found this surprising, because every single time they wanted to talk with me personally, they had always been waiting in that area. So I asked my bouncer, "Where are the cops at?" and then he told me that there waiting outside in their car. As we started walking through the dance floor, towards the back door that goes downstairs to the parking lot, I was thinking about this odd feeling I had, which I didn't find pleasant. (Remember I was high on 5 hits of LSD at the time, so I was very reflective, and spending much more time thinking about each possibility, about how I felt, then I normally would when I'm sober, and able to think about so many possibilities, in a very short period of time. In reality, I was likely thinking just as quickly, but just had a lot more thoughts going through my mind.)

By the time I got to the door at the top of the stairwell, just as I opened the door and was about to start walking down the stairs, I suddenly realized exactly what I was feeling inside that I didn't like. I was feeling insulted, very insulted. The reason why I felt insulted was that they came to *my* place to talk to me, and instead of having the respect and courtesy to come up like they had always done in the past, all of a sudden this time, not only are they interrupting my evening, but they want *me*... to walk downstairs... To talk to *them?* How rude and selfish of them I thought to myself. So just before I started to walk down the stairs, I stopped, turned around and went back into the club, thinking to myself, "I need to take a piss; they can fucking wait!"

After I finished in the washroom, I decided to go back into my office. When I got into the office, I hadn't been gone very long, so Karo and my 2 friends were looking at me, as though they were surprised at how quickly I was back. But I didn't say anything to them, and they were just kind of watching me to see what I was doing, as though maybe I'd forgotten something important. I hadn't forgotten anything, but I was doing something important. I just felt that my office was slightly dusty, so I walked around and inspected the dust, by sliding my finger across the different surfaces.

Once again, if there's any Star Trek fans out there, who like The Next Generation, you may know the particular episode that I'm referring to. The Captain was dealing with a particularly rude species, that kept hanging up on him throughout the whole episode, when finally, the Captain found some obscure law, within a treaty between the 2 species, that finally gave the captain the upper hand. After explaining that point to this rude species, suddenly they wanted to talk, but this time the captain, in a very uncharacteristic way, cut off the conversation with them. Immediately after, the other species called them back, but he just continued to ignore the call for quite some time. And similarly to my 3 friends in my office that night, his entire bridge crew just kind of looked at him, wondering what the heck he's doing, as he walked over to a plaque on the wall, and started inspecting how dusty the top of it was. Well that was my exact inspiration for what I was doing at that present moment, as I intentionally made them wait, until I felt like going down to talk to them.

Eventually, after a few minutes of some mild finger dusting in my office, I decided to casually make my way downstairs. Talked with a few people on the way, asked the bartender how sales were, walked down the stairs, asked the coat check the same question, and eventually made my way outside.

The door to the building exits directly into a parking lot, onto a short brick walkway, and is level with the lot. The back of my car is about five feet away on my right, closely parked alongside, and parallel to the building. The cop car is just to the left of the walkway, about 15 feet in front of me, facing in the direction of my car. I walk past the front of the cop car, turn left, approach the opened driver's side window, and bend down slightly; making eye contact with the driver. I'm certain I recognize him, but after seeing so many cops at the club during the previous two and a half years, usually while I'm intoxicated on one thing or another, I have no idea where I've seen him before.

I then ask the driver, "You wanted to speak with me?" He then says the very proper thing, by asking, "Are you the owner?" After I tell him, I am, he informs me that they had a noise complaint, and they are here simply to ask me to turn the music down. This is quite confusing, and sounds completely absurd, because the club has been here for about 8 years, and this is the first time there has ever been a complaint about the noise. Additionally, there are no residential homes nearby. The club is surrounded by government office towers and some light industrial buildings.

So I ask him, "Who made the complaint?" He says he doesn't need to tell me, so I explained: because there are no residential buildings nearby, in this case, I do have the right to know. Section 11 of the Charter says, if I am going to be charged with an offence, I have the right to be informed of the reason why, and considering nobody lives nearby, it's not at all reasonable for there to be a noise complaint, which goes against Section 1 of the Charter! Still, he keeps insisting he doesn't have to tell me, and says, "We've just had a complaint, but if you turn the music down, there won't be any problem." This only frustrates me even more, so I stand straight up, and take a couple steps back, because I know I'm about to raise my voice.

I begin shouting quite loudly, start pointing up at the buildings on the other side of the street, and tell him, "You've got government buildings there! You've got government buildings over there! You've got government buildings all around us! So who the fuck's complaining?!!" Finally, he admits: they are the ones who are complaining, "...on behalf of community." At that point, it finally makes sense! My face lights up as I'm understanding the extent of this absurdity, and now I'm shouting even louder, as I start telling him:

"Oh! You're the one who's complaining! I understand. So what you're saying, is if the two of you weren't complaining, then there'd be nobody complaining! And nobody be complaining, if the two of you stopped complaining!! And none of us would complain, if the two of you got the Fuck out of here! And stopped complaining!!!" At that point he looks at his partner with a rather uncertain look on his face, and then I ask, "Do you know Dan?" But he says, "Dan who?" So I point at the left side of my chest where Dan's military awards were, and repeat, "You know!.... DAN!" as I keep pointing at my chest. When he finally understands who I'm talking about, he says, "Dan's not here right now." Then I say, "Let's talk to Dan about this and see what he has to say!" He then repeats. "Dan's not here right now!" So I say, "But if he was here, I bet he'd be more *my* friend than Yours!" Then suddenly, with the sharp prick of that realization, it was clear that I punctured the balloon of his overly-inflated ego. So I say to him, "Fuck it! You want to give me a ticket? Give it to my bouncer, bitch!"

I then turn and start walking towards the door.

Just as I grab the door handle, he leans out his car window, mumbles something unintelligible, then points at my car in front of him, and says something about my license plate. (Oh! He does know who I am, despite pretending like he didn't when I first came out, and he asked, if I was the owner. Oops! Dumbass just fucked up a little bit there.) I immediately turn around, and say to him, "Yeah that's my car, registered in Ontario, private citizen. What the Fuck does that have to do with anything?!" What he says next, is so shocking, I'm initially in disbelief about what I hear. The idiot actually says, "Oh, I know where you live!" Stunned, I repeat what he just said, "You know where I live?" to make sure I heard it correctly. As I slowly walk back towards his open window, so I can look him in the eyes without the windshield in the way, I continue by saying: "You know where I live? Are you threatening me?" And then once I get around the other side of his car again and while looking directly at him, I repeat, "You know where I live?!" and then yelled, "YOU'RE A FUCKING POLICE OFFICER! I HOPE YOU KNOW WHERE I LIVE!... YOU DUMB FUCK!"

I then turned around, started talking with the people sitting on the guardrail, who were outside having a cigarette, enjoying the show the whole time, and rhetorically asked, in a voice easily loud enough for that moron to certainly hear, "How stupid do you have to be, to make a threat like that, in front of a bunch of witnesses?!" Then not long after, they start backing out of the parking lot, and for good measure, as they were backing out, I started pointing and yelling at them some more!

Once they were gone, I went back upstairs to my office, and immediately one of my friends says, "WOW! You were really giving those cops shit!" Initially, between the 5 hits of Acid that were in full effect, and still distracted by the parking lot excitement, I was a bit surprised when I heard him say that. So I asked, "You could hear me yelling? He didn't actually hear me, but they were watching the lively video feeds on one of my computer monitors, and because of how animated I was while yelling at them, the extent to how much I was giving them shit, was clearly evident!

House: 7: Visitors 0

A few weeks later, I got a 641$ fine in the mail for a noise violation, but this was a good thing! Because of this noisy stupidity of his, by sending me a fine, he also gave me his name and badge number! This also told me where I knew him from; he was the exact officer who initially grabbed me at the casino illegally! He was also at the club both days when they came in illegally! Now, not only did he come and harass me again, he threatened me as well! It gets even better though, because the name on the fine says: "Legal Entity: BPM NIGHTCLUB". The dumb ass, either didn't realize, or was too stupid to remember, that this was a private club, without a business license, and therefore there is no such legal entity called BPM NIGHTCLUB. Because of this, if I were to have actually went to pay the fine (which I obviously didn't do) I would in fact be committing fraud since I knew there is no such legal entity called BPM NIGHTCLUB. So thank you Simon for the wonderful souvenir, it is now sitting on my bookshelf next to the piece of Flex's car!

One point for giving me his badge number and more documented proof of harassment...

House: 8, Visitors: 0

...and then another point for giving me the wonderful souvenir, which I can't legally pay.

House: 9, Visitors: 0

ILLEGAL ARREST AND ASSAULT

The following weekend, around midnight, as Karo and I pulled up into the club parking lot behind the building, there was a police car waiting on the street that immediately followed in behind us.

When we got out, I purposely left my bag in the car and locked the door behind me. The officer approached me, and demanded to see my ID. I then asked why I was being detained and being asked to show him my ID, which I have the right to know under Section 10 Subsection a, of the Charter of Rights. The answer he gave me was, "Because I'm telling you to." I then told him that's not a valid reason under the Charter because that violates Section 9, which is the right against being arbitrarily detained or imprisoned, him just "telling me to" is obviously completely arbitrary. It also violates Section 1, because limiting my rights in such a way would not pass the test for "reasonableness".

He then changed his reason, by telling me it was because he saw me driving my car, and that's reason enough. Of course, it isn't, since that is also arbitrary. So I insisted that he call a supervisor, which of course he also refused to do. He then told me that if I didn't show him my ID, I was going to be arrested. To which I responded by telling him, I don't have to legally show him my ID unless he has a reason, that's not arbitrary.

Then he said I was being arrested for not cooperating with the police, so at that point I said I'd show him my ID, but he said it's too late, which it obviously was not, and is another arbitrary thing. Then he immediately grabbed me in an aggressive way, all of which was completely illegal and against the Charter. Just like at the casino, I immediately tensed up to protect my shoulder.

Despite the fact that neither he nor is partner called for backup on their radios, which can be clearly seen from the security videos, somehow 4 cop cars knew to suddenly show up, and you can also see on the videos that the cars were coming down the street well before he decided to arrest me. At which point, all of the officers got out of their cars and rushed at me. Even though I was already on the ground and being securely held by 4 officers, the last officer that showed up, felt for some reason that he needed to start punching me on my lower back, which happened to be exactly where the damaged joint is from the other cops stepping on my back at the casino, and has only caused it to hurt a little more since.

Ultimately, I was charged with resisting arrest, and after they searched my locked car illegally using my keys to unlock it, they found my bag of drugs, and once again I was charged with possession for the purpose of trafficking.

In this case, because of the evidence that I have which shows their wrongdoing, I consider this to be a point for the house. When it comes to assault causing bodily harm, there is no statute of limitations regarding how long you have to press charges or sue. The only reason why I haven't filed a lawsuit yet, is because I simply haven't been able to afford it.

I initially filed a lawsuit shortly after the casino incident, because of the damage they caused to one of my facet joints, and as I mentioned not only did the MRI show the damage shortly after the incident, but it's continued to get worse over the years, just as the doctor predicted. The reason why I didn't follow through with the lawsuit, was because I was waiting until the outcome of the trial was determined. By the time I was finally acquitted of the charges, I was already having difficulties with the same cops at the club, but because they had started to leave us alone, and my natural tendency to avoid conflict if it's not something I'm being actively faced with, I decided not to do anything that would likely cause them to start harassing us again.

This kind of behavior is obviously not acceptable. The police are supposed to be there to stand up for people who have their rights violated and not be the ones who are violating people's rights, and with the indictable evidence I have, justice will eventually be served.

House: 10, Visitors: 0

A few days later, two detectives stopped by the club to talk to me, because the city had finally decided to give me two fines for operating an illegal "nightclub", which were 600 dollars each. If it wasn't for what happened with the cops over the last two weekends, first with the one threatening me and then the following weekend when they basically followed through with the threat, then I would've fought those tickets in court, because like I said before, I'm sure that those bylaws are unconstitutional, but at that point, I had already decided I'd be closing the club.

I'm sure they probably feel like it was their point, but I'm sure they won't feel that way after I finally file a lawsuit, which for any sort of indictable offenses such as assault causing bodily harm, there is no statute of limitations in Canada (or in simple terms, there is no time limit).

CHARTER APPLICATION – ROUND DEUX

Just like the first time when I was charged with trafficking, I also admitted to the charges this time as well, even though they didn't have a book proving it. I even knew I could file a Charter application under Section 8, because they searched my car illegally, but I didn't want to fight it that way. When I was first arrested that night, I told them to look into my bag, and they would find that laminated business card of the Federal Prosecutor who dropped the case the first time, which I still had in my bag all those years for just such an occasion. I told them to give him a call, and he would explain to them why it's futile to prosecute me for drug charges. I highly doubt they ever called him, but considering this happened on the weekend, he wouldn't have replied until after I was already charged.

This next bit may seem like a random tangent, but it quickly relates. Something I have slowly noticed since I moved to Ottawa almost 20 years ago, is a subtle, but unspoken rivalry between Gatineau and Ottawa. I'm sure nobody in any kind of official position would ever admit to that, but it's obvious to anyone that pays attention to the subtle, but noticeable signs. I've been living in the area long enough to realize the type of pride that the people of Québec have. I'm not saying there's anything wrong with that, quite the opposite. I'm actually half French Canadian myself and I wish I knew how to speak fluent French. People should generally be proud of their heritage, and it's understandable that they would feel particularly protective of theirs, knowing how it's slowly being changed and influenced by the mostly English country they find themselves surrounded by.

I have no doubt, at least in some way, this influenced the way the prosecutors in Quebec proceeded differently than the federal prosecutor in Ottawa did. If for no other reason, there's also the language difference. Every prosecutor I dealt with while I was fighting these new drug charges on the Québec side, was obviously very French and even though all of them could speak fluent English, it was still clear it wasn't their first language, and the Charter Application that I wrote is obviously not a simple document to quickly understand, even for a lawyer who is fully fluent in English.

Since I knew I was facing a slightly more difficult situation this time, I got back to work, and because of all of the times I thoroughly explained the first Charter Application to hundreds of people while I owned the club, I already knew of ways to make it even more bulletproof. As I mentioned previously about the first Charter Application, I was planning to rely on a bunch of scientific evidence, which would've required me to find expert witnesses to support the evidence that I was planning to use, and that would've cost a bunch of money. So this time I decided to take a completely different approach.

Rather than relying on any scientific evidence at all, I decided to focus my research on the debates in the House of Commons and the Senate that occurred when the Bill was first introduced, which eventually got passed, and became the Controlled Drugs and Substances Act. Ultimately, that is what I was being charged under, and is also the act which fundamentally places unconstitutional restrictions on the drugs that it deems to be illegal. Initially I knew I had my work cut out for me, and was expecting to be spending a lot of time at the National Library; spending countless hours, going through all of the Hansard records of all of the past debates. But to my surprise and delight, I discovered that the entire Hansard collection is not only available online, but the text has been indexed, which means it's searchable. Over a period of many weeks, I very thoroughly found every single reference pertaining to Bill C-7/Bill C-8, which ultimately became the Controlled Drugs and Substances Act. Eventually, I found almost 300 examples that overwhelmingly prove drug laws are unconstitutional.

I fully explain everything on my site, www.daffa.org. The website contains the actual case files, the source files for all the evidence, and a number of other things as well. I explain the legal details in a simple and easy to understand way; if you are able to read this book, you should just as easily be able to understand the simple explanation I wrote on the site. If you'd rather listen, I included a few short videos that also explains everything. Since this is an issue that affects us all, even non-drug users, I recommend everyone spend a few minutes to understand for yourself.

By using evidence from the lawmakers in Parliament, no witnesses are needed to testify to the validity, accuracy or merit of any of that evidence, since lawyers and judges in a Court of Law, are already expert witnesses.

After I compiled all the evidence into 3 coil bound books, I had to make five copies, due to the nature of the argument I was going to be presenting in the Charter Application. I was required to submit a copy of the evidence to the Federal Prosecutor, the Attorney General of Québec, the Attorney General of Canada, a copy for the court file for whatever Judge that would preside over the case, and finally a copy for myself.

Eventually a hearing was held this time, but to my surprise, the Superior Court Judge, essentially refused to even listen to the Charter Application and the case that I put together, on the grounds that she didn't understand how any of my rights were being limited, and that unless I could convince her of how my rights are being limited, she wasn't required to listen to the argument in the Charter Application. Yes, that's right! Let there be no misunderstanding about what I just said there! Somehow she was unable to understand that drug laws place limits to our rights. The very fact that I was required to be in court to defend myself, should be self-evident to even somebody in grade 8, that rights are being limited! Even the prosecutor from the Attorney General's office of Québec, agreed that rights were obviously being limited!

She did mention that even if she did see how rights were being limited, that she wouldn't have the jurisdiction to hear that kind of constitutional argument anyway. I didn't know that at the time, but it actually made a lot of sense as soon as she said it, and supports my previous belief that I expected it to eventually end up in front of the Supreme Court. She could have just said that from the beginning, instead of the two hours of us basically going around in circles, while I was trying to explain to her the obvious fact that the prosecutor even agreed with; that there's no question about rights being limited! The very fact that the Judge said that she couldn't see that obvious fact, essentially says one of three things: either she really couldn't see the obvious, or she did see the obvious, and was just lying and pretending that she didn't, or the Charter application I wrote was too complicated for her to understand; regardless of what the reason was, anyone of those, shows a level of gross professional incompetence that makes me think she should not be a Judge at any level of court, especially not at the Superior level!

My dad came from Detroit to watch the hearing, as well as two other friends, and all of us felt what she was saying was absolutely absurd. After the absurdity of that hearing, that only further convinced me of the merit of the case that I'd put together. Personally I don't believe that she didn't understand what I wrote, but rather, the way she was that day, just made me think that they were afraid they would lose, because the only reason that I can think of which explains why she didn't just say from the start she didn't have the authority to rule on that issue, is to try to discourage me from appealing the decision. I wasn't discouraged though, but rather I was even more determined than ever to see it through to the Supreme Court. The next step though, would've been the Québec Court of Appeal, and after going around in circles with her for two or three hours, I even told her I thought what she was saying was ridiculous, and if she was refusing to listen to the case, then I would be appealing it right away, and that ended that hearing right then and there.

As I mentioned, I knew the cops searched my car illegally in the first place, but I didn't want to fight it that way, because I was pretty sure I would win. If I did, I knew I would feel the same way I did after the first time, when they dropped the first drug charges a few years before that. I never did stop feeling that way, which was the reason I wasn't concerned about spreading the rumor about my license to sell, when I owned the club. At some point after that farce of a hearing, my dad ended up asking me to at least try challenging the validity of the search, and after asking me a few times, his concern was quite noticeable, so eventually I did file a motion under Section 8 of the Charter, but I didn't really feel it was something I was doing for myself.

A trial date was set after that ridiculous Charter hearing, and the prosecutor also knew I was going to be filing another motion under Section 8, and the Charter hearing for this new motion was going to occur the same day, directly before the trial. When that day finally came, Karo came as well, as a witness, since she was with me and also got arrested the same night at the club. On the prosecution's side, the Crown had as her witnesses, four of the cops that were there the night I got arrested. During any kind of hearing, witnesses that haven't testified yet, or may need to testify again, are required to stay out of the courtroom, as to not create any kind of bias or influence in their minds.

As soon as the Charter hearing began, the Crown called her first witness, which was the initial officer that wanted to see my ID, and after about ten minutes of asking him questions, it was then my turn. The first few questions that I had, related to some contradictory things he said in his statement, and were intended to get him to commit to those specific details. I intentionally designed these questions, to seem as unrelated to each other as possible, and after he committed to those answers, that's when I was going to really dig into him, and expose his contradictions in a completely obvious way. After asking only my second question to that first officer, the Judge apologized for interrupting me as I began my next question, because he wanted to ask the Crown something. He then asked the Crown, if all of her other questions for her other witnesses followed the same kind of theme. After she told the Judge, yes, the Judge then said: "Ok, what I'm going to suggest then, so that were not wasting court time, or anybody else's time that's here right now, because it's not as though I don't have other things to do, I actually have a lot of things to do, as I'm sure you do as well, is that we take a short recess, so that you can re-evaluate your position, and then decide if you still want to proceed." Needless to say, I was absolutely stunned at what he just said. And try as I may, I don't think I was able to completely prevent a little smirk from appearing on my face, as I saw the Crown's jaw drop to the floor!

After being in the courtroom for only about fifteen minutes, when we should have been in there for 2-3 hours before the first break, as we walked back out of the courtroom so soon, Karo, as well as the three other officers sitting outside the courtroom, all looked equally as surprised to see us coming back out so soon. After the Crown went into a little room with the four cops, I explained to Karo what just happened, and that I was pretty sure I had just won!

In terms of the cops and the club…

House: 11, Visitors: 0

… and with respect to my legal career

Unlisted: 2, Her Majesty the Queen: 0

(I don't count the farce of the Charter hearing as a loss, because she refused even listen to the argument; you can't really lose, if a game was never played.)

As a final note, even though I was eventually charged with trafficking again, I never once felt that I may have been wrong in thinking the cops knew they couldn't come after me for drug issues while I owned the club. When I did consider that possibility while I was in jail for the few hours after being arrested, it was immediately apparent that there was just too much evidence supporting my initial conclusion. From the numerous tips I heard from various sources, to the overall pattern how the cops were towards me, all the way to when Dan the cop pointed to a pile of different drugs on my desk and told me I wasn't being charged. If you ask any professional that routinely deals with needing to decide what is accurate when faced with many possibilities, they will all agree that the simplest explanation is usually the correct one. In this case, the simplest explanation is that I likely pissed off the local street cops to the point where they didn't even care what they may or may not have heard, about why I was never charged when they found drugs on my desk, and figured they had nothing to lose from at least trying to get some drug charges to stick. Obviously the look on their faces when I successfully defended myself after only 15 minutes into that final hearing, was clearly priceless.

LOVE AND REGRETS

I initially met Karo within the first year of owning the club. At first, she could barely speak any English, and because I didn't speak any French, we never had any kind of significant conversation; the little bit of communication we did have was mostly nonverbal. Because I'm an avid people watcher, I noticed right away that she was a very respectful and considerate person. She also wasn't like the majority of the girls that were persistently flirting with me, despite making it obvious to them that I wasn't interested. Eventually, after watching her a little bit each time she was around over a period of many months, I started feeling like there was something uniquely different about her, which caught my attention long before there was any kind of romantic interest. At one point during the times that I'd be DJ'ing, I started noticing that I would always look around to see if she was there and dancing. Initially, I wasn't even sure why I would look for her, but like any question that my mind wants to know the answer to, eventually the answer popped into my mind, even though it wasn't something I was actively trying to think about.

The reason why I would look for her while playing, was because I felt it gave me a reference to how good I was mixing. I've been told countless times that I have a very unique style of mixing, which I've never fully understood, but I'm sure it's partly related to the way I like to experiment and mix tracks that you might not think would work well together. Most of the time these unconventional mixes are decent and even good, once in a while they don't work at all, but then sometimes it ends up creating something special and unique, quite like her. But just because I think something sounds amazing, doesn't mean anybody else does, and that's one of the reasons why I'd look for Karo. I could tell just by the look on her face how much she was enjoying what I was mixing, and when she thought it was excellent as well. That's when I'd see that big contagious smile of hers, that would light up the darkest of rooms, and it would put an equally as big of a smile on my face too.

Our romantic interest didn't begin to develop until much later, when we were both recently single, and both of us had previously been in relationships that didn't end well. Her previous relationship didn't end as abruptly as mine, but had ended not long before mine. When my relationship ended, Karo and I were already hanging out at the club the same day, that I broke up with my girlfriend over the phone. It was purely just a friendship between Karo and I, and was just a coincidence that she was the only one left from the party the night before. She didn't want to go back to her place, since her ex was there, and hadn't moved out yet. After that point, we started spending all of our free time together at the club, usually mixing music. I had no interest in quickly getting involved in another relationship, and only saw her as a friend.

I've never been a serial dater before, but 6 months after I took over the club, I got back together with that same ex-girlfriend from the casino, only for things to end again about a month later. Not long after that, I ended up dating one of the staff for about 6 months, until the end of January the following year. Less than two months later, I got back with that same ex-girlfriend again, and that time, we ended up dating for about 6 months until this day when I was at the club with Karo. So after having that serial dating experience for the first time, I was in no rush to get involved with anybody else, so that was the last thing on my mind.

Over the next couple of weeks, Karo and I continued to hang out almost daily. I started teaching her how to DJ and mix music, which she picked up impressively quick, and she actually taught me a bunch about music theory that I didn't know. She also seemed to enjoy learning about any other thing that I would teach her, and similar to how I am, she seemed to absorb it all like a sponge. I could tell she obviously enjoyed learning all sorts of stuff because I kept seeing that same amazing smile each time I taught her something new. Some days we would even hang out for more than 24 hours at a time. I also noticed that her English was getting better by the day, although I don't think I've ever told her how impressed I was by that.

Between how quickly she was learning how to DJ, and the daily improvement with her English, as well as how much she loved learning about all sorts of stuff, it was very apparent to me she was exceptionally intelligent and I realized the impression that I had of her, not long after we first met, was quite accurate. Then one day, while we were in the DJ booth, about two weeks after we had been frequently hanging out with each other, I abruptly realized a few things; one thing directly after the other.

The first thing I realized was how incredibly attracted I was to her. I was quite stunned by this, because I hadn't felt any attraction slowly building before that moment. As soon as I realized that, I quickly thought about all the time we'd spent together over the last couple of weeks, and I could actually see all of the little moments when I slowly became more attracted to her. During that brief moment when I was completely distracted by those intense thoughts, I didn't realize the distinct expression those intense feelings created on my face. Karo clearly noticed and immediately asked what I was thinking about with that same intoxicating smile.

Obviously that was an awkward moment, because I wasn't about to tell her exactly what I was thinking. She obviously understood it was something really pleasant, because of her smile and the excitement she had. As soon as Karo noticed my expression, even before she'd said anything, not only did she still have that smile, but she also had her own distinct expression, that told me she knew I was thinking about something *really* special. After seeing how quickly she noticed my expression, I realized she was much more intuitive and sensitive then I had realized before.

As I reflected upon this, I suddenly had an even more profound realization, when I suddenly felt like I was falling in love with her. The moment I thought that, she instantly saw yet another distinct expression on my face, and became even more excited and curious, insisting even more that I tell her what I was thinking about. Obviously I wasn't about to tell her something as profound as that, especially considering that we had never even kissed before. Instead, I simply said to her, "I'll tell you at some point… maybe."

I then asked her to turn around and close her eyes, because I was going to do something to remind us of this moment, that I would share later, if it ends up making sense at some point. After she turned around and closed her eyes, I went over to where the controllers were for the lighting. I had made a very intricate, interlocking wood system, that held down the controllers to prevent anybody from stealing one. So I slid out the piece of wood that locked it all together, and drew a heart on the backside of the piece of wood. I then slid the wood back into place, and then put the marker where she couldn't see it. I told her she could open her eyes, but it was pointless to try to convince me to tell her right now, so let's just play some music.

Not long after that moment in the DJ booth, Karo and I started dating. Initially we didn't tell anyone at the club, because neither of us wanted to deal with the gossip. It didn't take long for me to realize that I was indeed in love with her. But rather than only being thrilled and happy like one would expect, I was also concerned.

My main concern had to do with how quickly it all happened, and also so soon after breaking up with my ex. Even though I felt like I was certain that I loved her, I was worried that I might only be feeling that way because of the bad relationship that I just got out of. I didn't want to be hurt again; more importantly I didn't want to hurt her either, if I started realizing these feelings were going away. But as time went on, the feelings didn't go away, and instead only grew stronger. Ironically it was because of the first few arguments and fights that we had which made me realize just how much I love her. Usually such fights so early on would have been a red flag for me, but they always seemed clearly related to partying and being awake for excessively long periods of time. Because I knew the club was never going to be a long term thing, I didn't feel those fights were a long term issue either.

Still, with every other relationship that I've had, if I said it was over, it was. So when we had a fight that finally caused me to say that it was over, I was quite surprised when I was the one coming back to her less than a day after I said it. Although that was a first for me, I would soon find out, it would be far from the last.

Ever since that first time I broke up with her, and then quickly went back, I don't know how many countless times I foolishly did that again. The reason why I would usually threaten to break up with her was because of what happened with my ex, who had a really serious speed addiction. Even though we were all doing drugs at the club at the time, Karo definitely liked taking speed. I'm not saying this to judge her, because I'm not, and it would be hypocritical of me to do so considering how much drugs I was doing at the time too, although speed was never something I did very much of. But it didn't change how I felt, which was fear that she would start doing as much as my ex did, even though she wasn't doing nearly that much. Most of the times when I threatened to break up with her, in a conditional way, I can't think of any time that wasn't related to drug use.

Understandably, I can see how something like that could seem manipulative, but it was purely motivated from a genuine concern for her wellbeing. For the most part, the threats to break up with her for such reasons, didn't really become a regular issue until after the club closed. There were many times when we would have a fight and she would leave, not threatening to break up, but just leave our place while we're both high, and then she'd often disappear for a few days. Often, when I finally saw her again, it definitely seemed like she hadn't slept for days and had done a whole lot more drugs since I had last seen her. So this quickly turned into me threatening to break up with her if she didn't leave those parties and get some rest, but she rarely ever would, almost never actually. When I think about things now, it's hard for me to separate how much of it were legitimate concerns from whatever bias I had from the experience with my ex.

Despite my threats, I never could break up with her, even though I was serious when I said it. Because of how much I was in love with her by this point, eventually, most of the times I'd threaten to break up with her, I'd already be emotionally overwhelmed, because of how afraid I started becoming that she's going to destroy herself like my ex did. I was also overwhelmed by the very new experience of realizing just how madly in love I was with her, and how much control that had over my choice about not being able to break up with her. It didn't even matter that she did not seem to really care, since she almost never left those parties or wherever she was. Overall, I was so overwhelmed with my own emotions, I never realized the way it was affecting her and making her feel, each time I threatened to break up with her.

About a year before she finally left, we broke up for about a month and a half, but then I quickly realized how deeply I missed her, and immediately tried to get her back. However, unlike every other time before, it wasn't so easy that time. We finally had a very productive conversation about a month and a half later, and that's when I found out that she did take it seriously, each time I threatened to break up with her. I had no idea how much it hurt her each time, because of the way she usually didn't seem to care. She told me that was one of the biggest concerns about getting back together. So I promised her that I would never threaten to break up with her again, and from when we got back together until she left recently, I kept that promise and I never did that again; I knew by that point, I never wanted to lose her.

Even though I did keep that promise and I never made those threats again, I realize because of how long I had been making the threats to break up with her, and then not following through with them, that only further reinforced the perception she had of me, that makes her think I am sometimes manipulative.

Of all of the mistakes and regrets I have about things I've done in my life, it's quite bewildering that most of my regrets, involve things I've done towards the most beautiful girl I've ever dated, and the only person I ever met that made me feel excited about having a family, and felt happy thinking about spending the rest of my life with. Sometimes I feel like it's some kind of twisted game the universe is playing, because of the tragic irony that these regrets are directly related to how deeply I love her. It would take the trauma of losing her to finally be able to figure out what I have, since she left.

Another reason why I sometimes feel like it's some kind of twisted game of the universe, is because of why I have so many regrets towards Karo. As I mentioned, most, if not all, of those regrets, were actually caused by the same issue I've never been able to figure out and change, which I've struggled with most of my life. Because of experiences I've had, such as the group home, going to jail, and with the countless social workers, therapists, counselors, and all sorts of different types of doctors, due to my social difficulties and behavioral issues as a kid. For the most part, I consider myself to be one of the rare success stories.

Most of the people that go through programs like that, statistically speaking, usually go on to have most of those same problems as an adult. If I've done a good job writing the stories I've shared in this book, then you should have a fairly good idea at how different I was as a kid. Obviously, it's impossible to paint a perfect and complete picture, which shows all of the problems that I use to have, but because of all the programs that I had gone through, I was essentially able to change pretty much all of those unhealthy behaviors.

Because of how keenly aware I am of all of those permanent changes that I've made, and how different of a person I am today as a result of those changes, I'm also very aware there's always been this one remaining issue. This has continued to cause problems in my life, despite all my attempts to try to figure it out and change (even before meeting Karo), just as I have done many times in my past.

Before I bought the club and met Karo, this issue would usually only cause problems a few times a year, at most, and each time it would come up, I'd always spend weeks thinking about it later, and never quite fully stop thinking about it. Often when I drive by where such an issue happened in the city, I'll still think about what had happened there, since it's always been something that I've desperately wanted to change and have never liked about myself. Until recently, anytime in the past when it has caused issues, none of them have resulted in any sort of loss or trauma, that would cause my mind to start endlessly obsessing about the issue, until it figures it out; so no answer was ever found, and the problem continued.

Further making me feel like it is some twisted joke the universe is playing, is because I've never met anybody before Karo, that has caused me to struggle with this issue so often, and the twisted part is knowing that it was because of the intense love for her and fear I had of losing that love, that was directly related to why I eventually ended up losing her. If it wasn't for the choices and actions of all those bullies that caused me to express my vulnerable emotions as aggressive emotions, and I had learned to deal with those emotions in a healthy way, instead of suppressing and hiding them, even from the person I love the most, then I'm sure I never would have scared her away. Of course, if I had never been bullied like that in the first place, my life would have likely been so much different, then chances are Karo and I never would have met in the first place. Either way, I wouldn't be left with this painful loss which only has one cure that I doubt I will ever see.

Since the bullying first started in kindergarten, expressing vulnerable emotions as aggressive emotions became more than just a habit; instead it evolved into instinct, and eventually I had no difficulty at all controlling my anger. Because of how much bullying I've experienced, I'm not easily overwhelmed by fear. In fact, until I fell in love with Karo, there was really nothing I was afraid of that was capable of overwhelming me.

If you think about some of the stories I've told, and fights that I've been in, having knives pulled on me, or even representing myself in court the way I did; all of those things caused some fear in me, but never anything close to being overwhelming. Interestingly, of those 3 examples, I'm sure most people would be most afraid of having a knife pulled on them, but I've become so comfortable with the risk of physical pain, I'm really not afraid of being physically hurt any more, at all. The fear and anxiety I had relating to court, was much more intense than any fear of being physically hurt, since I had zero experience representing myself in court; I also knew the significance of what I was attempting to do, but that still wasn't even close to being overwhelming.

The fear I had of losing Karo, was an entirely new kind of fear that scared me in a way I was completely unprepared for. I've never met somebody that made me feel so vulnerable, and sadly, out of instinct, too often I hid it. I don't think she even knows just how vulnerable my love for her made me feel. After about 35 years of experience hiding my vulnerable emotions, I did what I would always do, and expressed my feelings in an aggressive and defensive way, unaware of the emotional time bomb this choice would eventually cause to explode. I've never hit her or been abusive in anyway, and even though I knew I never would, regardless of how upset I ever got, clearly she had no way of knowing that, and considering how many times I definitely scared her, it's sadly understandable that this could be a concern of hers.

I've mentioned how much I love her smile, but I love her laugh even more. I'd even go as far to say I was addicted to those things, and that addiction often motivated me to do silly things, just to invoke those reactions from her. I'd do things I would never have done before, because

I would've felt awkward and uncomfortable doing them, but the potential reward of seeing her face light up, far outweighed any anxiety I would have.

One such time, while at a thrift store, as we were walking by the hat section, I noticed the things next to the hats, were not at all hats, and it gave me a bright idea. So when she wasn't looking, I tried on one of the unusual "hats", went up behind her and got her attention by asking, "How do you like my hat?" But of course it wasn't a hat, and was actually a lampshade! I never would've done something like that with anybody else before, because the illogical social anxieties that I've always had, anticipating a whole bunch of people in the store may start looking at me funny, because of how loud Karo may end up laughing. But that was the very motivation for doing something like that, and that reaction it invoked, instantly made me completely forget about any anxiety I had been feeling. But still, each time I'd do those things in public, I always felt a little vulnerable, but would still do them anyway. I also felt vulnerable because of the power she had over me, knowing how easily and deeply I could be hurt because of this most precious love.

Not even the bullies from my childhood had that kind of power over me, because I wouldn't allow myself to expose any vulnerabilities at all the way I would with Karo. Even when we weren't in public, I'd constantly be doing things to make her laugh and smile, and sometimes the things I'd do, or blurt out of my mouth, were so unexpectedly funny, even to me, we'd end up laughing until our stomachs hurt. These details about vulnerability and Karo, is just one little thing that I've realized recently, that I was completely unaware was contributing to why I was so easily overwhelmed towards her. Again, something that seems so obvious now, but not at all obvious after spending a life time hiding vulnerability.

Another type of regret that I have, involves how I would sometimes react to other drivers, which would scare her at times. The most recent example I can think of, and definitely one that really scared her, happened on the highway coming back from Montréal.

A van came up behind us fairly quickly, and then just started following behind way too close, despite there being no other cars around on the road. I tried to slow down a bit but they just slowed down as well, and still stayed too close to my car. I then downshifted into a lower gear, so that I knew I could accelerate quickly after tapping the brakes. Usually that works with drivers like that, but not this driver, and a moment later that driver was tailgating us again. So this time I hit my brakes really hard. The whole time Karo was asking me to stop but obviously I didn't. Things continued for a bit with the van, and eventually when she got quite scared, I accelerated down the highway, knowing the van couldn't keep up.

I'm sure it could have easily seemed to her that I didn't care about how she felt, but that really wasn't the case at all. As soon as I saw how upset she eventually became, I was immediately upset with myself that my actions scared her that much, which is the exact opposite of her smile and laugh I love so much. I'm not even sure if I apologized, but I don't think I did. I know I had thought about it a lot, but I was mostly distracted with the regret I was feeling about not stopping sooner, when she first started asking me to. It wasn't that I didn't notice or care at first, but was one of those unintended consequences from all the years I've been redirecting emotions into anger.

Even though I didn't intentionally redirect the compassionate emotions and concern I had, but because I already allowed myself to get aggressive towards the driver of the van, seeing how upset she initially was, only made me angrier towards the driver and that caused me to become more aggressive. This is a great example of one of the harms caused from the way I'd redirect emotions, that I wasn't even aware of until recently.

After thinking about the issue with the van recently, I realized something else that hadn't even occurred to me at the time, that I am particularly bothered by now. Not only did I ended up scaring her, but if I was the passenger, and suddenly the driver hit the brakes without any warning like I did, I would definitely be upset from being jolted so hard, and it likely would have bothered me enough to say something about it. Not only do I realize how hypocritical this is, but it's even more upsetting knowing that Karo surely found it unpleasant that way too, in addition to being scared. Again, this is another one of those things that seem obvious, but wasn't to me until writing about it now, because of ways I've been redirecting emotions without even noticing.

The specific thing that caused me to start thinking about the time with the van, and all of the different times I've caused Karo to feel uncomfortable in the car, happened about a month ago while I was driving around doing some errands one night, weeks before I even got to this chapter. I noticed some car do something stupid that I always would have notice and likely react to, but not only did I not react to it, surprisingly, I barely noticed at all. The only reason why it even caught my attention, was when I realized that I usually would have reacted in some way.

After how surprised I was, I've spent a lot of time thinking about it since. I realized it is related to some of the changes I've started noticing, specifically relating to the ways I was subconsciously redirecting emotions. After I first noticed that, I started noticing other similar examples, and unsurprisingly, I've been much more relaxed while out doing errands. As with all the times in my past during other moments of fundamental changes, now that I'm aware of it, it's ever present in my mind; just like I still smile to myself sometimes while I'm out dancing, remembering how afraid I used to be.

I just realized something else while writing this, relating to the "…obsessiveness as a defense against emotional distress.." quirk about my personality. I've written about it quite a bit, and have been thinking about it even more, because of how it relates to the negative ways I'd often react towards Karo, or became obsessive about past problems when I was younger; until now, I was only seeing it as a liability. Because of how much torment that quirk has caused me, I never made the completely obvious connection, which is that same quirk also helps *reinforce* a new change and cement it into my mind, to leave a very lasting change. Regarding the examples of the different things that don't upset me anymore, I kind of feel like my mind never seems to quite stop obsessively thinking about them, at least subconsciously, as a defense against *future* emotional distress. Similar to how my past fear of dancing will randomly pop into my mind while out dancing, and still continues to reinforce that change that happened 20 years ago.

Getting back to the topic of regrets I have towards Karo, sadly, there are many, but because they pretty much all relate to the same basic issue, it wouldn't add anything to this book to write about them, but there is one more I want to share. It was the last fight we had about a month before she left, and even though she hasn't mentioned it at all since she left, I can't help but feel it was shortly after this fight when she started making plans to leave.

OUR LAST FIGHT; MY CATALYST TO CHANGE

During the months before she left, things at her job were getting progressively worse, and I knew it was stressing her out. I have no idea how much it was stressing her out because we didn't really talk about it, but I could tell by the way she was often a bit irritable after work, it was definitely bothering her a lot.

About a month before she left, we were sitting in my living room listening to music, chatting, and having a couple of drinks, not long after she got off work. Neither of us were drunk, and the two drinks I had, wasn't even enough to feel a buzz. All of a sudden she got really upset, got up and started walking out of the living room. I had no idea why she got upset, even to this day, and for a moment I just sat there confused, trying to understand what just happened and what I said or did to upset her.

At the time it didn't seem like a big deal, because nothing I said or did seemed like anything anyone would be upset about, and the only thing I could think of was maybe she misheard something I said and it was really just some kind of misunderstanding. But then when I saw that she was going to leave, combined with the fact that I didn't even know why, I was rapidly filled with fear quicker than I had ever been, and I immediately started panicking *inside*. But because of the way I generally hide my vulnerable emotions, the only thing she would've seen was confusion.

Of all the fights we have ever had, I can't even think of a single time when she ended up leaving so suddenly like that. It would always be after we had been arguing for a while and things got progressively more intense. Usually I'd get frustrated at first and become more and more frustrated the longer the fight would go on. Eventually, the frustration would turn into aggression, and eventually anger, but because of how sudden this happened, and not even knowing what the issue was, my usual pattern of behavior didn't occur, and I found myself experiencing an unfamiliar intense mix of emotions.

As she was getting her shoes on, I just looked at her, completely confused, and calmly asked, what just happened and why was she leaving? She just looked at me and said "You know why!" But I didn't, and because I knew I didn't say anything that would make sense for her to be upset, for a brief moment I thought it might be some weird joke, but as soon she opened the door I realized it wasn't, and the panic instantly became worse.

Usually, I don't have a hard time remembering details about something that happened, even from when I was really young, but when I started writing this story down, and I got to the next part, I was suddenly surprised that I could barely remember any of the details. This should give a good idea about how completely overwhelmed I would eventually become. Despite this story not even being very long, it actually took quite a while to write. Initially, I just kept focusing on the few details I could remember, then slowly, as I started remembering more, and I had more details to focus on, eventually I was able to remember enough to write down into a story. By the time I finished writing, I was shocked at what I remembered, and that caused me to spend a lot of time thinking about it until I finished the last remaining chapters. I had already done the initial edit of most of what I had written already, so only about a week passed until I came back and started editing this chapter. As I began reading about this fight, more details quickly started coming to my mind. It didn't take long for me to remember the entire fight quite clearly, and I was horrified at what I recalled.

I still wasn't angry or aggressive, just full of panic, fear, and completely confused. As I went down the hall to try and talk to her, that brief thought this may be a joke, led to me thinking how silly it all seemed. By the time I caught up to her at the elevators, some more emotional redirection took place and I also had a slight bit of a joking, laugh it off, dismissive kind of emotion that was now mixed in with the intense confusion, fear and panic. Since I still didn't know why she was upset, I had no way of knowing the extent of how upset she was, or how she would end up reacting, but I would soon find out. Because of the unfamiliar mix of emotions I was experiencing, which I was completely overwhelmed by, I didn't even realize how I was about to unexpectedly, and regretfully react.

When the elevator door opened, the panic suddenly became terror, and all I could think of doing, was holding her and giving her a warm hug, hoping it would somehow help. To my complete horror, instead of a warm hug, all I ended up doing was the "holding on to her" part. In a panic, as I grabbed her in a tight bear hug sort of way, she immediately screamed! Shocked by what I just did and frightened by her scream, all I could think about was not wanting to lose her and I held her even tighter.

Externally, I'm sure it didn't seem that way at all. Instead, the joking, laugh it off, dismissive emotions became more pronounced, and when she started screaming for police, I was so completely overwhelmed, I responded by saying the most irrational thing possible in that moment, and I also shouted out "Yeah, call the police", just as loud as she'd said it. As I said that, and noticed there was almost a laugh in my voice, the instant I realized that, I understood how fucked up and out of control the whole situation was, and I instantly let her go.

After I suddenly realized all of that, knowing that I only meant to give her a gentle compassionate and warm hug, to try to calm the situation down, and reassure her that she didn't need to leave. Instead of that aggressive bear hug I gave her, I then tried to give her the warm hug I meant, and told her I didn't mean to grab her the way I just did. But she didn't believe that at all, and considering that all my fear and panic was completely locked up inside, in some kind of instinctual protective bunker, completely hidden from her, I'm not surprised she didn't believe me.

Even as I'm writing this now, and reliving those horrible moments, I can't even begin to imagine what she was thinking about me at that point. After what I did, and only reacting as though I felt it was just some big funny joke… …. as I was writing that sentence, the rest of the words were suddenly gone, and were replaced with emotion. I've been sitting here for the last 20 minutes or so, thinking about that night. There's so many ways I could complete that sentence, each one feeling just as horrible as the next. Reading this for a third time now, as I'm doing another edit, each time it's definitely been the most difficult part of the book to write.

When Karo first left, I didn't think this fight had much to do with her leaving, if at all. For the same reason why I initially had a hard time remembering the details, I realized after I wrote this story last week, that was also why I didn't feel it had much to do with her leaving. But It was so upsetting even to me, no doubt that is why I somehow blocked most of it from my memory.

After I was able to remember enough to be able to first write this story down, I went from not thinking this fight was a big issue at all, to thinking it was certainly a factor. When I first edited it, and remembered the rest of the details, I suddenly felt like it was definitely what caused her to leave, and she likely started thinking about leaving right away. I also think I have a good idea what might have been going through her mind when I started shouting, "Yeah, call the police". Considering my facial expression, tone of voice, and my entire demeanor as I said that, I must have looked like the most careless asshole ever….

As I've been sitting here for a couple hours since writing that last line, I have been writing a bunch, then erasing it, writing some different stuff, deleting it, and then just sitting and thinking for a while; then repeat. I don't think there is really anything else that needs to be said about that.

By the time I started writing this book, I didn't think I'd ever end up finding out why she decided to leave the way she did, but at least that makes sense now, and I won't be left forever wondering why. Even though it was the only fight when I didn't express any anger, or even frustration, I definitely feel this last fight was by far the worst we've ever had. It was the only time with her, I ever really lost control of my emotions the way I did and caused me to react in such a regrettable way.

Over the last 6 weeks or so, since I started figuring things out, and noticing positive personal changes as I've realized more and more, I know I wouldn't undo that last fight, even if I could. I know how grateful I am that I finally figured out this last haunting issue, which has continued to cause issues in my life. I'm certain this is one of those moments of fundamental and lasting changes, so I'd be a fool to want to change that. It only would have prevented me from realizing all these things, I have wanted to change for a very long time. Even if it means I've lost Karo forever, I realize if she hadn't left when she did, then I wouldn't have figured any of this out, my book may never have been written, and because of how much I have obviously hurt her, I have no doubt I would have ended up pushing her away eventually.

MOMENTS OF TIME

As you can obviously tell from the amount of pages that are left, we are getting close to the end of the story. But before I get into the details about everything that's happened over the last few months since she left, I want to take a moment to explain a few things about time. At first it might seem like a complete tangent, which has nothing to do with the story, but the reason I'm sharing this, is to help illustrate my perception of time and the way it's been influencing the events over the last few months.

As I'm writing this, it's now July 12, 2020, and as of today, she's only been gone 138 days, but because of how much has happened, and how much I've gone through since she left, it feels like years have passed; many, many, years.

There's actually a scientific basis for the way time seems to go slower sometimes, and faster at other times. Fundamentally, time is related to change. The more change that occurs, the more time you experience. Conversely, the less change you experience the less time you also experience. Our perception of the length of time, how much time there is, or has passed, only begins to form in our minds when we look back to the past. If time suddenly stopped, and we found ourselves stuck in a single moment, then suddenly the whole concept of time would become completely meaningless, and we would have absolutely no concept of time at all. There would be no time, because there would be no change. This isn't just a philosophical concept, it's part of Einstein's Special Theory of Relativity.

If we didn't understand these principles, our global GPS system would not work. The GPS system relies on very accurate atomic clocks. For increased accuracy, each GPS satellite has multiple atomic clocks, and because of how fast the satellites are moving relative to the clocks on the earth, the clocks on the satellites actually tick a little bit slower, since they're experiencing so much more change, in their positions, because of how much faster they're moving.

Thoughts and perception are no different. I'm sure everyone is aware of how our perception of time can drastically change from one moment to another. In a way, if you want to live a longer life, all you need to do is experience more change; learn new things, constantly, experience new things, and try new things, instead of getting stuck in the same old routine.

Because of how often I am constantly learning many different things, on so many different subjects, all of those different things are equivalent to changes. Changes that happen within the mind, and as a result of that, it feels like I've experienced a lot of time in my life. Of course it is impossible to directly compare my own perception of time, to the perceptions of anyone else, but it's not actually necessary to make a direct comparison between people, to understand this is true. All I need to do is compare moments in my life when I learned a lot or did a lot of different things, to other moments when I barely did anything at all.

When Karo first left, for the first 2 weeks I pretty much did nothing at all, and mostly just slept the whole time. The reason why I wanted to sleep as much as I could, was because I understand time goes by really quick when doing very little. But of course I couldn't continue to be like that, so after two weeks, I picked myself up off the couch and joined a gym; then 3 days later the world shut down due to the COVID-19 virus. At first glance, it is easy to think that being stuck at home suddenly, with nothing to do and little change occurring, would make time fly on by, like when I slept for 2 weeks straight. But of course everybody knows this isn't true, because when you're stuck with nothing to do, it usually feels like time goes by very slow. This may seem like it contradicts what I previously said about the nature of time and change, and even though it seems like you're not actually experiencing much change, when you're bored with nothing to do, as you examine it closer, often the opposite is true. Usually when we are bored, a lot of time is spent thinking about all sorts of different things that we would like to do instead. Well that's actually a whole bunch of mental change that is occurring.

Consider a clock for example, as you watch it go Tick, Tick, Tick. The change of the ticks are not the only things that you're thinking of. Go watch a clock tick, and pay attention to what's going through your mind, as you wait and anticipate for the next tick to occur. If you're really concentrating on the clock, to the point where it seems to be moving so slow, you're actually concentrating on the moments of nothingness between the ticks as well. Even though it may seem like you're concentrating on nothing, nothing is still something. Even if it isn't noticeable, not visible, not tangible and is actually invisible, you're still experiencing those moments of change. Unless you are a Zen master when it comes to meditating, you'll likely find it very difficult to focus on those moments between the ticks, without random thoughts constantly getting in the way of your view of nothingness. You may even start to realize; how many thoughts are actually going through your mind when you're not distracted by anything else.

Usually, when we are doing something fun, "time flies", which makes sense, because most fun things that cause time to fly by are generally not very complicated, and usually involves a few things being done again and again. Most sports, simple games like Tetris, and even most TV series almost always follow the same basic format that result in not much change occurring in our minds. Other things like homework, trying to learn or do complicated things that require lots of different steps, or problem solving, all tend to make time feel like it goes by much slower. Because of how fast our minds can think about different ideas, simple things that can effectively distract us from our thoughts, generally results in less mental change. This makes time feel like it passes quickly, whereas things that are complicated and difficult, can easily make our minds consider more different things as it tries to figure out the problem and make time feel like it passes very slow.

Over the last few months, there have been some periods when I was so mentally exhausted, that time seemed to just pass by without realizing it, but for the most part, my mind has been in obsessive overdrive, as it has been relentlessly searching for answers. The only points in my life when my mind has got into a state like that, has only ever been during those other moments that eventually led to some kind of fundamental and lasting change. Because of how quickly my mind starts thinking about as many different possibilities as it can, it has the side effect which makes time feel like it's passing very, *very* slowly. On one hand, that's a wonderful thing in a moment like that, because essentially your thoughts become more efficient, since you're processing a lot more ideas in the same amount of time. But on the other hand, during these dark moments of despair, that often trigger my mind to start thinking obsessively, that also effectively increases how long I'm experiencing that pain and despair.

ETERNAL LOVE; FOREVER LOST, A TRAUMA LEADING TO CHANGE

Until recently, I've felt that I knew myself exceptionally well. The reasons I felt that way is because of how important learning and self-improvement has always been to me, the countless hours I spend thinking about and reflecting upon every single mistake; especially the painful ones, since I'd never want to make such mistakes again, and knowing how many times this has led to moments of fundamental and lasting changes.

After Karo suddenly left, near the end of February without explaining why, followed a few weeks later by the forced isolation due to the COVID-19 pandemic, it set off a chain of events over the following 4 months, which ultimately led to the most grievous pain and sadness I have ever felt.

Completely isolated, with nothing that could distract me from my thoughts, alone in my apartment I dwelled, as my mind grew completely consumed by this burning question of why. A slave now, powerless to extinguish the expanding blaze raging in my mind, and unable to escape this growing inferno of hell, I was helplessly forced to watch; as I melted, and I deformed into a turbulent river of molten salty ooze. Over the next few months, as this burning pain continued to fuel the flames of despair, this molten mass of me, was carried away with the turbulent river of thoughts, as my mind relentlessly tried to understand why.

Further fueling the fire, were a few other questions my mind was relentlessly thinking about. Why did I keep doing those same few things, over and over again, that ended up pushing her away? What caused me to act that way? Most importantly, how do I prevent it from ever happening again?

Because of other times in my past during other traumatic moments, I knew my mind would not stop thinking about these questions, and would go into hyper-drive until it found the answers. There is even that phrase, from the psychological assessment, that perfectly illustrates why I knew my mind wouldn't stop thinking about it. The phrase that mentions how I sometimes use "…obsessiveness as a defense against emotional distress…."

All of those moments in my past, when I went through a lot of positive changes in a short period of time, has always begun after a period of intense trauma, when my mind wouldn't stop thinking about the problem, just as it did after I realized I had lost Karo. It's the very fact that my mind will not stop obsessively thinking about a problem, and how to fix it, to prevent it from happening again, that has always allowed me to finally figure out what was causing me to be a certain way, which caused the pain in the first place. But even though I've been able to make lasting fundamental changes to my behavior a number of times in the past, I knew that wouldn't guarantee I'd be able to figure out the questions that were on my mind relating to why Karo left; in fact, as the months went by, and I fell deeper into the hell I was in, I started becoming very concerned I may never find these answers.

After I fell deeply in love with Karo, there was nothing else that has ever been in my life that I had ever been so afraid of losing. That fear had such a reoccurring and constant emotional influence on me, and was capable of overwhelming me emotionally, that I suddenly found myself frequently overreacting towards Karo, and it would often turn a minor argument, into a big fight. Because of the way I was usually expressing my fear as anger, there was no way for her to realize how much I was bothered every time something like that happened, or how much I would think about it afterwards. The fact that I continued to overreact the same way, likely seemed like it wasn't that serious to me. Even though I was upset with myself each time I would get that way, because she had always stayed with me, none of those times created enough emotional distress, to cause my mind to start obsessively thinking about the issue, until she finally left.

During the first few weeks after she left, I was feeling like I was going to lose my mind, because I was unable to find anything that could successfully distract me from my thoughts. At one point I started thinking about this book, and the title that I'd thought about back in the fall. I thought about many possible titles over the years, but when I first thought of this title, I knew right away it was perfect. I knew the book was going to be a collection of stories that involve moral questions, just like the topic of drugs and the Charter issues are. Towards the end of March, when I seriously started questioning whether or not I was a good person, I started thinking about the title of my book, and decided to sit down at my desk and start writing about how I was feeling at the time. Because I knew Karo still loved me, but decided to leave anyway, all I could think about was how horrible of a person I must be, knowing I had obviously scared her, and hurt her a whole lot more than I realized.

As I started writing on March 22, I realized it was helping a bit, and I also realized why I wasn't able to distract myself with anything else. The other things I was attempting to distract my mind with, were all unrelated to what I was obsessively thinking so intensely about, and because of the intensity of my thoughts, it was impossible for anything unrelated to be able to distract from them. As I was writing, I quickly noticed that it was helping me to think about things more clearly and in more detail. As soon as I realized this, I was immediately hooked, and I spent most of my free time over the next 2 weeks continuing to write.

Around the time when I first started writing, Karo and I also started chatting fairly regularly through text messages, and I was at least able to find out more details about why she left, some of which were things I never would've thought about, since many of them were not even related to my past behavior, but of course I still knew my behavior, even though it was not a frequent issue, but the times when it was, it was obviously a big factor. That was clear from the beginning, but it had been almost a month before she left since we had that last fight, which I didn't remember being a very big issue, and further seemed confirmed by the fact that she didn't even mention it, so I knew there was a lot more to it.

As she told me about the other reasons why she left, I realize those were all things that were easy to change. I also made a comment to her about, "I wish we would've moved out west a while ago, like we talked about so many times." And because of her response, "Yeah, we should have." a plan started forming in my head.

I knew certain stresses in our lives were causing some of our problems we were having, because they were often the initial things that started the minor issues, which would end up getting much worse because of the way I would react. One of the stresses that I've always felt since the club closed, is how I didn't feel welcomed at certain parties that she would go to, since a lot of the people at those parties, knew me only from the club. Some of those people definitely do not like me, either because they were personally disrespectful to the point that I had to deal with their behavior, as a club owner, or else they are friends with somebody that I had to deal with that way.

Most of the time, when these kind of confrontations occurred, there was usually only a few other people around, and most of the details others would hear, came from people gossiping with each other; of course everybody knows how distorted facts get, very quickly, even after being passed between only 2 or 3 people. I don't know how many times I've heard people who were upset with the way I dealt with a situation, but were not there to witness what actually happened, tell me I didn't need to react that way, and I could have just asked politely for the person to obey the rules. Then after explaining the other side of the story, their opinion would quickly change, but most people wouldn't ever come talk to me about things after, so unsurprisingly, such distorted opinions remained.

Because I had almost 40 cameras around the club, usually the video footage itself was enough to show, I usually wasn't in the wrong for needing to deal with someone the way I did. Something most people didn't seem to realize, is that I always attempted to address any problems politely first, ALWAYS! Even my highest test score relates to an "…ability to respond and adapt to situations by dealing with a specific problem in an efficient and socially acceptable manner." The only times when I wouldn't start by being polite, are a few times when the issue started as a physical confrontation or fight, and at that point it's already beyond words, but those types of situations didn't occur that many times. The point is, because most of the people in the community only ever knew me as a club owner, who often had to deal with very disrespectful people, a lot of them have this very specific idea of me in their heads, which isn't how I am, as an individual.

Realistically, I have no idea who doesn't like me and who does, other than perhaps a few that I'm sure don't like me. And technically, I don't know if I was ever welcomed at any of those parties or not, but I was never invited to any of them, and Karo never invited me either; this further reinforced the feeling I had that I wasn't welcomed, which only added to the stress I would feel and was definitely a factor that made some of our fights worse.

Another issue that was causing stress in our relationship, was related to our work schedules, because we often wouldn't wake up until one or two in the afternoon. Then immediately she'd have to get ready to go work at the restaurant. Before she left, she was even talking about getting a normal 9-5 kind of job. After thinking about all those things, I felt like things could be a lot different if we moved away, got day jobs and could have a fresh start.

By that point, I'd already been writing every day for 2 weeks, and had written about 30,000 words. Because I started writing about my childhood first and had written up until I recently got out of jail, and I'd already started realizing some very significant things, which related to those questions I was trying to figure out. One of the significant things I first started realizing by that point, was how much more affected I was from all the bullying, than I had ever realized before. That was also the first time I ever realized I had any suppressed memories at all, and because of how well I remember so many details about most of my life, I was quite shocked to find out when I first discovered that. I also pulled out the psychological assessment off my shelf, when I was writing about the time when I first started learning about the Charter while I was in jail, since I wanted to quote my highest score because of how it relates to being good at understanding law.

After I had the report in front of me, I also decided to read the whole thing again, hoping that I might find some other insightful things that could help with writing the book. But because of how many times I had read that report in the last 20 years, I didn't expect to learn anything new and significant about myself. When I came across the paragraph that mentions I can become obsessive as a defense against emotional distress, I was suddenly shocked. Each time I had ever read the report, I always mostly dismissed that part, because even though I saw some truth in it, I realized that 99.xxxx% of the time, nothing about that paragraph is true about me at all.

After what happened recently, not just with Karo leaving and all of the thoughts that were on my mind, but also the few things that I started realizing about my childhood, being bullied, and the suppressed memories, when I read that paragraph again, with those things on my mind, it felt like I just ran straight into a brick wall. As I read it, again and again, I realized every single word about that paragraph was 100% true about the state of mind I was currently in, as well as the way it related to the fights between Karo and I; suddenly I had another little epiphany, and immediately the puzzle became a little bit clearer.

After thinking about all this for a while, and ways to eliminate a lot of stress from our lives, I came up with a plan and suggested it to Karo. Because she agreed that we should have moved out west a while ago, I suggested to her that I would sell all of my stuff which I wouldn't want to bring. I have a huge electronics collection, circuit parts and things like that, because after going to school for Computer/Electronics Engineering, even though I dropped out of the program, it's still been a hobby and interest of mine since. Even though it's something that I enjoy, I realize it's also a stressful hobby, and more importantly, it takes up a lot of time. Because I have so many interests, and there's not nearly enough time in a day to spend on all of them, I knew I could happily sell all of my electronics stuff. I also know that having all this stuff causes a very mild but constant anxiety in my life, there have been a lot of moments when I've thought about selling it all, because it would be one less distraction that would allow me to spend more time on other healthier interests, like biking and other physical activities that I rarely do anymore.

After explaining all this to her, suggesting I sell everything and we move out west, get day jobs and have a fresh start with much less stress around, I was obviously disappointed when she didn't agree to what I suggested. At least she did say, "You would need to be at a very different point in your life, for me to even consider giving us another chance." At the time this still seemed encouraging, and at that point, I stopped writing, and immediately started organizing things that I was already planning to sell, but have just been procrastinating about.

Over the next couple weeks, I spent most of my free time organizing what I wanted to sell right away, taking pictures and posting ads online. When I gave her updates as I sold big things, she seemed very pleased when I told her news like that, and that started giving me hope.

At the time, we had been using WhatsApp to text to each other, which allowed me to see when she read my messages. During the next couple of encouraging weeks, she would usually respond either right away, or at most within a few hours. Then one day for no apparent reason, I saw that she read one of my messages, and didn't reply right away. I did notice that she would come online a number of times, because the texting app also showed when she was last online. After a day or two without any kind of response, I started panicking more and more. Eventually I became so overwhelmed, I started messaging her a lot, with a bunch of stress fueled messages. Still not getting a response, I started calling her many times in a row. While I was calling her, instead of getting her voicemail, I suddenly heard a message that the number I'm trying to call is out of service. In that moment, my heart sank. I knew it could only have meant one of two things. Either her phone had suddenly been disconnected, because of nonpayment, which was a possibility since she was not working, due to the lock-down, or else she decided to change her number.

As the days went by, I eventually found out that she did change her number. Suddenly I felt all hope was lost, and realized I just did the same thing again, that caused her to leave in the first place. And then the protective shield of hope, that was sheltering me from the emotional inferno that was still raging all around me, which was slowly allowing me to regain form and structure, was suddenly gone. As the fuel of this additional regret made the fire even hotter, I could feel myself quickly melting away again, and the additional heat made the river even more turbulent; abruptly, I was swept away once again, and the ride was about to become much worse.

Initially, I tried to start writing again, because of how much it was helping me before, but at this point, the turbulence was too much to allow me to get any kind of grip on anything, including the keyboard, and no matter how long I sat in front of my computer, the only thing I could do was sit and stare; I lost all sense of time, as I felt I was endlessly flowing down this river of hell.

Once I knew she had changed her number, I felt like I would never hear from her again. As the days went by, the ride down the river became progressively worse, the longer I didn't hear from her. Finally, the little bit of motivation I still had to do anything, was quickly diluted from the turbulent ride, and all motivation had dissipated, and I found myself with none. As I slowly started shutting down, I turned the ringer off on my phone and didn't leave my apartment or talk to anyone for the next 10 days. I slept as much as I could, and barely ate. Even when I would make something to eat and sat down with the plate of food in front of me, I would suddenly realize I had been staring at it for hours, and hadn't even taken a single bite; I was completely lost in my own thoughts, and my ability to focus had been completely washed away. I weighed around 160 lbs when Karo left, but after being unable to eat for so long, my weight dropped as low as 134 lbs.

I started smoking not long after the lock-down started, and by that point I was smoking over two large packs a day. I don't remember much during those days, because I really didn't do much. During those 10 days, I don't think a whole minute went by without me thinking about her and feeling the torment of how much I miss her. I mostly just wandered aimlessly around my apartment. I'd end up going into my office and sit down in front of my computer, intending to try to do something, but then hours would go by, and again, I would suddenly realize I had been sitting there the whole time, helplessly staring at the burning thoughts raging through my mind.

So I'd get up and go back into the living room to watch something. Just like in the office, at some point, I'd suddenly realize 3 whole episodes had played, and I hadn't watched a single moment, even though I was staring directly at the screen. My eyes might've been looking at the TV, but no matter how many times I tried to pay attention to what my eyes were seeing, almost immediately, my attention would quickly drip away and further down the river I went. Looking at me in that state, I was so calm externally, you would never imagine, the endless raging torrent of traumatic thoughts I was unable to escape from, as my mind desperately tried to find the answers, which would allow me to escape this river in hell.

Thoughts of my childhood were common, as it was understood already that more answers were to be found there. After I recently understood I was more affected by my childhood than I had previously realized, and I wasn't even fully aware of the different ways I had been negatively affected by those past traumas, it's not surprising that so many people who know me, including my own family, would have some of the misconceptions they do of me. Despite how many times I've attempted to explain things such as, I don't think I am always right about everything, or I'm not being manipulative, no one ever seemed to believe what I was saying.

Karo specifically, would often make the same dismissive comments about how, "I'm smarter than that", simply because my highest score just happens to relate to things that are very noticeable during any kind of social interaction. Additionally, because of how quickly apparent that very specific type of intelligence is, no one ever seems to stop and take into account what my weaknesses are, or how very aware I am of many of those weaknesses. It also doesn't help that I've spent most of my life hiding them, even from myself, and in the same way I will express sadness or fear as anger or aggression, until recently, I didn't even realize I was doing the same kind of thing with all emotions in general. Depending on the situation, I could easily express any emotion as any other emotion at times, if I felt it would best protect me from some *perceived* danger.

Even though I generally forgive the bullies, because I don't think most bullies would bully other kids if they realized what they were really doing. I have no doubt that such intense and frequent bullying would leave a lasting effect on anyone. But between the extreme emotional sensitivity which is common with autism, combined with my rare and specific strengths as well as weaknesses, I'm sure the bullying affected me a bit differently than it would affect most people.

The reason I believe this, is because my outstanding ability with "… Practical social judgment, the ability to organize facts and relationships, and superior abstract thinking….. The ability to respond and adapt to situations by dealing with a specific problem in an efficient and socially acceptable manner." When I first started getting picked on in kindergarten, I engaged my practical social judgment superpower, and thought about how to adapt to the different bullying situations in an efficient way. I organized all those facts and relationships, used my superior abstract thinking, and mastered the ability to express any emotion as another; after doing it for so long, from such a young age, it's not surprising it became so natural, that I wasn't even aware of the extent in which I was doing that. But not just that, something else I realize recently relating to expressing one emotion as another, is that I actually took it a step further. I learned to do this so efficiently, the reason I didn't even notice it, despite even actively looking for different ways I have been affected as an adult due to those childhood traumas, is because sometimes I wouldn't just knowingly *express* one emotion as another, but I learned to do this so completely, often I would actually *feel* one emotion as another.

If it wasn't for the trauma from losing Karo, followed by the lock-down, and then deciding to write this book at this point in my life, I'm not sure if I would have ever even realized any of this. For someone who always felt they understood themselves very well, realizing such a thing at my age, has understandably been a very shocking and humbling realization. As soon as I realized I've been turning all sorts of emotions, into all sorts of other emotions, anytime I felt overwhelmingly threatened or vulnerable, more pieces to the puzzle were suddenly found buried under the debris of the past; but where did they fit in?

Being so humbled during this turbulent ride, only further diluted any sense of self that I still had. Feeling even more alone now than before, because of the strength that was found believing that I knew myself so well; more than ever, I was a stranger a within myself. After first realizing I've lost Karo, which already made me feel more alone than ever before, after this new humbling realization, suddenly I wasn't even sure who I was. With the other thoughts in my mind, of the things that I don't like, about that person who scared my love away, I suddenly found myself sharing a body with a complete stranger, I've seen do things, I absolutely despise.

When thoughts of suicide first entered my mind, not long after I realized Karo wasn't coming back, that was the exact moment I knew I needed to make some kind of change, which is why I joined the gym. I knew I wouldn't act on them, but had little control of them randomly popping into my head, and all I could do, was dismiss and distract myself from them; joining a gym seemed like the perfect solution. But then a few days later, when the lock-down started, and the gym was closed, dismissing that idea of suicide, became progressively harder to do.

After all that had just happened since then, and now finding myself trapped in this mental hell, tied to a stranger that scared away the only person I've ever wanted to spend the rest of my life with, all I could think about was how to escape; the potential consequences no longer mattered.

Although I'm not a religious person, I am deeply spiritual. Simple physics tells us that energy is neither created nor destroyed, and I do believe, there are parallel universes with other "me's" and other "you's". Our most accurate physics theory predicts this to be true, and basically, anything that *can* happen, *does* happen, but this doesn't mean that anything is possible. This is one of those examples that could easily be seen as the same things, but upon realizing the subtle distinction, they clearly mean two very different things. If it is actually true, then it answers an age-old question about choice. Is choice real or just an illusion? I thought about this question a lot over the years, before I even learned about what physics says about parallel universes. After I learned that our most accurate physics theories predict parallel universes, it made me think of that question about choice again. In order for choice to be real, there needs to be a place for that choice to occur.

Think about a worldly example such as coming to a fork in the road. Suddenly we are presented with a "choice" about which way to go. If either one of those two paths weren't there, then obviously there wouldn't be a choice; now let's think about this on another level. The reason why there is this age-old debate about choice, is because no matter how many forks in the road we come to, ultimately, we can only ever choose one of them. If there are no other parallel universes, just like if there wasn't really a fork in the road, then similarly, choice could not be a real thing, and would simply be an illusion.

That alone isn't very convincing, until we consider the other possibility. If there are parallel universes with other "me's" and other "you's", then we know there is really a place for a choice to occur. The same theories that predict these other universes, also state that not only do they exist as real choices, but in that moment, when we are first presented with a choice, both choices are actually made. The you that made the choices *you* remember making, is the you that *you* are now; the you that made the other choices, was the exact same you before *you* made that choice; there wasn't two of you, but only one. The moment after you made that other choice, that other you became slightly different, and not quite you anymore, which is why you are not even aware of it. According to physics, this same process takes place every time we are faced with a choice, and every day, we are faced with many countless choices.

The reason why I explained all of that, is because I truly believe in this theory. I could write a whole book about why I believe that, but obviously that's not what this one is about. I also believe in karma, as well as reincarnation, but my belief in reincarnation isn't like any religious theories talk about. My belief in reincarnation is based on things I know about physics, which have been proven to be facts, and I would believe this even if the parallel universe aspect is not true. The physics that cause me to believe that we experience other lives, is based on experiments done over 100 years ago, and has been proven to be true from countless more experiments since. The explanation isn't important here, because just like with any religious belief, personally, I have faith in the science.

Similar to a lot of religious teachings regarding suicide, the physics that supports my belief in reincarnation also gives me concern relating to suicide. I don't believe it is some kind of sin, like some religions teach, and I don't think somebody goes to hell if they commit suicide, but I do think there's a good possibility that killing oneself leaves some kind of imprint on the energy which makes each of us who we are. Based on what I believe about physics, I think the most likely effect from suicide, would essentially mean that in the next life, we would still need to deal with a similar problem next time around.

So to get back to where we were, being stuck in the mental hell, tied to a stranger that scared my deepest love away, the pain I was feeling was unlike anything I imagined was possible, which says a lot considering the painful life I have had. Suddenly I found myself not caring if I needed to go do it again, and that's when I seriously started researching different ways to escape the hell I now found myself in.

On June 3, after thinking about a number of ways to end the pain, I suddenly started thinking about being in grade school, when kids would take turns standing up against the wall, while someone else would put both of their hands on the side of their neck and push until they pass out and drop to the ground. I've had this done to me a few times, and it was always rather interesting, and never in any way painful. It simply felt just like falling asleep suddenly when you're really exhausted, but even quicker than that. So eventually, I took a winch that I have and bolted it to the wall in the hallway. I hooked up a pulley in the ceiling, tied myself a noose and put a clip on the end, to attach to the cable of the winch, and then slowly began to prepare myself.

I wrote a rather long letter to my family, explaining some things that I don't think they know about me, particularly about how hard I've always felt my life has been, and some of the things I don't think they realize have always been a struggle, in the hopes that they would understand. I then wrote a letter to Karo, telling her it's not her fault, and I don't want her to blame herself, because her leaving was just a small aspect of a much larger struggle, that I finally had enough of. I also sent her all the money I had in my bank account, and also made a little will indicating that I wanted her to have the rest of the money I had here, as well all my other things that she could sell, to help her with this new life that she wants.

After sending her the email, sending the money transfer, and having the letter to my family where it would be found, I went over to where the winch was set up and started hooking everything together. After everything was hooked up, with the rope around my neck, I pressed the button on the winch controller that would slowly lift me up. In those brief moments, as the rope slowly started tightening around my neck, all I could feel was unbearable guilt and selfishness, thinking about how much this choice would destroy Karo for the rest of her life; then suddenly I let go of the button.

The only thing I wanted most, was to have one more chance with Karo, but knowing that wasn't a possibility, the only other thing I wanted, was to get away from this stranger I was tied to in that mental hell. But despite how desperately I wanted to escape, I just couldn't do such a selfish thing, knowing how much pain I would cause her for the rest of her life.

Eventually, Karo ended up replying to me because of that email and money transfer. Even though I'd already given up the idea of committing suicide, I was still ignoring my phone, and not talking to anyone. When somebody did message me, I'd still see the light flash and look at the message. Eventually I saw a number I didn't recognize, from the Québec city area, and it was from Karo. At first I wasn't going to reply, and because I was out of smokes at that point, I took a walk to the store to grab some more, because I knew it was going to be hard not to reply, without the comfort of chain-smoking. Even though I knew that my email would have only made her only less likely to want to give me another chance, I still wanted nothing more than to talk to her, even if it was just for a few minutes. By the time I got back from the store, I realized no matter how long I delayed replying to her, ultimately I would at some point, and because of the message that I'd sent her, I didn't want her to worry about me.

When I finally replied, it was just a very simple "hi..", but if I'd known how she was going to respond, I don't think I would've said anything at all. As soon as I replied, all she said was, "Great. You're alive! Have a good night!" All that made me think, was maybe she didn't really care the way I thought she did, or else she was thinking I only sent the message to be manipulative, and was just a way to get her to message me. It wasn't that at all, but I didn't want to hurt her anymore, so I wasn't about to explain how close I actually was, or what made me stop.

After she unexpectedly responded that way, I started spending a lot of time trying to figure out how to interpret it. But because I was in an almost perpetual state of being emotionally overwhelmed, which was now even worse because of the way she responded, it was completely impossible for me to come to any kind of rational conclusion. In that moment, because my thoughts were irrational, it was surprisingly easy, to irrationally dismiss the rational possibility, that I was likely thinking irrationally.

Eventually I gave up trying to figure out how to interpret her message, because I realized it didn't matter either way; so my mind went back to obsessively trying to figure out the answers it's been obsessing about for months.

A few days after I almost ended it all, I hung out with my buddy Issa, that I've known since I moved to Ottawa, for the first time since the lock-down. After being up all night having very long conversations about all sorts of stuff that had been going on, initially before he went home, I thought I was feeling a little better. But not long after he left, things got even worse than before we talked, and once again in a complete state of overwhelming panic, I sent two very long, stressed fueled messages to her, despite having a fairly good conversation with her a few days before, when she kindly asked me to give her some space. During that conversation, she said she didn't want to block me again, but if I continued the way I was, she would change, not just her number, but her email addresses, and any other way I had to contact her. After I sent those stressed fueled messages, within a few minutes, I suddenly thought about what she'd said a few days before, and then immediately after remembering that, I sent another message. But somehow, despite the mental state I was in, I was able to calm down enough, and wrote what I felt was a thoughtful and calm message.

I knew her summer tires were still in my storage unit, so I started off by apologizing for the stressed out messages, I just sent previously, quickly explained that I was really emotional after talking with Issa all night, and that I'd like to do something nice for her. I suggested I could bring her tires by her place and put them on her car, it would only take 10 minutes, and she wouldn't even have to come outside of her apartment. And then I added if she didn't want me to do that, to let me know and I could just bring the tires over to her sister's place.

I then tried to fall asleep, because I'd been up all night, but that was impossible with so many thoughts going through my head so quickly. Because of all those thoughts still racing through my mind, 5 minutes seemed like hours. As I was laying down on my couch trying to fall asleep, I was still staring off into space, and not seeing a thing that was happening around me. When I suddenly realize how much time had passed, I would check my phone, thinking maybe I didn't hear the sound while I was lost in my thoughts, and disconnected from the world around me. Yet each time I looked at my phone, I was shocked that only a few more minutes had gone by. What's even more shocking, about being so shocked about that, is how often I felt like that since she first left, but every time I would still be surprised, because of how sure I was it had been hours, rather than just minutes; when I say it feels like it has been years since I've seen her, it truly does feel that way.

After a few days went by without any response at all, I assumed the worst, and that she actually changed her number again. But I didn't dare call just to see if it was true, because if she hadn't changed her number, calling would just make it that much more likely she would. Three days later, I sent her an email, expecting it would be the last thing I ever said to her, and I didn't expect a reply. Then a few hours after I sent the email, I found out from my buddy Issa, Karo had messaged him on Facebook early in the morning. She told him that she was packing, then suddenly found herself staring at the wall for hours and couldn't stop crying, and she just wanted to know if he knew how I was doing.

As soon as I found out what she had said to him, I became even more angry with myself, knowing I had made things so bad, she wouldn't even message me to ask how I was. Suddenly the anger towards myself, that I had been suppressing ever since she left, was no longer something I could suppress. I had been intentionally redirecting the anger into sadness, because I knew the sadness and depression was so intense and already overwhelming, and it would not be good at all, if I allowed myself to feel anger at the same time.

I started pacing around my apartment, chain-smoking for hours, just trying to dissipate the energy. Normally I'm not a clumsy person at all, but over the previous two months, I had been uncharacteristically clumsy, because of how consumed I was with my thoughts. As I was pacing around that day, I was even more clumsy. Banging into one thing after another, and then finally, after I smacked my bare foot into a fairly sharp object, which hurt quite a bit, I became even more angry with myself, followed a few moments later by banging my elbow really hard on a railing. Suddenly in that moment, that anger turned into rage, and I suddenly wanted to destroy everything in my apartment. Normally I'm not one to break my things, no matter how angry I get. But in that moment, I wanted to completely destroy, Every.Single.Thing!

Despite the fact that I wasn't just feeling anger, but went past that simple intensity and turned into rage, because of how much forced experience I have from dealing with bullies, I still wasn't concerned I'd actually lose control of it and start breaking things, because that just isn't in my character to do, but it was obvious I couldn't stay feeling like that and I needed to go get something to calm down to be able to sleep. At that point I'd be up for days until I was finally exhausted enough to be able the pass out for 12 to 18 hours, and then I would get up and that pattern would repeat. That went on for months, and no doubt made things worse. I don't like going to the doctors even when I'm really sick, and only ever go if I absolutely need to. I knew if I went to the hospital by myself for a mental health reason, I would almost certainly get frustrated waiting for hours and end up leaving, so I knew I needed to ask somebody to go with me. I don't like asking people for help to move something like a couch, I don't like asking people for help for any reason, so I knew how difficult it was going to be to ask Issa to go with me. I sent him a message on Facebook asking if he was busy after work, he said no almost right away. I sent "…", and then wrote a message asking him to go with me to the hospital, but then it took me well over an hour to finally press send.

Because of the mental state that I knew I was in, I decided to bring in the psychological assessment from jail, to show them that one paragraph about how I can become "obsessive as a defense against emotional distress". I realized how perfectly it explained what was going on in my head for the last few months, and the loop that I was stuck in; trying to find out the answers that I was looking for. By the time I ended up going to the hospital, I had already been thinking about that particular paragraph for a couple of months, but over the previous week I started almost obsessing about it, feeling like there were more clues within that paragraph; I don't remember how many times I read that paragraph, each day during the previous week, before going to the hospital. When I finally met with a psychiatrist, I started off by showing her that paragraph. As soon as she finished reading it, she looked up at me and asked, "Is there any history of autism in your family?"

Clearly anybody would be as surprised as I was, to hear that most unexpected of questions, but not only was I surprised, I was also very intrigued because of some research that I had done about 5 years before that. One day, years before, I was reading about A.D.D., because ever since I found out that I have A.D.D., every so often I'll start researching it again, to see if there's any new information about it. Because of how many different times I researched things like that, I was well aware of the fact that A.D.D., anxiety, O.C.D., and a whole bunch of other things often coexist, and if you have one, you're likely to have others. As I was on the wiki page for A.D.D., I saw a link to the autism page, and since I didn't really know much about that particular condition, purely out of curiosity and my enjoyment of learning, I clicked on it and begin to read.

One of the first things that I learned about autism, had to do with the spectrum of severity; ranging from being completely dysfunctional, to not even noticeable. As I started reading about some of the traits particularly to people who have a very mild form, there were a few really specific things that caught my attention. I then read about how most autistic children have delayed language development, as well as problems with pronouncing certain letters. There were also a few other very specific things relating to people with mild forms, that completely resonated with me, and perfectly described a few of my unusual personality quirks. At that point, I started feeling like I might be ever so slightly autistic, because when I was younger, I had to go to speech therapy for a few years, precisely because I had problems pronouncing certain letters. "R's" were especially difficult for me, and for the longest time I had difficulty saying certain words the "wight" way. Afterwards, I didn't really think much else about it, and it was essentially just a passing curiosity in my mind, since it didn't seem like it made any difference if I actually was or not. But then, when that psychiatrist asked me that question about a month ago, I immediately thought back to that suspicion that I already had.

Before I gave her that paragraph to read, the first question she asked me, is the reason why I was there. I was very clear that I was just there to get something to sleep, and help me calm down, because of how much I had been stressing over the last few months, and it was only getting worse. Next she asked all the standard mental health questions, and when she asked about any past suicidal thoughts, I was completely honest, but also stressed that I'd completely given up even considering the idea, after realizing I would completely destroy the most beautiful girl, that I love with all my heart, and always will until the day I die. I don't know how many times I stressed this point, because I wanted her to understand that it was not a concern she should be having, and that I was only there to get something to help me sleep and for the stress. She even asked my friend if he thought I was suicidal, and he also said no.

But as I would soon find out, her and the other doctor decided that they were going to force me to stay there for 3 days anyway. Of course I started explaining the Charter to them, but they were completely ignoring me at that point. I told them that they're breaking the Hippocratic oath, because they're only making my stress worse, when all I wanted was something so I can go home, relax, and sleep in my own comfortable bed. But no matter how loud I said it, because they were on the other side of their glass windows, it was like I wasn't even there. Obviously this wound me up even more, and understandably, made me angrier and more frustrated. When they gave me the form that they are required to give a person, any time they force someone to stay against their will, I noticed right above where I had to sign, it said, "You have the right to retain and instruct a lawyer without delay." As soon as I saw that, I immediately held it up so they could see it, told them that I wanted to exercise this right, immediately, without delay, and I'd like my phone back so I can call my lawyer. But still they ignored me, and never allowed me to call my lawyer. At that point, I was so angry with the situation, going in there just to get something to sleep, and suddenly finding myself locked up.

Before they took my phone away, I started messaging Karo, very angry messages, and for the first time since she left, I was telling her how I felt about the unnecessary way she left. And if she was unhappy, I would have helped her move to Montreal, which is where she ended up moving. But because of how shaky I was from the adrenaline flowing through my body, I used the voice-to-text feature while I was in one of the rooms, by myself, and out of view from the doctors. Because I use the voice-to-text feature so often, it didn't occur to me that the doctors might think, when they only heard me shouting by myself in the room, as though I was some crazy person.

Not long after that, the area slowly began to fill with a number of security guards, until there was about 8 or 9 of them. At that point, the doctors came into the room and told me, that I *had* to take some pills they were holding out in front of me. I asked what they were, and told them I want to research what they were, before putting them in my body, just like I would any other drug. I told them it would only take a few minutes, but they wouldn't even allow me to do that. I then told them that I was not going take anything without knowing what it is.

Then they threatened me, and told me if I didn't take the pills, they were going to strap me down to the bed, and stick me with the needle one of the doctors was holding in their hand. I protested until the very last moment, because even in that mental state, regardless of how emotionally overwhelmed I was, I've never become so irrational that it would qualify as being idiotic. I made sure to tell everybody, even though I was taking this myself, it was still against my will, since I clearly didn't have a choice in the matter. Not only did they cause me substantially more stress, but the issues I already had about seeing doctors, just became substantially worse.

The doctor that came to see me in the morning, was actually a very nice guy, and it was obvious he knew how to listen, unlike most doctors that I've met since I've been in Ottawa. Ultimately, he let me out instead of keeping me for the 3 days, and gave me some Seroquel, both to help me sleep, and every 4 hours as needed during the day for stress.

I dropped off the prescription they gave me at the pharmacy on my way home, and while I was waiting at home for the prescription to be ready, I was obviously more upset than I was before I went to the hospital. This additional emotion was mostly just anger towards how I was treated at the hospital and the completely illegal thing they did by not allowing me to call my lawyer.

This made it easy to ignore the anger I still had towards myself, because if there is one thing that should be obvious by now, unjust acts by someone which negatively affect others, is always something I don't take kindly to. Admittedly, if they had allowed me to call a lawyer, and not violated that very clear legal right, the reasons for keeping me in the first place, could be debated, since it was not completely without merit. But based on what both myself and my friend said, relating to the suicide issue, I still feel they were completely in the wrong, and also violated my rights by forcing me to stay there.

As soon as the prescription was ready, I wasted no time going to pick it up, and even bought a drink at the pharmacy, so that I could take a pill soon as I got in my car. The doctor in the morning suggested some other medications as well, but I picked Seroquel because I'd taken it before; although not for medical reasons.

Back when I owned the club, one of my weed customers, would regularly trade me large bottles of 50mg tablets of Seroquel, in exchange for weed. Because of the strong sedative effects Seroquel has, it was quite effective at putting us to sleep after parting at the club all night.

Normally with the types, and amounts of drugs that I would do at the club, even once they wore off, I felt exhausted and tired, when trying to sleep, I'd usually end up laying there half awake and half-asleep for 12 hours or so. This was obviously a problem when needing to get up the following night, and do it all over again. But no matter how recently, or how much drugs I'd take at the club, a couple of those 50mg pills, would put me to sleep within minutes. I had a regular supply of the pills, starting before owning the club, and still had some left after the club closed. I was very familiar with it, and knew I didn't have any kind of adverse reactions.

Even though I've taken more Seroquel than I can remember, during those years of the club, I'd only ever taken it to sleep, and was even surprised that the doctor gave me that for stress during the day. Within about 30 minutes after taking it that first day, not only did it immediately eliminate all the emotional spikes that I was having, but I also felt that it was doing something else as well.

That evening, somewhat coincidentally, my mom called me, which was the first time we talked in months. She already knew about Karo leaving and the abrupt way that she left. She also knew that I was having a really rough time with it, and the reason she ended up calling, was because of something I wrote, and posted to Facebook the day before I went to the hospital.

I posted this particular thing because I felt it was funny, despite how sad it was too. I've always been the kind of person that talks to myself out loud when I'm doing certain things, especially when I'm working on something complicated. I find it helps me focus better talking about the steps out loud to myself, so it's not at all out of character for me to do something like that.

I'm not sure how many people notice this about themselves, but I believe this is something that's true about everyone, and that we all have these 2 voices inside of our heads; cartoons often portray them as a Devil and an Angel on a character shoulders. Even though that only portrays the two voices in a moral context, in reality, I believe it's much more fundamental than that. Based on what I know of the brain and such things, I think it's really an issue of the left in the right brain having their own voices. This is another one of those topics I could write in great length about.

As far as how it relates to what I wrote on Facebook, these two voices in my head are both very loud, are a fundamental part of why am so good with law, as well as any other task that requires one to debate with themselves, to be able to come up with the correct answer. One voice will try to disprove a point, while the other voice attempts to prove it. Normally this is a very enjoyable quality that I like, but is also quite stressful and annoying; during these rare periods of intense trauma, when my mind won't stop obsessively trying to find an answer, because of something I did.

The day before I went to the hospital, I was allowing those voices to be spoken out loud. They had already been arguing with each other for months, and it had long passed the point of being annoying, so instead of trying to fight the impossible, instead of trying to shut them up, I decided to have fun with it. One voice kept saying, "She's going to come back;" the other voice, "You'll never see her again." After listening to this argument for so long, when I finally started saying it out loud, I found myself using slightly different voices for each. Then quite quickly, because I'm a fan of The Lord of the Rings, I started imitating Gollum's and Schlegel's voices. After a few minutes of this, I thought about this funny truth: *"When you start arguing with yourself like Gollum and Smeagol, you can be pretty certain it's because something precious was lost."*

The purpose for my mom's call, was obvious to both of us, and was understood without anything needing to be said. I know my mom well enough, that I even knew the exact words that she would start off with, as well as the tone of voice she would have. A soon as she asked, "So... How you doing?", I already knew I was going to tell her most of the details about how I've been over the last few months. Initially, I wasn't going to tell her about the suicidal details, because I didn't want to worry her. There were also a number of questions I wanted to ask her about when I was younger, that I thought about while I've been writing.

One of those questions led to her sharing something that I never knew about, and was something she had always felt very remorseful about. I always assumed the reason I was sent to the hospital and the group home, was because I threw a paint can at her, which was technically assault. But after I first got to the hospital, and explained to the doctors that it was just a small quart sized paint can, the expression on the doctor's face quickly changed, and it was quite obvious to me, he suddenly didn't see the incident nearly as serious as he initially did. I was still told I was going to be kept for 24 hours, and then the next day I was told for 3 days, and eventually a month later, I was transferred to the group home. I didn't know until my mom told me this on the phone the other day, that they were going to release me after observing me for 3 days, because they didn't feel I needed to be there.

The reason why they ended up keeping me and sending me to the group home, was because of what my mom said when she was meeting with a Judge and the doctors. When they told her they saw no reason to keep me longer, she lied to them, and said if I went back home, she would hurt me, which is something I knew she would never have actually done. I had no idea about that before, and from the way she was crying as she told me, it was quite obvious that she'd been carrying around this guilt for the last 25 years. I told her I wish she would've told me that 20 years ago, after I got out of jail, because I would've told her the same thing I told her last month; "Thank you! There's no reason for you to feel guilty. I'm glad you lied to them, because if I hadn't gone to the group home, I'm sure I'd either be in jail or living on the street right now, because of how many problems I had that the group home helped permanently change.... "

The question I wanted to ask her about the most, was about autism. Because of how open and honest my whole family is with each other, and how often we still continued to talk about things from the past, as soon as I thought about asking my mom, after the doctor mentioned autism, I figured if anybody had ever considered that about me when I was younger, I would have heard about it at some point. But to my surprise, when I specifically asked, "With all the things I went through when I was younger, all the counselors, doctors and everyone I saw, did anyone, at any point, ever once suspect that I might be slightly autistic?"

She replied in a very energetic, *matter of fact* way and said, "Oh yeah! We definitely thought that! We even tried to get you help with it, but every doctor we went to, just dismissed it, because the way autism was looked at back then." As soon as she said that, suddenly a whole bunch of things from my childhood made complete sense. When I first thought about asking her, I hadn't spent any time considering how I was going to feel about it if she said yes, because I wasn't expecting her to say that. Initially I wasn't quite sure how I felt; I knew I felt a little odd, but then the conversation quickly carried on and I was distracted from those thoughts for a while.

Another question that I asked her, that ended up having a big impact on me, was when did I start having a temper issue. It was one of those questions I thought about while I have been writing. Because of how vivid my memories start from such a young age, I knew it started suddenly, and before that point I was a very calm, gentle, emotionally sensitive little kid, who was always very polite and hated confrontation; I wouldn't even hurt a fly. I always assumed my temper issues started about half way through kindergarten, and was a result of being bullied, but I didn't have any specific memories of that negative change. But when I asked my mom, she immediately knew exactly when, and told me it began as soon as I started school. After asking why she was so certain, she said it started because of the teachers. Obviously that left me with more questions, but before I was able to ask any, suddenly, I saw another suppressed memory vividly appear in my mind.

The memory was from the first day of kindergarten. I remembered sitting on the floor of the classroom playing with some toys. I remembered other kids around me as well, but I was only interested in playing with the toys, because I knew I still had difficulties pronouncing things properly. When any of the other kids would say something to me, I wouldn't say anything, replied with body language, and was kind of dismissive, because I was nervous about talking to anyone; I only wanted to keep playing with the toys. Then eventually the teacher said playtime was over, and all the kids got up, except me. I clearly remember the teacher saying it the first time to everyone, then a few more times directly to me, since I wasn't getting up.

Initially, I wasn't sure why I didn't get up, especially considering I was always a very polite and respectful kid. Even though I heard her every time, I was completely unresponsive to her. When I first started thinking about this memory, I didn't remember feeling any emotions at all, but after thinking about it for a while and writing some more, I realized that I was actually so overwhelmed with fear, I completely disconnected myself from those feelings, and obsessively continued playing with the toys. I was so fixated on playing with the toys, when she came up and gently touched my arm to get my attention, I instantly, and completely, freaked the fuck out! I knew right away this was another important piece of the puzzle, and my mind took it out of the vault and set it next to where the puzzle was slowly being put together.

If a kid were to do that in the first day of kindergarten now, at the very least, it would definitely raise some kind of red flag, and would be further investigated, but most likely the first thought any kindergarten teacher would have these days, would almost certainly be about autism.

As the conversation with my mom continued for hours, I kept thinking about that odd feeling I had when I first realized that I'm definitely slightly autistic, but again I'd quickly be distracted with something else in the conversation. Towards the end of the conversation I started realizing what I was feeling, and I knew it wasn't good. I knew as soon as I got off the phone with my mom, I was going to have an emotionally rough night. After the months of turmoil that I just went through, which wasn't even over, being a spectator in my own mind, as it relentlessly obsessed over the questions that it was desperately determined to answer, because if it didn't, then there would never be a possibility that things could even change between Karo and I, even if we did end up getting back together.

That hope of having one last chance, already felt slim at best, but after I freaked out on Karo while I was in the hospital, and started blaming her for the way she left, it just so happened she was having a really bad night too. When I message her that night, she obviously had no sympathy at all, and told me, "NEVER FUCKING MESSAGE ME AGAIN!" So not only did I no longer have any hope of ever having another chance together, but now I just found out that I have this incurable condition, and I started thinking I would probably never find the solution to that last behavioral issue I've continued to be haunted by.

All these thoughts started coming together as I was listening to my mom, and towards the end of that conversation, I was already struggling to hold back tears. I just wanted to get off the phone, take a few Seroquel's, and pass out for as long as I could. Thoughts of suicide immediately came to my mind, but were just as quickly dismissed, for the same reason I let go of the button a week before. It didn't even matter if Karo hated me, I just knew I'd never be able to hurt her like that. Even if there's nothing after this life when you die, I'd rather suffer the rest of my life feeling the way I do right now, then that brief moment of overwhelming guilt I started to feel while I was holding onto that button.

As all those thoughts were quickly going through my mind, while I was trying to pay attention to what my mom was saying, it was all suddenly interrupted, when my phone made the most unexpected sound. For a moment, I thought I must've heard the sound wrong, and was some other alert on my phone instead. But when I pulled the phone away from my ear to look at the screen, I realized it was actually Karo's unique ring tone that I heard. I was in such disbelief, I initially brought the phone back to my ear quickly, so I didn't miss anything my mom was saying. A moment later, I abruptly said, in a very mundane tone, "Karo just texted me."

Initially, I was so stunned to get a message from her after what I said to her from the hospital, I was going to continue talking with my mom, but then I kept thinking about the message preview I briefly saw at the top of the screen, and I started thinking that it seemed like a positive message, so I decided to say good night to my mom, and read what Karo had sent. She actually said quite a few things, and even though we ended up chatting longer than we had in a long time, it didn't restore any hope that she would ever give me another chance. At least she did respond to something I said in the email I sent her, she told me, "I will read your book.... OBVIOUSLY Adam." Just hearing that, suddenly made me feel a lot better, because I was finding it quite upsetting, thinking about the few reoccurring misunderstandings she seems to have of me, and I just didn't want her to remember me that way.

When I woke up the next day, I was surprised at how motivated I felt to start writing again, and besides one day when I needed to work on my car, I've spent almost all my free time over the past month entirely on writing. Not only am I surprised that I've written over 100 000 words in the past month, but I'm also completely shocked at the unexpectedly wonderful thing that has happened over the last few weeks.

A quick moral note: even though I still don't feel Karo needed to leave the way she did, especially considering I had driven her to the airport one time during another long break up, I still regret blaming her while I was at the hospital. Considering the unexpected way I reacted during that last fight, it's definitely understandable that she would feel unsure about how I would react to her breaking up. Even though most people have told me similar things contrary to how I feel, blaming her like I did will likely bother me for a while, because the idea of dismissing how I act because of any state of mind; to me, this just feels like I wouldn't be taking any responsibility, and then there would be absolutely no sub-conscious motivation to change.

BITTERSWEET CHANGES; MUSICALLY MINOR IN KEY

During the first couple of weeks, after the incident at the hospital, I found myself in a very reflective state of mind. Even though I knew I still had this deep sadness inside, now that I was taking the Seroquel regularly, I suddenly found myself being able to think about all these new things that I've been realizing about myself recently, and focus clearly on the puzzle before me.

One of the first important changes that occurred, happened suddenly, and I only noticed it about a week or two later. As soon as I did, I felt like this change happened directly after asking my mom about the autism. After she told me they definitely thought that, I can't think of any point after that when I felt any kind of anger at all. The main reason why I was so angry with myself, was because I was blaming myself for a lot of things, but as soon as I learned I'm a bit autistic, that blame and anger towards myself suddenly went away. Initially I had mixed feelings, because I've always been taught that a person should always take responsibility for their own actions, but on the other hand, I knew I never meant to hurt her, and the related things from my past, were outside of my own control.

Even after I started dating Karo, and it became a much more frequent issue, despite how hard I tried to change that behavior, it now makes sense why I have never been able to. I don't think the autism caused the problem, but I also don't think I would've struggled with that issue my whole life, if I wasn't autistic at all. This may seem like a contradiction, but this isn't an issue of logic; but is a rather emotionally sensitive issue. Slight wordplay aside; essentially every big fight her and I've ever had, are all moments when I became emotionally overwhelmed. The emotional intensity was very apparent in those moments, and when I became overwhelmed, it was often so intense, that it would end up scaring her.

It's the same emotional sensitivity I have, as result of being slightly autistic, that essentially forms a core part of the underlining problem I was having. Interestingly, I also feel it's that same emotional intensity responsible for the intense intimate bond I've always felt with her. The reason why I pointed out those two contrasting examples, is because it shows that the emotional intensity isn't really the problem. When I first found out about having autism, I initially thought that the emotional intensity was the problem, and because it's a core part of the autism, I realized it would be an impossible thing to change.

Thankfully, I've realized a lot of other things as I've been writing, and that's when a wonderful and unexpected thing happened, that puts a smile on my face, even as I'm thinking about it now. The reason why I'm smiling is because my mind has finally stopped obsessively trying to find the answers to those questions, because all of the answers have been found! Finding out about the autism was a big piece of the puzzle, because of that emotional intensity. The rest of the little pieces that finally completed the picture, are all related to the defensive habits I developed as a result of being bullied, and remembering all those suppressed memories.

After writing so much about those experiences, and realizing even more than what I've shared, I finally understand why I've never been able to change this one big issue I've struggled with most of my life. Part of the reason I failed is because I was focusing on the wrong aspect of it. Because of how well I can control my anger, I didn't see that as a problem. So during those moments when these types of fights and issues would happen between Karo and I, I would *always* attempt to control the intensity or suppress my emotional sensitivity. Because I know I'm definitely able to do that a lot of times, it seemed perfectly reasonable that I should be able to during those moments Karo and I would be fighting. There were definitely plenty of times when I was able to control the intensity and emotional sensitivity, and prevented a minor issue, from turning into a big serious issue. But I wouldn't call that a success, because it was more like putting a Band-Aid on a gunshot wound, when in reality, the wound won't heal until you take the bullet out.

Even though I realized that my anger in those moments, was mostly redirected sadness or fear, that was pretty much all I was aware of in terms of redirected emotions. If I hadn't written this book, I never would have realized all of the other different ways I was redirecting any emotion and expressing them as another, and more importantly, feeling different emotions differently at times. Also, after learning about the autism and the related emotional sensitivity, I realized I was essentially attempting the impossible by trying to control the intensity of my feelings.

Instead, if I simply would've stopped expressing my vulnerable emotions as anger, the problem would have been possible to effectively address. The reason why I'm certain of that, is because it was something I knew I was doing willingly. Ever since I first started doing that to protect myself from those bullies and learned to control it, over the last 30+ years, it had always protected me. In a way, anger was like a friend I would turn to when afraid, but now, after everything I've realized, I feel quite betrayed and no longer want anything to do with that angry person. Thankfully, because of how well I can control anger, I'm sure it will be easy to decline any future invitations to hang out.

Of course, I'll now have other emotional friends to deal with more often, but at least now I'm sure I'll know who's at the party, and if any of them get a bit rowdy, I have no doubt that I'll be able to quickly learn how to deal with them "…in an efficient and socially acceptable way."

Part of me feels like Karo left at just the right time, because if I wasn't suddenly forced into isolation from the lock-down soon after, I'm sure I never would have started this book, may never have figured out this problem I've been struggling with, and instead would have distracted myself with social activities, redirected my sadness and depression into other emotions, and that would have protected me from this pain and loss; but only in the short term.

At least now, I've finally figured out this problem I have been trying to solve for so long, and my book will finally be done soon, but now that I realize how harmful and dangerously unhealthy redirecting emotions have been, it's something I'll no longer choose to do regardless of how much I hurt. This is also the exact reason why I decided to share the intensely personal things that I've shared in this book. After I initially wrote this chapter, and started thinking about everything that I've written, I started thinking about how close the book was to being published, and all the people I have been telling. After writing a whole book, and just getting in the flow of things, while attempting to be as open and accurate as possible, initially when I wrote some of the details, I didn't really think about what I was about to share. Once I did start thinking about it, I had thoughts about removing some of the things, but then I immediately realized that would be no different than suppressing emotions, in that moment I knew I wasn't going to remove any of it. I know I'm still going to be nervous when it is published, but after what I realized lately, knowing it was that very thing that was related to pushing Karo away, there's no way I can keep doing something like that.

After writing in detail, and reliving my past to the extent that I have, I'm feeling surprisingly humbled by its unexpected effect upon me. I assumed I would learn a few things by digging through my memory, but I didn't expect writing would end up leading to another fundamental change. Like every other time I've experienced such changes, I'm sure it will still continue to affect me in surprising ways. I most certainly didn't expect it to lead me to the answers I've long been searching for. Overcoming my fear of dancing is a perfect example, because of how simple and sudden it was. But every time I've had a moment like this, there has always been a common feeling, regarding the uncertainty about the extent of how it is going to affect my life, that has always been purely exciting and positive. But this time I don't only feel excitement, and I think I know why.

First, there is the uncertainty about publishing this book. If it is successful, then hopefully I'll have enough money to go start a new life. If it's not successful, obviously that would be very disappointing, and am not quite sure how that would end up affecting me in the long term. There's also the question about what's going to happen with the Charter and drug laws, after I follow through with my plans on Parliament Hill to make it public. Again, it could be as successful as I hope it will be, or it's possible, despite all my efforts promoting the day on social media, and through the regular media, that very few people will show up, or even none at all. And then most concerning, is the uncertainty about my love. If all of those things go as well as I hope, I'll be the happiest person in the world, and I'll almost certainly be moving out of Ottawa, but more often than not, things rarely turn out the way I like them to. If none of these things work out, I'll probably still leave Ottawa. Time will tell, but one thing I'm sure of, no matter what happens, I still wouldn't ever do anything ever again to hurt the most precious person I've ever loved, regardless of if we even see each other ever again.

As I'm writing this, I'm also looking at the psychological assessment in front of me, from twenty-one years ago. One of the tests that I haven't mentioned so far, involved a series of cards she showed me with different pictures, which I was asked to make up a short, paragraph sized story about for each picture. What I said twenty-one years ago when asked to make up a story, is just as true today, as it was then. I only have her summary of what I said, so it's in her words, but it still illustrates the point:

"Card sixteen is a blank page and therefore is entirely subjective. Adam told, in minute detail, the story of his offense, changing only the names of the characters involved. It seems significant to note, that while this was a 'story', Adam nonetheless absolutely refused to summarize an ending for it. When pushed, he gave his characters 'wish' for the future, but insisted he could not create an ending to the story. The character's wish was that he would become a computer engineer who will 'one day settle down with a wife in a small house with a nice, white picket fence..... He will take it one day at a time."

The white picket fence detail, was just a funny cliché I threw in there because she was insisting. The computer engineering thing didn't work out, even though I do stuff like that as a hobby, but as I mentioned before, I could easily live without it because it's also a stressful hobby. As far as the settle down with the wife part goes, I genuinely meant that when I said it when I was eighteen, and it's never stopped being true. Even though I only recently found out I'm slightly autistic, I always knew I was a bit different than most people, because of the way kids would react to me, and for a long time, I wasn't sure I ever would find someone I felt so strongly about.

After the dancing epiphany, when I overcame that fear, I also had a new confidence about myself in general, and after I broke up with the girl I started dating, a week after the dancing epiphany, soon after when I discovered meeting people online, I was hooked. I probably met close to a thousand girls from online over the years, but not with any kind of sexual intent. I just found it extremely fascinating talking to people online and seeing how my impression of them compared to how they are in person. Most of the girls I met, I knew I had no interest in dating. But ultimately that was what I was looking for, just that one girl.

Of all the girls I've ever met, Karo was the only one that ever made me feel like I finally found her, and I still have hope that she is.

If she isn't, then I know I'll be faced with a moral dilemma.

I know my feelings for her will never change, and because of my memory, and the way my mind works, those feelings are not going to fade in time, like people keep telling me; that I'm certain of.

The moral dilemma I'd be faced with:

Is it morally okay to date some other,
knowing I have such feelings for another?

It's honestly hard to say, but it definitely seems, quite Morally Grey.

www.ingramcontent.com/pod-product-compliance
Lightning Source LLC
Chambersburg PA
CBHW030902080526
44589CB00010B/106